Poverty and the Poor Law in Ireland

Reappraisals in Irish History

Editors
Enda Delaney (University of Edinburgh)
Maria Luddy (University of Warwick)

Reappraisals in Irish History offers new insights into Irish history, society and culture from 1750. Recognising the many methodologies that make up historical research, the series presents innovative and interdisciplinary work that is conceptual and interpretative, and expands and challenges the common understandings of the Irish past. It showcases new and exciting scholarship on subjects such as the history of gender, power, class, the body, landscape, memory and social and cultural change. It also reflects the diversity of Irish historical writing, since it includes titles that are empirically sophisticated together with conceptually driven synoptic studies.

1. Jonathan Jeffrey Wright, *The 'Natural Leaders' and their World: Politics, Culture and Society in Belfast, c.1801–1832*

2. Gerardine Meaney, Mary O'Dowd and Bernadette Whelan, *Reading the Irish Woman: Studies in Cultural Encounters and Exchange, 1714–1960*

3. Emily Mark-FitzGerald, *Commemorating the Irish Famine: Memory and the Monument*

4. Virginia Crossman, *Poverty and the Poor Law in Ireland, 1850–1914*

Poverty and the Poor Law in Ireland

1850–1914

VIRGINIA CROSSMAN

LIVERPOOL UNIVERSITY PRESS

First published 2013 by
Liverpool University Press
4 Cambridge Street
Liverpool
L69 7ZU

British Library Cataloguing-in-Publication data
A British Library CIP record is available

ISBN 978-1-84631-941-9 cased
ISBN 978-1-78962-055-9 paperback

Typeset by Carnegie Book Production, Lancaster
Printed and bound in Poland by BooksFactory.co.uk

Contents

List of Figures

List of Tables

List of Maps

Acknowledgements

This book could not have been written without the assistance and support of a number of funding bodies, institutions, and individuals. The archival research on which the study is based was a funded by a research grant from the Economic and Social Research Council for the project 'Welfare Regimes under the Irish Poor Law'. I am immensely grateful to the three project researchers, Georgina Laragy, Seán Lucey and Olwen Purdue, for their painstaking research, their ideas, and their enthusiasm. Additional research assistance was provided by Richard Biddle and Ceci Flinn. I am also grateful to all those who contributed to the three workshops that formed an essential part of the project and helped shape the project research. Particular thanks in this regard are due to Ciara Breathnach, Larry Geary and Cormac Ó Gráda. Peter Gray and Queen's University Belfast supported the project throughout and hosted the final conference. Sabbatical leave granted by Oxford Brookes University and a Research Fellowship from the Leverhulme Trust gave me the time to analyse the research data and write the manuscript.

I wish to thank the staff of all the libraries and archives that I and the project researchers worked in. Particular thanks are due to the National Archives of Ireland, the National Library of Ireland, Ballymoney Museum, Cork City and County Archives, Donegal County Library, Dublin Diocesan Archives, Kerry County Library, Laois County Library, Limerick County Library, Tipperary Local Studies Library, the National Folklore Collection at University College Dublin, and the Public Record Office of Northern Ireland. I am grateful to the Deputy Keeper of Records at PRONI for permission to quote from material in his care.

Colleagues at Oxford Brookes past and present have provided invaluable support throughout the process of research and writing. Anne Digby, Steve King and Elizabeth Hurren shared their knowledge of poor law practices and ideology. Glen O'Hara read part of the manuscript and provided sound advice and comparative perspectives. Thanks are also due to Carol Beadle, Joanne Bailey, Tom Crook and Alysa Levene. Brian Griffin and Des

Marnane were generous with their knowledge of local sources. Stuart Basten produced the maps. Alison Welsby at Liverpool University Press has been an exemplary editor. My greatest debt, as ever, is to Maria Luddy who lived with the project, and the book, and read each chapter as it emerged. The manuscript was immeasurably improved by her suggestions.

Introduction

The focus of this study is the poor law system, and the people who used it. Modelled on the English poor law of 1834, the Irish Poor Relief Act of 1838 established a nationwide system of poor relief based on the workhouse and financed by a local property tax.[1] The poor law system remained the primary form of poor relief in Ireland until the 1920s, and in Northern Ireland until after the Second World War.[2] From its inception, the poor law was the focus of criticism and complaint. As the author of an anonymous pamphlet published in 1857 declared, the poor law was 'an acknowledged grievance, and complained of by all classes of the community, those who support it by the imposts levied on them, those who are forced to seek aid from it, and even the conscientious among the staff who are employed for, and so well paid to carry out the system'.[3]

Accusations that the system was expensive, ineffective and pernicious were heard throughout the period of its existence. In 1886 the nationalist newspaper, *The Nation*, published an article by a workhouse physician lamenting 'the deteriorating influence of workhouses'. He called for the poor law to be modified 'in the direction of home relief', which was less demoralising and more just to the deserving poor. This article was welcomed by a correspondent to the paper as highlighting 'the glaring defects of this most expensive, ineffective and degrading system'. 'Poverty in Ireland', the writer claimed:

> is condemned to starvation or imprisonment ... No free people would tolerate such an unjust, cruel and costly system. It has been used as a

---

1 Irish Poor Relief Act, 1838, 1 and 2 Vic., c. 56.
2 For a concise history, see Virginia Crossman, *The Poor Law in Ireland 1838–1948* (Dundalk: Economic and Social History Society of Ireland, 2006).
3 *Poor Rates: A Simple, Truthful Tale, Illustrating Some of the Wrongs of Ireland in the Nineteenth Century* (Dublin: Madden and Oldham, 1857)

political machine to effect purposes which are altogether outside the scope of Christian charity.[4]

The political argument against the poor law was taken up the following year by the land campaigner and nationalist MP, Michael Davitt, who identified one of the most urgent tasks facing an Irish Parliament, as 'the abolition, root and branch of the workhouse system'. Describing the system as 'the bastard offspring of landlordism', Davitt claimed that Irish workhouses were filled 'with the hapless victims of social wrong and landlord greed. The poor we may always have with us, but it does not follow that they must be so numerous, and remain as paupers.' Put an end to evictions and increase employment and industrial development, he argued, and 'the workhouse will disappear from the social life of Ireland', to be replaced by a system that did not degrade, but would provide succour 'for the helpless and deserving poor against the inevitable misfortune of life'.[5]

A common theme in such critiques was that the workhouse system was an alien imposition unsuited to Irish society and culture. As one poor law guardian commented in 1892, workhouses were foreign to the sentiments of the Irish people, who favoured almsgiving rather than state relief.[6] Thus while there was no shame attached to accepting private charity, entering the workhouse was seen as disgraceful. Following a visit to Ireland in 1883, the English Jesuit, Richard Clarke, had noted that the impersonal, institutional character of Irish workhouses was 'especially hateful to the warm-hearted and sensitive Irish'. The workhouse, he suggested:

> was bound up in their minds with the patronizing ascendancy of English rule. The feelings they bear to the latter attach to every Government institution. Everyone hates to receive charity from an enemy.[7]

It is tempting, therefore, to see the poor law system and the institution of the workhouse in particular, as an exemplar of colonial modernity, one of a number of institutions established in Ireland that exploited violence and poverty in order to safeguard the imperial order.[8] As with the introduction

4 *The Nation*, 27 March and 3 April 1886.
5 *Munster News*, 19 November 1887.
6 *The Irish Peasant: A Sociological Study by a Guardian of the Poor* (London: Swan Sonnenschein and Co., 1892), p. 69.
7 Richard F. Clarke, *A Personal Visit to Distressed Ireland* (Dublin: M. H. Gill and Son, 1883), pp. 33-4.
8 See, for example, Anna Clark, 'Wild Workhouse Girls and the Liberal Imperial State in mid-Nineteenth Century Ireland', *Journal of Social History*, 39 (2005), pp. 389–409.

of the national school system and the Irish constabulary force, the aim of the poor law, it could be argued, was to impose order on the unruly natives. But while the political context in which the workhouse system was introduced and operated was clearly crucial to its character and development, it was only one element of a broader picture. Issues of control and domination were central to the perception of and debates over the workhouse system, but the ideological roots of these debates lay as much in class and religion as in politics and ethnicity.

Concepts of entitlement and deservingness shaped welfare provision throughout this period. Generally associated with middle-class values and perceptions, and often assumed to be an English importation to Ireland, the concept of the deserving and undeserving poor became deeply rooted in Irish popular culture. The respectable poor, those who had fallen on hard times through no fault of their own, such as the elderly and disabled, were regarded as deserving of sympathy and relief while those lacking respectability, such as vagrants and prostitutes, were felt to deserve not assistance but punishment. One of the main criticisms of the poor law system in Ireland was that it failed to discriminate adequately between the respectable and the non-respectable, since all destitute people were eligible for relief within the workhouse. Speaking at a meeting of the Granard Board of Guardians in 1885, a local Catholic priest asserted that workhouse system had 'failed miserably. The old and the young, the sane and the crazy, the impure and the virtuous were all huddled into the one institution.'[9]

Rising levels of expenditure on poor relief in the post-Famine period, together with the growing predominance of the elderly and sick amongst workhouse inmates, paralleled developments in England.[10] But in Ireland poor law boards acquired a far wider range of functions than was the case in England. Their responsibilities encompassed the administration of a dispensary medical service and the provision of social housing, as well as the implementation of public health legislation.[11] Poor relief became one

---

9 *Freeman's Journal*, 22 September 1885.
10 For England, see Anthony Brundage, *The English Poor Laws 1700–1930* (London: Palgrave, 2002); M. A. Crowther, *The Workhouse System 1834–1929: The History of an English Social Institution* (London: Batsford, 1981); and Lynn Hollen Lees, *The Solidarities of Strangers: The English Poor Laws and the People, 1700–1948* (Cambridge: Cambridge University Press, 1998).
11 For the dispensary system, see Ronald D. Cassell, *Medical Charities, Medical Politics: The Irish Dispensary System and the Poor Law 1836–1872* (Woodbridge: Boydell Press, 1997); and Laurence M. Geary, 'The Medical Profession, Health Care and the Poor Law in Nineteenth-Century Ireland', in V. Crossman and P. Gray (eds), *Poverty and Welfare in Ireland 1838–1948* (Dublin: Irish Academic Press, 2011), pp. 189–206. For social housing, see Virginia Crossman, *Politics, Pauperism and Power in Late Nineteenth-Century Ireland* (Manchester: Manchester University Press, 2006), pp. 144–82; and

element of a general system of health and welfare administration. The character and evolution of this system reflected both the particular circumstances of Ireland and the efforts of the British Government to counter the appeal of Irish nationalism through the promotion of social and economic development. In England the growth in state spending in the late nineteenth and early twentieth century, reflected a developing consensus around the benefits of centrally-sponsored welfare initiatives. In Ireland state spending was associated with waste and inefficiency, and widely regarded as a tardy and inadequate response to centuries of neglect and misgovernment. Despite general agreement on the evils of the workhouse system, there was little public debate on the kind of welfare system that should replace it, or how this should be financed.

One of the characteristics of the new English poor law was the creation of a new machinery of poor law government. In place of the voluntary, part-time overseers of the poor who had distributed aid under the old poor law, the new poor law was administered by a professional corps of officials including relieving officers, medical officers and workhouse officers, all appointed by and responsible to the local authority: the board of guardians.[12] At the same time a new central authority, the Poor Law Commission, was established to provide supervision and guidance. Responsibility for the Irish poor law was initially entrusted to the English Poor Law Commission to be exercised through a resident commissioner in Dublin aided by a team of assistant commissioners. Four assistant commissioners were brought over from England with further appointments being made in Ireland.[13] A separate Irish Poor Law Commission was established in 1847. This was replaced in 1872 by the Local Government Board for Ireland which assumed responsibility for all aspects of local administration. Central oversight, independent from local interests, was seen as essential to the efficient running of the new system. This was to be achieved through a system of local inspection and supervision, each assistant commissioner (or local government inspector from 1872) being responsible for a designated area.[14]

The overriding rationale of the new poor law was to establish a clear distinction between the independent labourer who supported himself and

Murray Fraser, *John Bull's Other Homes: State Housing and British Policy in Ireland, 1883–1922* (Liverpool: Liverpool University Press, 1996).

12 Crowther, *The Workhouse System* pp. 113–34.

13 Peter Gray, *The Making of the Irish Poor Law 1815–43* (Manchester: Manchester University Press, 2009), pp. 284–5.

14 Crossman, *Politics, Pauperism and Power*, pp. 16–26. For the English Local Government Board, see Christine Bellamy, *Administering Central-Local Relations, 1871–1919: The Local Government Board in its Fiscal and Cultural Context* (Manchester: Manchester University Press, 1988).

his family through waged labour, and the pauper who was dependent on handouts. This distinction is also evident in historical writing which has tended to treat workers and paupers as two distinct groups. The early history of poverty and poor relief concentrated on examining administrative provision for the poor.[15] As attention has shifted from how the poor law worked to how the poor experienced and utilised the poor law, it has become increasingly clear that poor relief was only one mechanism by which the poor obtained support, and that the division between workers and paupers was far less clearly defined than the framers of the poor law had intended or envisaged.[16] Recent studies have expanded the focus of historical enquiries to investigate local communities, exploring the various strategies adopted by poor people to provide for themselves, including growing food, gleaning, pawning items, poaching and stealing, as well as seeking help from family, friends and the community.[17]

There has been much emphasis on examining the lived experience of the poor. Pauper letters have proved a rich source for historians of the English poor law and the history of the poor in England is now told, at least in part, from the perspective of the poor.[18] It remains the case, however, that historians of poverty are forced to rely largely on sources produced by the middle classes, whether in the form of administrative records of the poor law system, court records, literary accounts or political enquiries into poverty and the problems associated with it. Such records were produced for a particular purpose and were shaped by and reflect the perceptions, assumptions and agenda of their creators. Even when the voice of the poor is heard in court records, or in giving evidence to official inquiries, it is a voice that has been transcribed and in some cases constructed. This does not make such sources invalid. All historical evidence, as Tim Hitchcock reminds us, is constructed.[19] But the historian must be alert to the process of construction and be willing to read between the lines, and against the grain.

---

15 The classic work in this genre remains, Sidney Webb and Beatrice Webb, *English Poor Law History* (London: Longmans Green, 1927–1929).

16 Hollen Lees, *The Solidarities of Strangers*; and Steven King and Alannah Tompkins (eds), *The Poor in England, 1700–1850: An Economy of Makeshifts* (Manchester: Manchester University Press, 2003).

17 See, for example, Samantha Williams, *Poverty, Gender and Life-Cycle Under the English Poor Law 1760–1834* (Woodbridge: Boydell Press, 2011).

18 For recent research on pauper narratives, see Andreas Gestrich, Elizabeth Hurren and Steven King (eds), *Poverty and Sickness in Modern Europe: Narratives of the Sick Poor 1780–1938* (London: Continuum, 2012). See also Steven King, 'Friendship, kinship and belonging in the letters of urban paupers, 1800–1840', *Historical Social Research*, xxxiii (2008), pp. 249–77; and Thomas Sokoll, *Essex Pauper Letters, 1731–1837* (Oxford: Oxford University Press, 2001).

19 Tim Hitchcock, *Down and Out in Eighteenth-Century London* (London: Hambledon,

Until recently, research on the Irish poor law system had focused almost exclusively on the framing and introduction of the 1838 Poor Relief Act and on its operation during the Great Famine.[20] Studies of poor relief in the post-Famine period were severely limited in number and scope. Works by Helen Burke, Ronald Cassell and Laurence Geary had highlighted the importance of the Famine in bringing about change, most notably in the introduction of outdoor relief and the expansion of poor law medical services, but these studies had not extended beyond 1872, leaving later developments unexplored.[21] Pioneering work by William Feingold had demonstrated that the period from 1877 to 1886 saw control of the majority of poor law boards pass from the landed elite to Irish tenant farmers.[22] Irish historians were quick to appreciate the significance of Feingold's conclusions for an understanding of nationalist politics, but they appeared largely uninterested in their implications for social history. There had, for example, been no attempt to test Feingold's theory that the rise in expenditure on outdoor relief in the later part of the nineteenth century could be linked to the rise in the number and influence of tenant guardians. It was not until my research on the politics of late nineteenth-century relief administration was published in 2006 that Feingold's work was taken forward.[23] But while my analysis of the often contentious relationship between local and central poor law authorities highlighted some aspects of local decision-making, the full range and variety of local relief practices remained unexplored.

Since research for the current study began in 2007, our knowledge and understanding of the evolution of social welfare and health care in nineteenth and early twentieth-century Ireland has advanced significantly. We know far more about the regional character of poor relief and the differences that existed between the administration and use of the poor law in large

2004), p. 234.

20 R. D. C. Black, *Economic Thought and the Irish Question 1817–70* (Cambridge: Cambridge University Press, 1960); Peter Gray, *The Making of the Irish Poor Law*; Timothy W. Guinnane and Cormac Ó Gráda, 'Mortality in the North Dublin Union during the Great Famine', *Economic History Review*, lv (2002), pp. 487–506; Christine Kinealy, *This Great Calamity: The Irish Famine 1845–52* (Dublin: Gill and Macmillan, 1994); and Gerard O'Brien, 'The Establishment of Poor-Law Unions in Ireland, 1838–43', *Irish Historical Studies*, xxiii (1982), pp. 97–121 and also 'Workhouse Management in Pre-Famine Ireland', *Proceedings of the Royal Irish Academy*, 86C (1986), pp. 113–34.

21 Helen Burke, *The People and the Poor Law in Nineteenth Century Ireland* (Littlehampton: Women's Education Bureau, 1987); Cassell, *Medical Charities, Medical Politics*; and Laurence M. Geary, *Medicine and Charity in Ireland 1718–1851* (Dublin: UCD Press, 2004).

22 William L. Feingold, *The Revolt of the Tenantry: The Transformation of Local Government in Ireland 1872–1886* (Boston, MA: Northeastern University Press, 1984).

23 Crossman, *Politics, Pauperism and Power*.

urban unions, such as Belfast and the two Dublin Unions (North Dublin and South Dublin), as compared to predominantly rural unions. By the end of the nineteenth century, a large proportion of inmates of provincial workhouses were casual, peripatetic visitors who stayed for a single night. Longer-term residents comprised mainly children, the elderly and the sick, and infirm. In the major cities where substantial numbers of people existed on the margins of economic independence, workhouses were more closely integrated into the local landscape of poverty and welfare providing a regular resource for people affected by temporary want.[24] We have a clearer idea of the structures of poor relief and medical relief, and the challenges facing poor law medical officers.[25] We also have a good understanding of particular aspects of the poor law system, such as the care of children. The boarding-out system whereby children could be removed from the workhouse and supported in a domestic environment, has attracted particular attention. The motivation and aspirations of reformers and professionals have been scrutinised, and the practical impact of the policy explored.[26] Many issues remain unresolved however, including basic questions concerning how the relief system operated.

This study is an attempt to answer those questions. It is not a history of the poor law.[27] It is an extended reflection on the understandings of poverty in Ireland and how these influenced relief practices. Exploring relief as a process, it is based largely on records produced by poor law adminis-

24 Georgina Laragy, 'Poor Relief in the South of Ireland 1850–1921', in Crossman and Gray (eds), *Poverty and Welfare in Ireland 1838–1948* (Dublin: Irish Academic Press, 2011), pp. 53–66; D. S. Lucey, 'Poor Relief in the West of Ireland 1861–1911', in Crossman and Gray (eds), *Poverty and Welfare in Ireland 1838–1948* (Dublin: Irish Academic Press, 2011), pp. 37–52; and Olwen Purdue, 'Poor Relief in the North of Ireland 1850–1921', in Crossman and Gray (eds), *Poverty and Welfare in Ireland 1838–1948* (Dublin: Irish Academic Press, 2011), pp. 23–36.

25 Catherine Cox, 'Medical Dispensary Service in Nineteenth-Century Ireland: Access, Transport and Distance', in Catherine Cox and Maria Luddy (eds), *Cultures of Care in Irish Medical History, 1750–1970* (Basingstoke, Palgrave Macmillan, 2010), pp. 57–78; and Geary, 'The Medical Profession, Health Care and the Poor Law'.

26 Anna Clark, 'Orphans and the Poor Law: Rage against the Machine', in Crossman and Gray (eds), *Poverty and Welfare in Ireland*, pp. 97–114; Virginia Crossman, 'Cribbed, Contained and Confined? The Care of Children Under the Irish Poor Law 1850–1920', *Eire-Ireland* (spring/summer 2009), pp. 37–61; and Caroline Skehill, 'The Origins of Child Welfare under the Poor Law and the Emergence of the Institutional versus Family Care Debate', Crossman and Gray (eds), *Poverty and Welfare in Ireland*, pp. 115–26.

27 There are now a number of short but comprehensive histories of the Irish poor law available and I do not intend to repeat that material here. See Crossman, *The Poor Law in Ireland*; Crossman, *Politics, Pauperism and Power*, pp. 6–35; and Crossman and Gray (eds), *Poverty and Welfare in Ireland 1838–1948* (Dublin: Irish Academic Press, 2011), pp. 1–20.

trators. As the scope and functions of the poor law became more extensive, so the process of central information gathering and monitoring became more elaborate and complex. Local officials were required to complete a bewildering number of forms and returns. A workhouse master, for example, was required to keep fourteen different registers or account books including the workhouse admission register; an admission and discharge book; a record of births and deaths; a weekly relief list; a provision check account; a provision receipt and consumption account; a clothing materials book; a clothing receipt and appropriation book; an inventory book; and a labour book.[28] These records were intended to provide an accurate and comprehensive account of the operation of every aspect of the poor law system, as well as a record of the central-local relations. By amassing this material the central authorities hoped to monitor what was happening throughout the country, assess the effectiveness of the system and measure the impact of changes and reforms. In reality, the appearance of comprehensiveness was always an illusion. As Ann Laura Stoler has observed, 'the seemingly panoptic glare of a vacuous stylized official gaze' is a 'fragile conceit'. The 'ethnographic space of the archive' she argues:

> resides in the disjuncture between prescription and practice, between state mandates and the maneuvers people made in response to them, between normative rules and how people actually lived their lives.[29]

Returns were completed and statistics compiled, but it was impossible to ensure uniformity in the way the information was recorded.

The records for one poor law union often bear only a superficial resemblance to those of another. Workhouse admission registers share a basic format but their contents can vary widely depending on the diligence of the workhouse master or his assistant. In some cases information was entered only in the most cursory manner and in others omitted altogether. The impact of such local idiosyncrasies is compounded by the uneven survival rate of poor law records. For many parts of the country the only records that survive are the minute books of boards of guardians. All other records, such as admission and discharge registers, relief lists, diet lists, punishment books, report books, accounts and letter books, having been destroyed. However, rather than lament the records that have been lost, it is important

28 General Order dated 8th April, 1853 for Regulating the Keeping and Auditing of Accounts and Prescribing Forms of Accounts to be Kept by Officers of Unions, in Thomas A. Mooney, *Compendium of the Irish Poor Law* (Dublin: Alex, Thom and Co., 1887), pp. 316–19.
29 Ann Laura Stoler, *Along the Archival Grain: Epistemic Anxieties and Colonial Common Sense* (Princeton NJ: Princeton University Press, 2009), pp. 23, 32.

to recognise the potential of those that have survived. Minute books, which were kept by the clerk of the union, contain notes on the proceedings of the board of guardians, together with officers' reports and a summary record of correspondence sent and received. They also contain tabular statements showing the number of people admitted to and remaining in the workhouse at the end of the week in which the board meeting was held and the number in receipt of outdoor relief. The figures for workhouse inmates are broken down by age, sex and infirmity. It is therefore possible to chart the changing population of the workhouse and to identify seasonal, as well as more long-term relief patterns.

Poor law records reflect the bureaucratic nature of the poor law system which recognised neither individuality nor personal circumstances. Nevertheless, poor law officials were required to reconcile lived experience with regulatory classification on a daily basis, struggling to make the variety of personal experience they encountered fit into the limited range of categories they were allowed to recognise. Compiled by the administrators of relief, poor law records are often assumed to present a one-dimensional account; a story from which the experience and perspective of the poor is excluded. But this is not the case. The voices of the poor are faint, but they are not absent. They make themselves heard through letters to relief committees and boards of guardians, comments to relieving officers and evidence given to official inquiries. Such material provides an insight not only into the lives of poor people, but also into the ways in which they sought to establish a claim to assistance. As we shall see, the records reveal the poor to have been active agents of their fate making calculated choices about how, when and where to apply for aid.

One of the problems facing any poor law historian is how to integrate the local and national. Until now, the historian of the Irish poor law has been forced either to focus on a particular poor law union, and run the risk of generalising from a very narrow base, or to adopt a generalised approach that glosses over local differences. It was not feasible for one historian to encompass the whole country.[30] This study breaks new ground by combining a national and a local perspective, both of which are securely rooted in extensive archival research. This was made possible by substantial project funding from the Economic and Social Research Council which provided for a team of researchers who mined the national and local archives to produce an indispensable body of datasets.[31] These include a database of

30 Mel Cousins makes a valiant, but ultimately unsuccessful, attempt to do this in *Poor Relief in Ireland 1851–1914* (Bern: Peter Lang, 2011). This work exemplifies the dangers of attempting a national survey from an inadequate research base.
31 The datasets have been deposited in the UK Data Archive.

annual poor law statistics for every poor law union in the country for the period 1850–1914. This provided the basis for a detailed, comprehensive analysis of national and regional trends in relief provision and expenditure. At the local level, thirteen poor law unions were selected as case studies: Ballycastle; Ballymoney; Belfast; Clogher; Cork; Glenties; Kilmallock; Kinsale; Mountmellick; North Dublin; Thurles; Tralee; and Westport. The aim was to provide a broadly representative sample embracing a range of characteristics – urban, rural, industrial, agricultural, core and periphery – from different parts of the country.

The final selection of case-study unions was determined by the availability of source material. Thurles and Kinsale were chosen, for example, as they are virtually the only unions in the far south of the country for which workhouse admission registers are available. Admission registers contain the details of every person admitted to or born in the workhouse. Analysis of this data can reveal patterns of usage, showing how people moved in and out of workhouses on a regular basis, as well as providing important insights into the operation of familial and social networks among the poor. The nature of the sources also determined the research methods used for different poor law unions. Where workhouse admission registers were available, details of all admissions in as many census years as possible were recorded on Excel databases.[32] Where workhouse admission registers were unavailable, the weekly number in receipt of relief, broken down by age and sex, was extracted from the minute books of the board of guardians, together with other relevant information. Local newspapers were consulted for reports of board meetings. The resulting data was analysed to explicate national trends, and to identify local and regional variations in the provision and utilisation of poor relief. This book is a distillation of that material. It does not claim to be definitive, but it does provide a fuller, deeper and more wide-ranging assessment of the Irish poor law than any study previously undertaken. As such, it represents a major milestone in Irish economic and social history.

The analysis that follows becomes progressively more tightly focused as it proceeds. The opening chapters provide a conceptual and analytical context for the more detailed discussion of relief practices that make up the remainder of the book. Chapter 1 examines concepts and understandings of poverty in Ireland, while Chapter 2 provides an overview of and proposes an explanation for national and local trends in poor relief and expenditure.

32 Unions with admission registers were Ballycastle; Ballymoney; Belfast; Clogher; Cork; Glenties; Kinsale; North Dublin; and Thurles. All entries for the administrative year (1 October to 30 September) were entered. The registers for Belfast, Cork and North Dublin 1900–1901 were sampled as the number of admissions made it impractical to enter the details for every inmate for the entire year. For a note on statistics and sources see below, pp. 230–34.

Chapters 3 and 4 explore the nature and operation of the relief system, examining firstly outdoor relief, relief provided outside the workhouse and then indoor relief, also known as workhouse relief. The Irish poor law as first introduced in 1838 made no provision for outdoor relief. The only relief available was within the workhouse. By the later decades of the nineteenth century, however, outdoor relief had come to form a significant element of the system. From the 1880s, only a minority of people receiving relief were required to enter the workhouse; most received relief in their homes. Any investigation of the relief system as a whole must, therefore, start with an analysis of outdoor relief. The institution of the workhouse, its function and operation, is the subject of Chapter 4. How people entered the workhouse is examined and the factors that determined how long they remained. The final three chapters focus on particular groups within the workhouse population. Chapter 5 assesses provision for the sick and infirm, and lunatics, and charts the increasing medicalisation of the workhouse in Ireland in the late nineteenth and early twentieth century. Chapters 6 and 7 investigate the reception and treatment of unmarried mothers, prostitutes and vagrants, and consider the ways in which those on the margins of Irish society utilised the poor law system. The aim throughout is to integrate analysis of contemporary understandings of poverty and welfare with evaluation of local relief practices, exploring the attitudes and responses of those both giving and receiving relief, and the active relationship between them. In so doing, the book provides a new interpretative framework for conceptualising and understanding the Irish poor law, and the society that produced it.

1

Concepts of Poverty and Poor Relief

Pre-Famine Ireland was a country seemingly defined by poverty.[1] The condition of the people shocked travellers and reinforced a sense of a place that was separate, different and foreign, not an integral part of the United Kingdom. Writing in the late 1830s, French social and political commentator, Gustave de Beaumont remarked that misery, 'naked and famishing', was evident 'everywhere, and at every hour of the day, it is the first thing you see when you land on the Irish coast, and from that moment it ceases not to be present to your view'. Irish poverty, de Beaumont asserted, had 'a special and exceptional character, which ... can be compared with no other indigence. Irish misery forms a type by itself, of which neither the model nor the imitation can be found anywhere else.'[2] To British observers, poverty in Ireland was a product and a reflection of the backwardness of the country and the character of the people. The poor were represented almost as a different race, closer to savages than to civilised people. Furthermore, as Glen Hooper has observed, while the poor in England were described as being part of British society and British life, the poor in Ireland were 'an ethnologically intriguing, but frequently detached community separated from the upper classes not just on social but on religious, cultural and sometimes linguistic grounds'.[3] The mass of the Irish people seemed to occupy a space outside civilised society.

Post-Famine Ireland seemed like a different country. Death and emigration had removed so many people that in many districts the countryside appeared deserted. The impression now conveyed to travellers was of a virgin land

---

1 For a discussion of the 'semeiotics' of Irish poverty, see William H. A. Williams, *Tourism, Landscape, and the Irish Character: British Travel Writers in Pre-Famine Ireland* (Madison, Wisconsin: University of Wisconsin Press, 2008), pp. 80–104.

2 Gustave de Beaumont, *Ireland: Social, Political and Religious*, edited and translated by W. C. Taylor, with an introduction by Tom Garvin and Andreas Hess (London: Belknap Press, 2006), pp. 128, 130.

3 Glenn Hooper, *Travel Writing and Ireland, 1760–1860 Culture History, Politics* (Basingstoke: Palgrave Macmillan, 2005), p. 127.

ripe for development.[4] The poor had not disappeared completely but they were less numerous and less visible. Irish society remained deeply divided. Community leaders, politicians and churchmen aligned themselves with the poor and pledged to advance their interests condemning the impoverishment of Ireland by rapacious landlords and the sufferings of the Irish tenant. Living standards improved, but Irish tenants felt poor in relation to their landlords. From being a condition of the entire population, extreme poverty was now mainly confined to the far west of the country, and to the major cities. Where previously visitors had expressed disbelief at the extent of poverty, they now expressed disbelief about its existence, often doubting whether the distress they encountered was genuine. An Irish landowner, George Hill, for example wrote to the London *Times* in 1880 denying reports of extreme distress in the far west of Ireland and claiming that smallholders had fooled philanthropist James Hack Tuke, amongst others, by hiding their possessions in order to appear poorer. The people, he maintained, were 'consummate actors and impostors'.[5]

When visiting Gweedore in County Donegal in the mid-1880s, The American, William Hurlbert, was pleasantly surprised to find little genuine distress. 'What distress there was in Gweedore', he declared, was due 'much more to the habits the people have been getting into of late years, and to the idleness of them, as to any pressure of the rents you hear about, or even to the poverty of the soil.' Having found the stone cabins he entered to be warm and comfortable, and greatly preferable to wooden cabins in the United States, he concluded that 'a great deal of not wholly innocuous nonsense has been written and spoken' about Ireland by 'well-meaning philanthropists' who had 'gauged the condition of the people here by their own standards of comfort and enjoyment'.[6] These comments were a reaction to the politicisation of Irish poverty during the period of the Land War. Distress had been the impetus and the backdrop for the land campaign and remained the subtext for much nationalist rhetoric. The Irish people, it was claimed, were poor because they were oppressed politically and economically. Divergent views of the causes of poverty reflected and reinforced a fundamental divide in Irish politics and society between those who saw the poor as innocent victims of the British imperial enterprise and those who saw them as agents of their own misfortune whose willingness to abuse any relief system made them almost impossible to help.

4 Hooper, *Travel Writing and Ireland*, p. 145.
5 Sara Smyth, 'Tuke's Connemara Album', in Ciara Breathnach (ed.), *Framing the West: Images of Rural Ireland 1891–1920* (Dublin: Irish Academic Press, 2007), p. 127.
6 William H. Hurlbert, *Ireland Under Coercion: The Diary of an American* (Edinburgh: David Douglas, 1888), pp 91–2, 103.

Historians of the new poor law in England have traced the ways in which attitudes to and interpretations of poverty changed over the course of the late nineteenth and early twentieth century.[7] The assumptions that lay behind the new poor law, that the poor were responsible for their own circumstances and that opportunities for improvement were available to all who sought them, increasingly gave way to more objective, evidence-based interpretations which stressed the importance of structural factors, such as population growth and unemployment, low wages and lack of education. Accounts of the poor became less anecdotal and more 'scientific', reflecting a growing interest in statistics and social surveys which sought to provide an objective basis on which to formulate policy. Social investigation techniques provided what appeared to be hard facts to support the structural interpretation of poverty, enabling investigators to distinguish between different types of poverty and to begin to quantify these in terms of income and expenditure. Poverty came to be seen not as a static, permanent condition but as a permeable, relative state. Social surveys revealed the crucial role of familial and life cycle factors, demonstrating that people became poor because the family lost a bread winner through death or illness, or old age and that many families relied on wages that were irregular and often insufficient to provide for the size of the family, particularly where there were young children.

It was perfectly possible however, to advance a structural interpretation of poverty whilst holding behaviourist views. Recent work by John Welshman and Katherine Callanan Martin has emphasised that all poverty theorists of the period fell back on behaviour to explain certain aspects of poverty.[8] Thus, Charles Booth developed the idea of a 'residuum mentality' that kept people in the poorest classes dependent on casual, irregular work, while Joseph Rowntree distinguished between primary poverty, which was structural, affecting families whose total earnings were insufficient to provide food and other essentials; and secondary poverty, which was generally behavioural caused by drink, betting, gambling and improvidence, affecting families whose incomes were technically sufficient were it not for a portion being absorbed by other expenditure. But if the rise of structural

---

7 See, for example, Anthony Brundage, *The English Poor Laws, 1700–1930* (Basingstoke: Palgrave, 2002; Alan Kidd, *State, Society and the Poor in Nineteenth-Century England* (Basingstoke: Macmillan, 1999)); and Lynn Hollen Lees, *The Solidarities of Strangers: The English Poor Laws and the People, 1700–1948* (Cambridge: Cambridge University Press, 1998).

8 Kathleen Callanan Martin, *Hard and Unreal Advice: Mothers, Social Science and the Victorian Poverty Experts* (Basingstoke: Palgrave Macmillan, 2008); and John Welshman, *Underclass: A History of the Excluded, 1880–2000* (London: Hambledon Continuum, 2006).

interpretations of poverty failed to supersede behaviourist accounts, they did strengthen the case for targeting assistance to different categories of poor people. People whose poverty was essentially structural, it was argued, could safely be given assistance in their own homes, while those who were poor because of their behaviour and possibly their genetic inheritance could be dealt with by more punitive measures, such as labour colonies.

A growing awareness of structural factors did little to undermine the conviction that the key to understanding Irish poverty lay not in the Irish economy but in the Irish character. The confusion between cause and effect, which Callanan Martin sees as a legacy of social science fascination with facts and statistics, is characteristic of much contemporary writing on Irish poverty.[9] This is particularly evident in discussions of the relationship between drink and poverty. William O'Hanlon, who spent five years in Belfast in the early 1850s as minister of the Congregationalist Church in upper Donegall Street, produced an account of the condition of the poor in Belfast, in which he traced the roots of much poverty and deprivation to drink. He recounted entering a house occupied by a man and his son in full employment as shoemakers who admitted that they spent all their wages in the public house. The proof, O'Hanlon noted, 'lay in the bare, furnitureless room'. Whilst acknowledging structural factors, such as irregular employment, O'Hanlon maintained that it was behavioural factors that made the difference between poverty and pauperism, 'The truth is that not only work is needed, but the spirit and disposition to do it. Idleness is, after all, one of the fearfully begetting sins of the Irish poor.'[10] Fifty years later, the journalist, Robert Sherard, attributed much of the deprivation and attendant social problems he encountered in cities throughout the United Kingdom to the effects of drink. 'That there was much poverty and distress in Belfast,' he observed, 'few can deny ... Many told me drink was the cause of the trouble here also.' He did however acknowledge alternative viewpoints noting that Belfast town councillor, Alexander Taylor, maintained that it was poverty that drove people to drink rather than the other way around and that higher wages would mean less poverty. Taylor claimed that there were six main causes of the high death rate among the poor in Belfast: improper food; insufficient clothing; impure air; damp, cold houses; hard work; and intemperance.[11]

Within the administrative elite, evidence-based analysis coexisted with

---

9 Callanan Martin, *Hard and Unreal Advice*, p. 176.
10 W. M. O'Hanlon, *Walks Among the Poor of Belfast and Suggestions for their Improvement, Belfast 1853, republished with a forward by Andrew Boyd* (Menston: Scolar Press, 1971), pp. 8–9.
11 Robert H. Sherard, *The Cry of the Poor* (London: Digby, Long and Co., 1901), pp. 102, 104. For an assessment of the importance of drink as a contributory factor in poverty

behaviourist assumptions. Drawn from the landed gentry and the professions poor law inspectors, the senior officials in the field, were largely Protestant by religion and conservative in their views, a fact that did not go unnoticed by critics of the poor law system. In 1861, *The Nation* published details of the central poor law establishment in Ireland noting that of thirteen inspectors, nine were Protestant and only four Catholic.[12] By the first decade of the twentieth century, the balance had improved with six Protestants and three Catholics, but the disparity remained a cause of grievance that, according to John Redmond, was undermining public confidence in the Local Government Board.[13] Attitudes within the inspectorate were shaped by the ideology of class and by the principles of the new poor law. Inspectors adhered to a strict distinction between poverty and destitution, and between poverty and pauperism, regarding the workhouse test as the only effective means of identifying the truly destitute, and thus putting an effective check on excessive demands for relief. Reporting from Belmullet in County Mayo in May 1860, Richard Bourke noted that there were many families 'utterly without means', who were nevertheless refusing to enter the workhouse fearing that if they did so, they would 'become paupers for life, and in most cases they will die sooner than adopt such a course'. This, Bourke maintained, demonstrated the importance of having spare workhouse accommodation available. Had the spare accommodation in Belmullet been appropriated for other uses, the board of guardians would have been forced to resort to a system of outdoor relief. This would have been as:

difficult to restrain or regulate now as in 1847–8 ... It is not in the province of a Poor Law to meet more than the absolute destitution created by the vicissitudes of seasons or other visitation, but it is only by the maintenance of abundant workhouse accommodation available for such contingencies (and see how easily they arise) that this relief can be safely administered.[14]

Inspectors shared the assumptions and prejudices of their class, including a tendency to regard the poor as an alien species. Defending the management of workhouses in the west, in the closing stages of the Famine, a number of inspectors sought to blame workhouse inmates for poor conditions. If

in Dublin, see Mary E. Daly, *Dublin – The Deposed Capital: A Social and Economic History 1860–1914* (Cork: Cork University Press, 1984), pp. 81–3.
12 *The Nation*, 27 April 1861.
13 *Light on the Local Government Board*, National Library of Ireland (hereafter NLI), undated pamphlet; Redmond to Balfour, 26 April 1898, Balfour Papers, National Archives, PRO 30/60/15. See Crossman, *Politics, Pauperism and Power*, pp. 21–2.
14 Report on distress in Belmullet Union, 3 May 1860, Larcom Papers, NLI, MS 7783.

workhouses were dirty and disorderly it was because the people in them were dirty and disorderly, not because they were badly managed. J. Hall, the temporary inspector for Galway Union insisted that 'the greatest obstacle' to good management was to be found:

> in the paupers themselves ... I have seen many take their discharge in preference to putting on Union clothing; I have seen others go away, sooner than submit to be washed. Being deprived of the free use of tobacco has caused the departure of several; and some leave the house in consequence of being obliged to go to bed and get up at a regular hour.

William Clarke, who had been responsible for Ballinasloe Union, argued that it was misleading to compare Irish workhouses to those in England where the circumstances, social relations and the character of the people were totally different. 'The standard of comparison in judging of personal comfort in workhouses', he maintained, 'is the state in which the class of persons generally applying for relief existed previous to admission. Irish workhouses, with all their imperfections, afford a desirable change from the squalid misery which characterises the cottier class in the West of Ireland.' Bourke, whose district included Gort and Clifden Unions, insisted that sanitary arrangements were basic but adequate. He acknowledged that 'to very fastidious persons, a greater degree of seclusion and privacy might seem desirable', but explained that:

> the class of persons with whom the guardians have to deal, are the very persons among whom such refinement would be least appreciated and most abused. The poor in the West of Ireland are totally unacquainted with the ordinary conveniences of civilised life; and the greatest impediment to decorum and cleanliness in these matters arises from their own habits.

In stressing the difficulty of the task facing poor law guardians, he revealed where his sympathies primarily lay. Guardians, he explained:

> had to contend with an enormous amount of real destitution, resulting from famine on the one hand, and the grossest imposition attempting to take advantage of it on the other. They had to struggle with deficient resources, and had to deal with people in a state of ignorance as almost to amount to barbarism.[15]

---

15 *Copies of the correspondence between the Poor Law Commissioners of Ireland and their*

Inspectors were well informed about the immediate causes and consequences of poverty but their judgements were frequently based more on subjective assumptions than objective facts. Indeed, they often found it difficult to reconcile empirical evidence with their own prejudices. In 1859 inspectors were requested to supply detailed information about the diet of the poorer classes in the districts for which they were responsible. In their responses many commented on the generally healthy appearance of the people. William Hamilton, the inspector for the southeast, attributed the improved state of the people to the availability of employment and of cheap, abundant food, although he admitted that even in these more favourable conditions, 'where the family is large I cannot even now either explain or comprehend how they are provided with anything beyond food'. Bourke noted that it was 'difficult to conceive how, without some additional resource', many household heads were able to 'procure all the needs of life even of the commonest kind'. He proceeded to blame the conditions of many poor families on inept household management despite the clear evidence of skilful budgeting. 'The typical poor housewife', he declared, 'did not possess the skill in household management requisite for making small means go as far as possible.' Moreover, she was under no pressure to learn as:

> the Irish peasant seems to have no appreciation of comfort, and inured from early youth to long fasts and frequent deficiency of food, he grows up careless of what he eats, and capable of undergoing without inconvenience long periods of abstinence.[16]

From Bourke's essentialist viewpoint, the hardships experienced by the poor were evidence not of endurance but of limited sensibility.

Such attitudes prevailed despite detailed factual knowledge. Officials were aware, for example, that the poor were not a homogeneous group and that the local economy shaped social categories as well as household economy and diet. Reporting on the diet of the labouring classes in 1859, Henry Robinson, then an inspector of unions in the northeast, noted that people in his district

---

Inspectors, relative to... a book entitled 'Gleanings in the West of Ireland', House of Commons Parliamentary Papers (hereafter HC), 1851 (218), pp. 5, 16, 25, 28.

16 Report on the Subject of Workhouse Dietaries and the Dietary of the Labouring Poor in Ireland, *Annual Report of the Commissioners for Administering the Laws for the relief of the Poor in Ireland*, HC, 1860 [2654], pp. 67, 47. Bourke's 'colonialist' attitudes may have been acquired from his father, Sir Richard Bourke, who was Governor-General of New South Wales 1831–1838. His son, Edmund Bourke, was appointed a Local Government Board inspector in 1886. See Fergus Campbell, *The Irish Establishment 1879–1914* (Oxford: Oxford University Press, 2009), p. 87; and Crossman, *Politics, Pauperism and Power*, p. 21.

could be divided into three classes: those supporting themselves entirely by agricultural labour; labourers with family members engaged in weaving; and those who maintained themselves by weaving. The weavers were generally in the best circumstances, but only when trade was good. Their diet, he noted, 'both in quantity and description, is much more variable, as their income is more fluctuating'. Information provided for the same dietary survey by the relieving officer for Mullingar Union, Francis Kerr, referred to class one and class two families, the first being on the verge of destitution, while the second were slightly better off, and included tradesmen and labourers in regular employment. A family in class one that lost employment would be tipped into destitution. The key elements differentiating a class one from a class two family was the regularity of employment of the head of the household and the extent to which other members of the family were earning. According to Kerr, better off families could avoid the workhouse even if the head lost employment because other members of the family were earning. Nicholas Kelly, relieving officer of Drogheda Union, also distinguished between families able to remain independent and those who became a burden on the rates. He noted that labourers in regular employment with access to land on which to grow potatoes 'never apply for admission to the workhouse except by [reason of] severe sickness'. Other families moved between independence and reliance on poor relief. Where the head of the household was not in regular employment the family was liable to fall into destitution. Kelly cited one case where a man was:

> employed at nine shillings per week but is not constantly engaged; he is the same as the last case, totally destitute when a few weeks idle; he deserts his wife and children who then become a burden in the workhouse.[17]

Whilst clearly aware of the structural causes, and consequences, of poverty officials still applied strict moral criteria. Regularity of employment was understood to be a crucial factor in explaining poverty, but the reasons why someone was not regularly employed were assumed to be behavioural. Either they were not looking hard enough or they were too lazy to hold down a steady job.

Analysing the domestic economy of the Dublin poor in 1904, Sir Charles Cameron, Medical Officer of Health for Dublin, was careful to avoid blaming the poor for their poverty arguing that the attraction of the public house to a poor man was understandable, 'His home is rarely a comfortable one, and in winter the bright light, the warm fire and the gaiety of the public-house

17 *Report on the Subject of Workhouse Dietaries*, pp. 31, 56–7, 59–60.

are attractions which he finds it difficult to resist.' He questioned whether a poor man spending a reasonable proportion of his earnings there was more reprehensible than 'the prosperous shopkeeper or professional man who drinks expensive wines at the club or the restaurant'. He did acknowledge, however, that there was 'too much intemperance amongst the working classes', and that women, 'who formerly were rarely seen intoxicated, are now frequently to be observed in that state'.[18] Poverty, in Cameron's view, did not excuse people from taking responsibility for their lives and the conditions in which they lived. Rejecting a call for stricter enforcement of sanitary regulations in Dublin, Cameron insisted that the defective state of many Dublin tenements was not due to any failure to enforce the sanitary laws. 'If they had not been enforced', he observed, 'the state of many of these houses would be incomparably worse than is now the case.' The real problem was the difficulty of 'reforming the filthy habits of the adult persons who inhabit the tenement houses. The bad condition of the tenements is nearly altogether due to these filthy habits.' By adult persons he primarily meant women. It was, he declared:

> the duty of mothers to bring up their children in habits of cleanliness, but in Dublin this obvious duty is neglected. In my opinion the tenement houses will never become healthful dwellings solely by the action of the Public Health Authorities. The people must co-operate with the Authorities.[19]

If they failed to do so, they could hardly complain about their environment.

An overtly moralistic view of poverty, together with more discriminatory forms of poor relief, has been associated with Protestantism, and particularly evangelical Protestantism.[20] Central to this view was the concept of temptation. Poverty theorists, Callanan Martin notes, 'demonstrate a strong if unconscious belief that idleness and vice are so tempting as to negate the desire for family life, normal comforts, and decency among the poor'.[21] The importance of religious ideas and imagery in late nineteenth-

18   Sir Charles A. Cameron, *How the Poor Live* (Dublin: John Falconer, 1904), pp. 19–20; and Lydia Carroll, *In the Fever King's Preserves: Sir Charles Cameron and the Dublin Slums* (Dublin: A. and A. Farmar, 2011).

19   Cameron to Secretary of the LGB, 19 March 1897, Chief Secretary's Office Registered Papers (hereafter CSORP), National Archives of Ireland (hereafter NAI), 1897/4319. For an analysis of the assumed moral deficiencies of the slum mother, see Callanan Martin, *Hard and Unreal Advice*, pp. 134–58.

20   Callanan Martin, *Hard and Unreal Advice*, pp. 24–6. See also Brundage, *The English Poor Laws*, pp. 37–9; and Kidd, *State, Society and the Poor*, pp. 71–4.

21   Callanan Martin, *Hard and Unreal Advice*, p. 42.

century discussions of poverty can hardly be understated. Religious teaching shaped societal perceptions of and thus responses to poverty. Clergymen of all religious denominations acted as conduits of poor relief and as spokesmen of the poor, soliciting aid and organising and distributing relief. Religious faith and religious divisions had a profound impact on the organisation and administration of both private charity and public welfare. Fear of proselytism within Protestant-run charitable organisations was a major concern within the Catholic Church; this helps to explain the almost totally segregated nature of philanthropy in Ireland.[22] Writing in 1884, the philanthropist, Rosa Barrett, lamented the 'wasteful overlapping of certain [Dublin] charities ... and the possibility that exists at present of one person getting relief from several societies, while whole classes of others, equally needy, are entirely overlooked'.[23] While the Catholic hierarchy was prepared to cooperate with state initiatives, such as the creation of the national school system, they did so reluctantly and would have much preferred all welfare institutions catering for Catholics to be under clerical control, devoting much time and resources to the establishment of a range of charitable institutions for vulnerable groups, such as children, the sick and disabled, and 'fallen' women.

The belief that Protestants and Catholics in Ireland had different approaches to charity is long-standing and still widely held. The 'Protestant moralist', T. P. O'Neill observed, 'believed that all charity had to be carefully examined to ensure that it did not create a new class of beggars or endanger the economic framework'. The Irish poor, on the other hand, 'had different values and held different notions about charity. They regarded charity as a duty for the donor and all beggars were recognised as objects worthy of help.'[24] This view echoed that of nineteenth-century commentators who claimed the Irish people were against the workhouse system and in favour of almsgiving. Entering the workhouse was regarded as disgraceful, even though no shame was attached to accepting private charity or begging. But while Catholic teaching stressed the duty of charity, it did not advocate indiscriminate alms giving. The first president of the St Vincent de Paul Society warned members not to be 'content to dole out alms' but to identify suitable recipients and 'in all cases help them to help themselves'.[25] Even poor

22 Maria Luddy, *Women and Philanthropy in Nineteenth-Century Ireland* (Cambridge: Cambridge University Press, 1995).

23 R. M. Barrett, *Guide to Dublin Charities* (Dublin: Hodges, Figgis and Co., 1884), pp. v, 78. For similar comments made almost twenty years later, see, G. D. Williams, *Dublin Charities* (Dublin: John Falconer, 1902), pp. 1–2.

24 T. P. O'Neill, 'The Catholic Church and the Relief of the Poor', *Archivium Hibernicum*, xxi (1973), p. 134.

25 Report of St Vincent de Paul Society (1913), cited in Alison Jordan, *Who Cared? Charity in Victorian and Edwardian Belfast* (Belfast: Institute of Irish Studies, n.d.), p. 198.

people, as Niall Ó Ciosáin has shown, drew a distinction between genuine and fraudulent beggars.[26] Concepts such as the deserving and undeserving poor were common to all religions and all classes. Where they differed was in their understanding of the place of the poor in society and the role of charity.[27]

Poverty and a sense of victimhood, Marianne Elliott observes, came to define a particular strand of Irish Catholic culture. Rooted in a sense of oppression and persecution, and drawing on the privileged place afforded to the poor within Catholic teaching, the assumed sufferings of the Irish people, past and present, were believed to give Irish Catholicism 'a unique and superior quality'. Reacting against Protestant critiques which blamed Ireland's lack of development on the character of the Irish people and the malign influence of the Catholic Church, which was believed to discourage individualism and entrepreneurship, Catholics embraced the idea of the virtuous poor. Catholic priestly writing, she observes, promoted the view 'not only that Catholicism is a religion of the poor, but that social progress and education might endanger its essential characteristics and make people less receptive to Church teachings'.[28] While he was critical of the British state for failing to relieve poverty in Ireland, Archbishop (later Cardinal) Paul Cullen regarded the wealth of Britain as a mixed blessing, believing the British to be obsessed with material rather than spiritual advancement. As he wrote to a colleague in 1857, the 'over anxiety of England to make money will some day or other bring on great ruin; whilst the poverty of Ireland may be her salvation'.[29]

'Such sanctification of poverty and endurance', as Elliott acutely notes, influenced attitudes towards welfare. The Catholic poor felt, and were encouraged to feel, shame at seeking and receiving charity.[30] Confident that suffering on earth would be rewarded in heaven, Catholic clergy believed the virtuous poor to be those most reluctant to seek assistance. The act of entering a workhouse became an admission not only of failure, but also of unworthiness. A dominant theme within Catholic culture was the idea that the virtuous poor would endure almost any privation rather than enter the workhouse. It was, according to Cullen, 'the greatest insult you can offer to

26 Niall Ó Ciosáin, 'Boccoughs and God's Poor: Deserving and Undeserving Poor in Irish Popular Culture', in Tadhg Foley and Sean Ryder (eds), *Ideology and Ireland in the Nineteenth Century* (Dublin: Four Courts Press, 1998), pp. 93–99.
27 See Larry Frohman, *Poor Relief and Welfare in Germany from the Reformation to World War I* (Cambridge: Cambridge University Press, 2008), pp 24–31.
28 Marianne Elliott, *When God Took Sides: Religion and Identity in Ireland – Unfinished History* (Oxford: Oxford University Press, 2009), pp. 180, 186–7.
29 Cullen to Tobias Kirby, 6 December 1857, Irish College Rome, New Kirby Papers, Carton II, Folder II, 52. I am grateful to Colin Barr for providing me with copies of Cullen's correspondence.
30 Elliott, *When God Took Sides*, p. 188.

a decent poor person in Dublin to ask him to go into the workhouse'. They 'would rather die of starvation than go there'. As he explained to a parliamentary select committee in 1861, the poor were essentially honest. They did:

> everything in their power to assist one another; to a great extent, the poor support the poor in Ireland ... I think there is no great inclination to take relief; I think the people are rather too proud in that respect.

People whose behaviour contributed to or exacerbated their poverty were a different matter however. In itself, Cullen maintained, poverty was 'most honourable', but it was important to 'look to the occasion of it'. When brought on by 'profligate courses', poverty required correction not alleviation.[31] Writing to a colleague in 1872, Cullen contrasted the character of poverty in urban and rural areas of Ireland. Whereas in the country 'the poor people are well to do', in Dublin, he observed, 'the drinking reduces them to rags. In the city too we have a great many strikes which also impoverish the poor.'[32] By describing the rural poor as being 'well to do', Cullen appears to have meant not that they were well off but that they were able to maintain an outward appearance of respectability, unlike the urban poor who were more obviously impoverished. While pressing for a more extensive system of outdoor relief, he made it clear that such relief should be carefully targeted. It should not be given to:

> a drunkard, or a man who had led a reckless profligate life ... I would also exclude such as are able, but unwilling to work, and all vagrants and sturdy beggars. I would not give out-door relief except in cases where giving it would bring about the re-establishment of the person in his situation in life in a short time again, or where a person had led such as life that he was not deserving to be thrust into a workhouse.[33]

Cullen's diocesan clergy shared his views on poverty, combining a deep

---

31 *Report from the Select Committee Appointed to Inquire into the Administration of the Relief of the Poor in Ireland*, HC, 1861 [408], Q3997, 4098. For an analysis of Cullen's views on social welfare see, Virginia Crossman, 'Attending to the Wants of Poverty: Cullen, the Relief of Poverty and the Development of Social Welfare in Ireland', in Dáire Keogh and Albert McDonnell (eds), *Cardinal Paul Cullen and his World* (Dublin: Four Courts Press, 2011), pp. 146–65.
32 Cullen to Tobias Kirby, 12 June 1872, Irish College Rome, New Kirby Papers, Box 3, Folder 4, 137.
33 *Report from the Select Committee Appointed to Inquire into the Administration of the Relief of the Poor in Ireland*, Q4093.

compassion for the poor with a strong sense of the need for moral classification. According to one of his curates, P. O'Neill, 'the virtuous poor who have children are scarcely ever induced, under no matter what pressures of the most awful privations, to take their families to the Poor-house'. Like Cullen, O'Neill argued that the 'industrious poor who from illness or other cause may be in temporary distress', should be given outdoor relief. 'Hopeless poverty, resulting from permanent illness or inability to labour may be proper a subject for well-administered indoor relief.'[34] Another Dublin priest, E. McCabe, referred to 'the heroism of those afflicted creatures who prefer to endure the pangs of famine rather than qualify themselves for relief in the workhouses'.[35] Perceiving those who did enter the workhouse as having failed some kind of moral test encouraged the idea that they were in some way responsible for their poverty. Thus Thomas Greene, writing to Cullen from Athy in 1861, declared that, in his view, the 'best portion of the working classes, the small farmer and cottager classes, who upheld a decent principle of pride and a high standard of morals' had left the country for America. Those who remained had been driven into towns like Athy, where, 'degraded by poverty, [and] huddled into overcrowded lodgings where the influence exerted by the opinion of friends and relatives could not reach them, they yielded to the corrupting agency around them and the result is a quadrupled rate of bastardy in ten years'.[36] These were the people who ended up in the workhouse. Clergy from other dioceses wrote in similar terms. The chaplain of Ballina workhouse lamented the fact that while the respectable poor shunned the workhouse, there were many who, 'long inured to idle habits', preferred, 'though in health, to eat the bread of idleness rather than go out and earn an honest living for themselves outside'.[37]

Catholic clerics were persistent critics of the poor law system focusing in particular on the institution of the workhouse, which they criticised for its indiscriminate character as well as its harsh regime. Within the hierarchy, attitudes remained hostile but there appears to have been little appetite for active campaigning against the system. Writing to the Donegal-based philanthropist, Alice Hart, in 1896, the Archbishop of Armagh, Michael Logue, acknowledged that workhouse reform was long overdue:

I have been well aware for years of the disgraceful condition of things in the Irish workhouses. The sick, the infirm, the imbecile and the

34 O'Neill to Cullen, 2 May 1861, Dublin Diocesan Archives (hereafter DDA), Cullen Papers, 340/1/70.
35 McCabe to Cullen, 22 May 1861, DDA, Cullen Papers, 334/1/III/3–4.
36 Greene to Cullen, 12 March 1861: DDA, Cullen Papers, 340/1/28.
37 Reply to queries regarding Ballina workhouse, 8 April 1861, Elphin Diocesan Archives, Sligo, Section III C. Workhouses – Reforms.

aged to whom those establishments should furnish a home are so badly treated in them that I never could bring myself to advise them to enter the workhouse, no matter what misery they were suffering outside.

The system, he concluded, appeared to be 'one of universal waste and slovenliness'.[38] But while he was willing 'to co-operate with any movement for the reform of the very unsatisfactory state of things that now exists', Logue showed no inclination to take the initiative.

Clerical efforts to improve the condition of the poorer classes were given added impetus during the pontificate of Leo XIII, who put much stress on the need for Catholics to develop a social conscience. In 1914, J. R. O'Connell, director of the Association for the Housing of the Very Poor, reminded members of the Catholic Truth Society 'how deeply the Church has been concerned for the welfare and upraising of the poor', before calling for action to tackle slum housing. He read a letter he had received from 'a well-known Dublin Parish Priest', recalling:

with clinging realism my countless visits, at all hours of the night, to the pestilent slum-rooms, in each of which five or six poor creatures, and often more, would be found inhaling, through their sleep, the night through, the foul and fetid air that worsened hour by hour.

Poor housing threatened not only the health and physical welfare of the poor but also their moral welfare, propagating 'the vices of drunkenness, immorality, idleness, thriftlessness, [and] turbulence in all their forms'. It was pointless to deplore drunkenness among the poor, 'while the only alternative to the glitter and the glamour of the gin-palace is the pestilential and fetid room in an unsanitary slum, shared by the worker with a wife and perhaps half-a-dozen sickly children'. Tenements were harmful for the same reason that workhouses were harmful. They brought the respectable into close association with the 'degraded'. This had:

the most deplorable results on the self-respect and decency even of those who come to it fresh from the healthful atmosphere of the country. In such conditions all inducement and encouragement to

---

38 Logue to Hart, 12 May 1896, NLI, MS 13827. Cullen's successor as Archbishop of
    Dublin, William Walsh, is described by his biographer as having a particular concern
    for the poor, but does not appear to have spoken publicly on the workhouse system:
    Thomas J. Morrissey, *William J. Walsh, Archbishop of Dublin, 1841–1921* (Dublin: Four
    Courts Press, 2000), pp. 154, 242.

cleanliness, thrift and progress vanish, and the tendency is to sink to the level of the most degraded.[39]

Despite their sympathy for the sufferings of the poor, Catholic clerics remained convinced that it was possible, and indeed morally necessary, to distinguish between those struggling to maintain a sense of decency and virtue, and those who had fallen so far as to be unredeemable. Speaking at an anti-poor law meeting in 1917, Dublin cleric, Francis McKenna, complained that under the poor law system thieves, vagabonds and tramps 'were mixed in horrible promiscuity with people whose only crime was poverty'.[40]

With such views being espoused by the clergy it is hardly surprising that popular attitudes particularly in rural areas absorbed these ideas and reflected them back. Moral judgements and behaviourist attitudes were not confined to poor law officials and Catholic clergy. They were deeply engrained in rural society. While it is difficult to determine the attitudes of ordinary people, it is clear that the poor were expected to adhere to recognised codes of behaviour. This is evident from a series of official investigations into cases of alleged deaths from destitution in 1861–1862. At the end of the 1850s the country saw the return of economic distress. As economic conditions worsened in the early 1860s reports of the impact of distress began appearing in local newspapers. Such reports raised questions about the effectiveness of the safety net provided by the poor law; questions that had hardly been heard since the Famine. In their annual report published in 1862, the poor law commissioners included details of investigations into the deaths of a number of destitute people. The intention was to confirm that the deaths had not been caused by destitution or starvation, and that neither the poor law system nor its officials were at fault in any way. Notwithstanding the underlying agenda, the reports give vivid accounts of the circumstances of the deceased in the period prior to their death, providing a rare insight into the lives of people existing on the margins of society, and into relations between the very poor and their slightly better off neighbours.

One of the cases involved a couple named Prendergast whose baby son had died in December 1861, while the family was staying in Athlone.[41] The couple had come to Athlone from Tuam with their son and two daughters, aged eight and three. Anthony Prendergast was a confectioner by trade,

---

39 J. R. O'Connell, *The Problem of the Dublin Slums* (Dublin: 1914), reprinted in Donnchadh Ó Corráin and Tomás O'Riordan (eds), *Ireland 1870–1914: Coercion and Conciliation* (Dublin: Four Courts Press, 2011), pp. 198–202. Daly notes that the second decade of the twentieth century saw the Catholic Church adopt a more proactive approach to poverty in Dublin: *Dublin – The Deposed Capital*, pp. 114–16.
40 *Dublin Saturday Post*, 3 November 1917.
41 *Freeman's Journal*, 9 December 1861.

and was in search of employment. The family had begged a night's lodging at the house of a pensioner named Dechamp and were resting when they realised that their baby son, who had been ill for some months, had died. The parents went in search of the relieving officer in order to obtain a coffin but were informed that he could do nothing unless they entered the workhouse, 'outdoor relief not being given in Athlone'. Having been asked to leave by Dechamp, 'as he objected to their sitting up all night with the dead child', another local couple, the Goldens offered them lodging and the family stayed with the Goldens for several days. The couple told the Goldens that they had been living in Stockport, where two of their children were working in a factory. Workhouse officials stated that the couple had applied for a coffin, but not for admission, and that they had refused to be admitted. The *Freeman's Journal* reported the case as the death of a famine victim and condemned the poor law commissioners for letting the poor 'perish in the street, and remain unburied on our highways'. Having investigated the case, Medical Inspector John Hill rejected the *Freeman Journal's* interpretation pointing out that the child had not died of famine, that the family had found lodgings, and had refused relief in the workhouse. The workhouse master, he noted, could not legally comply with the request for a coffin. In the reporting of the case and in the family's own account of their actions, much stress was put on the fact that Anthony Prendergast was looking for work, and that the couple refused to enter the workhouse. By stressing his desire to work and to remain independent the couple was able to present themselves as respectable working people and being accepted as such were able to obtain lodgings within the locality.[42]

In another case, an old woman, Maryanne Wakefield, was found dead from exposure in Trim Union, County Meath on 30 December 1861. She was reported to have been well known in the locality having been 'for a long time totally dependent on the charity of the peasantry for her food as well as her lodging but had never been allowed to be in want of either'. Said to have been a person of strictly temperate habits, she was known to be 'simple and not quite in her right senses'. A local woman, Mrs Cormick, who had given her lodgings, said she had known her for the last thirteen or fourteen years:

> formerly she used occasionally to knit socks and make quilts for anyone who would give her board and lodging, but that of late she had become 'simple' and usually spent her days sitting at the side of the road receiving but never soliciting the alms of the charitable.

42 Correspondence and Reports relating to Alleged Cases of Death from Destitution, *Annual Report of the Commissioners for Administering the Laws for the Relief of the Poor in Ireland*, HC, 1862 [2966], p. 52–4.

Wakefield was said never to have sought poor relief in any form. In Mrs Cormick's view, 'the poor creature had not that much forecast'. Wakefield clearly fell into the deserving poor category. She was temperate in her habits, she worked to the best of her limited ability, she did not seek relief and she did not make a nuisance of herself.[43]

It was important to establish a clear entitlement to aid. John Meehan, who worked as a labourer in Clones Union, died in February 1862. He had been suffering from a stomach ulcer for some years. Due to the delicate state of his health he had been unable to work 'continuously for any length of time', and 'for the month previous to his death he was altogether out of employment'. Meehan's wife and two children were reported to have been 'reduced to great poverty; they had pawned or sold all their furniture to provide themselves with food, and for some weeks had been dependent on the wife's casual earnings, and the charity of their neighbours'. Meehan had been begging some time before his death 'under the plea of the want of employment', but had not applied for relief. His wife was reported as saying that 'she would rather suffer hunger than go into the workhouse'. The local constabulary inspector, Mr Kirwan, reported that he had often seen the man begging and had told him it was a shame to be begging, 'when there was absolutely a want of labourers in the neighbourhood'. Meehan had explained that he was not well and was unable to work. Kirwan advised him to go to the workhouse, but he repeatedly refused to do so saying he hoped to be able to work very soon. Meehan's problem was that his inability to work was not immediately evident so the police inspector assumed that his begging implied laziness rather than incapacity. His neighbours were more sympathetic however, enabling the family to remain in their home.[44]

In the above cases local people were willing to offer assistance. But there were other cases in which the behaviour of a poor person had led to their being ostracised. Owen Dogherty died at Glenarm on 11 March 1862, having resided for the previous three months with his mother, Mary, and three siblings in a pigsty. The family was living on the earnings of Owen's elder brother who was about fourteen years old. Mary had been urged to go to the workhouse, but had refused. Poor Law Inspector (PLI) Richard Hamilton reported that Mary was a woman of a 'violent temper, and addicted to habits of intemperance. She was turned out of her last lodgings for getting drunk and breaking the windows.' She had a brother living in Glenarm in comfortable circumstances but he said he had ceased to help her as anything

---

43 Correspondence and Reports relating to Alleged Cases of Death from Destitution, pp. 58–60.
44 Correspondence and Reports relating to Alleged Cases of Death from Destitution, pp. 70–2.

he gave her was used to buy whiskey. The inspector was of the opinion that Owen had died from exposure and want of nourishment, but that 'the mother is the only person to blame'. Mary was suffering from cancer of the face. Hamilton noted that the:

> smell from the cancer is very offensive, and independent of her bad character, I am not surprised at her finding it difficult to procure a lodging: very few people would like to take such an object into their house. I urged her most strongly to go to the workhouse but she positively refused to go. She is not a person to whom outdoor relief could be safely given, because, as her brother says, 'she turns all she gets into whiskey'.

The local police constable had told him that the distressed condition of the family 'arises entirely from their own bad conduct'. Mary had some pride, however. She stated that the family had a fire in one of the piggeries and a blanket and quilt to cover them. She claimed that they 'always had enough to eat, and that there was never any hunger among them'. This was partially confirmed by Hamilton who said that Mary's daughter was a 'strong, healthy-looking young woman'.[45]

Another case involving alcohol abuse was that of Mary Heath. She was described as a mendicant who 'had no fixed place of abode, and obtained her means of living from the inhabitants of Laurencetown and its neighbourhood, by going from house to house. She is stated to have been out of her mind for many years, and sometimes very noisy and troublesome, especially when she had been able to procure any spiritous liquors, to the use of which she is said to have been addicted.' She was seventy years of age and very infirm. Local people had tried to get her to go to the workhouse, 'for she was a great annoyance to the neighbours'. She had previously refused, but does seem finally to have agreed to go, and was being taken to Ballinasloe workhouse on an ass-cart on 24 December 1861 when she died. Local people clearly found her difficult. One said he had seen people 'run and shut their doors as soon as she was seen approaching'. She had, nevertheless, been able to get by and had been given a night's lodging in Laurencetown the day before her death.[46] These cases reveal important differences in the way people living on the margins of society were described and treated by their neighbours. Mary Dogherty and Mary Heath were seen as a nuisance, and

45 Correspondence and Reports relating to Alleged Cases of Death from Destitution, pp. 76–8.
46 Correspondence and Reports relating to Alleged Cases of Death from Destitution, pp. 65–6.

received little or no help as a consequence. Even though he and his family were strangers, Anthony Prendergast was able to get help by presenting himself as a respectable working man in search of employment. Maryanne Wakefield had worked in return for aid as long as she was able, and as a result was regarded more kindly by her neighbours. Refusal to enter the workhouse accorded some people a degree of respect, but in other cases it contributed to their perceived irresponsibility and incapacity. As far as poor law officials were concerned it was a sign of mental incompetence, reinforcing their view that these people had only themselves to blame for their situation.

The idea that entering the workhouse was shameful, which was of course by no means peculiar to Ireland, became deeply ingrained in rural society. When the Folklore Commission collectors asked people about attitudes to their local workhouse in the 1950s, the universal response from informants around the country was that it was regarded with fear and hatred. The workhouse was said to be 'the last resort for the people and they hated to go there'. It was said to be 'a disgrace' to say anyone belonging to you was in the workhouse, 'more so if a relative died in there'.[47] Michael Morris from County Tyrone described the general attitude as:

one of detestation; it symbolised a fear, and appeared to them to loom as a personification behind ill-times ... Only as a last and very distasteful resort would the people generally agree to consent to enter the workhouse. It brought a stigma upon them.

Significantly however, the real misfortune was not to have fallen on hard times but to have been let down. Citing the phrase, 'He'll land us all in the workhouse' to describe someone who was financially irresponsible, Morris stated that people ended up in the workhouse due to 'neglect of work or family by a responsible member of the family'.[48]

Attitudes to and understandings of poverty were complex and contested. How people thought about and responded to the poor in Ireland, as elsewhere, was influenced by class, religion and politics. It was not only elite attitudes that reflected class assumptions and ideology. This was equally true of other social groups. Moreover an identification with and sympathy for the poor did not preclude people from holding strongly judgemental views and advocating punitive action in response to particular groups or types of behaviour. Common to much contemporary commentary was a tendency to make sweeping generalisations about how poor people thought and behaved

---

47 Interviews with Richard Denihan, County Limerick; Michael Hanrahan, County Kerry; National Folklore Collection, University College Dublin, MS 1193, 1391.
48 Interview with Michael Morris, County Tyrone, NFC, MS 1221.

which were presented as universal, reluctance to enter the workhouse being an obvious example. Some poor people were reluctant to enter the workhouse. Others entered it willingly, and were reluctant to leave. Catholic clerics promoted the image of the virtuous poor. The governing elite propagated the image of the deceitful and duplicitous poor. Such images were not only unrepresentative and misleading and they contributed to the exclusion and marginalisation of anyone who did not conform to expectations. Assuming the poor that shunned the workhouse had the effect of marginalising those who did utilise the system. The implication that entering the workhouse was shameful influenced how people used the system and how they experienced it, as well as how they were perceived.

Factors signifying poverty were largely negative, relating to what people lacked: food; clothing; permanent accommodation; household goods; etc. Over the course of the nineteenth century a very restricted diet was increasingly seen as evidence of poverty, in addition to an insufficient diet. Clothing was a critical indicator. Judgements based on appearance and how people were dressed were fundamental to social interaction, as they were to the operation of the relief system, and played a vital role in determining entitlement to relief. As we shall see, people who did not appear poor, if they were too well dressed for example, could be refused relief. Conversely anyone appearing too dirty or ragged was liable to be assumed to fall into the category of the disreputable poor, and might be prosecuted as a vagrant. Since people had some control over their appearance, it was assumed to reflect not only their lifestyle but also their character. Cullen attributed the ragged appearance of the Dublin poor to their drinking contrasting this with the appearance of the rural poor, without considering the fact that the conditions in which the city poor lived made it more difficult to keep either themselves or their clothing clean.

In many ways social attitudes towards the poor remained remarkably constant, just as there was little difference in basic attitudes between classes or religions. What changed and where there were differences, were in rationalisations and responses. Protestants tended to adopt a less fatalistic approach and to place more emphasis on individual responsibility. They were wary of institutional responses unless these were small scale and aimed at helping people to be independent. Catholics placed more emphasis on external assistance, but here again the poor were required to earn it and, thus, demonstrate their entitlement by their behaviour. By the early twentieth century there was more awareness and understanding of the economic causes of poverty and less readiness to assume that poverty was a consequence of innate moral failings, but the poor were still judged by moral criteria and moral distinctions based on behavior and this determined the kind of help they received and how they were perceived and treated. The poor were rarely given the benefit of the doubt. The professional and upper classes were assumed to be honest, unless they there was clear evidence to the contrary; the poor were assumed to be dishonest. As we shall see, poor law officials who behaved irregularly or inappropriately were often let off with a warning. Such latitude was rarely extended to welfare recipients.

2

Context and Trends

The impact of the Great Famine (1845–1850) was profound and shaped attitudes to relief long after the crisis had passed.[1] Workhouses became associated in the popular mind with death and disease, while outdoor relief became associated in the establishment mind with widespread abuse and fraudulent claims. The introduction of outdoor relief, together with other reforms introduced during the course of the Famine changed the way that the poor law system operated. Before examining the nature and extent of that change and in order to provide a context for the discussion that follows, it is necessary to give a brief overview of social and economic developments in post-Famine Ireland. Population levels fell dramatically during the Famine and continued to fall well into the twentieth century, due primarily to consistently high levels of emigration. Having reached over 8 million prior to the famine, total population figures had dropped to 4.4 million by 1911.[2] Subsistence agriculture declined in the post-Famine period and the average size of landholdings increased. In 1845 holdings of between one and fifteen acres made up 55 per cent of farms. By 1853 this figure had fallen to 44 per cent and by 1902 to 37 per cent. Holdings over fifteen acres increased from 31 per cent of farms in 1845, to 51 per cent in 1902.[3] Changes in landholding were accompanied by changes in the type of farming undertaken. Pasture replaced tillage in many parts of the country.

---

1 For the economic consequences of the Famine, see Cormac Ó Gráda, *Ireland: A New Economic History 1780–1939* (Oxford: Oxford University Press, 1994), pp. 173–210. For the wider political and cultural legacy, see Virginia Crossman and Scott Brewster, 'Rewriting the Famine: Witnessing in Crisis', in Scott Brewster et al. (eds), *Ireland in Proximity: History, Gender, Space* (London: Routledge, 1999), pp. 42–58. For the poor law during the Famine, see Peter Gray, *Famine, Land and Politics: British Government and Irish Society 1843–1850* (Dublin: Irish Academic Press, 1999); and Christine Kinealy, *This Great Calamity: The Irish Famine 1845–52* (Dublin: Gill and Macmillan, 1994).

2 L. M. Cullen, *An Economic History of Ireland Since 1660* (London: Batsford, 1976) pp. 134–5.

3 Michael Turner, 'Rural Economies in Post-Famine Ireland, c. 1850–1914', in *An*

The number of agricultural labourers declined by 20 per cent between 1841 and 1851, and continued to decline in subsequent decades. Samuel Clark estimates that the proportion of labourers within the male agricultural labour force as a whole fell from 56 per cent in 1841, to 38 per cent in 1881, while that of farmers and farmers' sons rose from 42 per cent to 60 per cent.[4] Those who survived the Famine saw significant economic and social progress in subsequent decades but this was neither distributed evenly nor experienced equally. Despite their decline in numbers, the circumstances of agricultural labourers appear to have improved less quickly and less noticeably than those of farmers.[5]

As their numbers increased, medium and large tenant farmers came to dominate rural society and rural politics. In order to maintain their position, tenant farmers needed to hold onto the source of their power: land. Impartible inheritance thus became the norm in rural areas, leaving non-inheriting children with a stark choice between remaining on the family farm as an unpaid farm servant, seeking alternative employment within Ireland or emigrating. The high levels of emigration in the post-Famine period testify to the limited opportunities available in Ireland. Levels of emigration were highest in those parts of the country where there were few employment opportunities outside agriculture. Connacht had the smallest manufacturing sector; Leinster and Ulster the largest. Unlike Scotland and England where employment in manufacturing declined, but only gradually, in Ireland the rapid fall in numbers employed in agriculture was matched by a fall in those employed in manufacturing. Sectors where employment increased included transport and public and professional services, together with domestic and industrial services, but these were generally unskilled jobs and were largely casual and irregular.[6] The prospects for women were particularly bleak. Female employment in both agriculture and industry contracted over the second-half of the nineteenth century as less intensive farming spread, and Irish industry succumbed to competition from Britain. Women responded by emigrating in numbers that, unusually, matched those of men.[7] Those who

    Historical Geography of Ireland, B. J. Graham and L. J. Proudfoot (eds). (London: Academic Press, 1993) pp. 311, 316.

4 Samuel Clark, *Social Origins of the Irish Land War* (Princeton: Princeton University Press, 1979), p. 113.

5 J. S. Donnelly Jnr., *The Land and People of Nineteenth-Century Cork: The Rural Economy and the Land Question* (London: Routledge, 1975), pp. 240–43.

6 S. A. Royle, 'Industrialization, Urbanization and Urban Society in Post-Famine Ireland c. 1850–1921', in *An Historical Geography of Ireland*, B. J. Graham and L. J. Proudfoot (eds). (London: Academic Press, 1993), p. 265.

7 David Fitzpatrick, *Irish Emigration 1801–1921* (Dublin: ESHSI, 1984).

remained retreated into the home where, it has been suggested, they could exercise a level of independence and control rarely available to them outside.[8]

Output and productivity levels grew slowly in the second-half of the nineteenth century, and Irish farmers exported an increasing share of their produce. Total agricultural exports doubled in the period from the late 1850s to 1914. However, imports of agricultural produce more than tripled.[9] Irish agriculture became more commercialised and the economy as a whole more modernised. The retail and banking sectors expanded; transport and communications improved; and the population became more literate. Real wages rose. The weekly wages of agricultural labourers increased from five to nine shillings in the 1860s, from nine to twelve shillings by 1880, and the upward trend continued in subsequent decades. Skilled wages were comparable with those in Britain but unskilled wages remained considerably lower than British equivalents. Local and seasonal variations could be considerable. Many labourers were under-employed in winter while summer wages could fluctuate depending on the availability of other work.[10] Wages were generally higher in urban than in rural areas, and higher in the major cities than in country towns. In 1856, for example, skilled wages in Dublin city averaged a little over twenty shillings a week compared to thirteen shillings in County Dublin. Tailors were earning around twenty shillings a week in Cork city, compared to fifteen shillings in rural parts of the county; while masons and carpenters could achieve twenty-four shillings in the city, but only seventeen shillings on average in the county. The wages of agricultural labourers varied less than those of skilled craftsmen, but were higher in the south and east (where they averaged around seven shillings a week in 1856) than in the north and west where the average was six shillings a week.[11] Staple food prices fell from 1860s easing the pressures on low incomes and allowing consumption patterns to become more varied. Across the country there was a general improvement in living standards.[12] Between

8 Joanna Bourke, *Husbandry and Housewifery: Women, Economic Change and Housework in Ireland, 1890–1914* (Oxford: OUP, 1993).

9 Ó Gráda, *Ireland: A New Economic History*, pp. 261–2; and Peter M. Solar, 'Irish Trade in the Nineteenth Century', in *Refiguring Ireland: Essays in Honour of L. M. Cullen*, David Dickson and Cormac Ó Gráda (eds). (Dublin: Lilliput Press, 2003), pp. 284–5.

10 H. D. Gribbon, 'Economic and Social History, 1850–1921', in W. E. Vaughan (ed.), *A New History of Ireland: Ireland under the Union 1870–1921* (Oxford: OUP, 1996), p. 320. Agricultural wages rose by a further 30 per cent 1880–1914.

11 Abstract of replies received from Inspectors to circular relative to the existing Average Rates of Wages paid to Agricultural Labourers, and the principal Classes of Mechanics in the their respective Districts, *Annual Report of the Commissioners for Administering the Laws for the Relief of the Poor in Ireland*, HC, 1856 [2105], pp. 44–50.

12 Gribbon, 'Economic and Social History', p. 332; and Ó Gráda, *Ireland: A New Economic History*, p. 250.

1845 and 1914 average incomes trebled, while life expectancy increased from under forty years in the early 1840s to fifty-eight years by the 1920s. The percentage of families living in 'fourth-class' accommodation (single-room cabins or tenements) fell from 10 per cent in 1861, to 1 per cent in 1911.[13] By the early twentieth century the one-room cabins which had housed the majority of rural poor in the pre-Famine period had virtually disappeared.

The percentage of the population living in cities increased. The population of Dublin grew from 232,726 in 1841 to 304,802 in 1911, while that of Belfast increased from 75,308 in 1841 to 386,947 in 1911. The economies of Ireland's two major cities were however, very different. Belfast was a major industrial centre accounting for one-third of Ireland's net industrial output. Textiles and shipping employed around three-quarters of the working population. In Dublin the proportion of the working population employed in industry in 1881 was 55 per cent, and most were in food processing which required largely unskilled labour much of which was casual and seasonal.[14] In Belfast the majority of working families lived in their own (rented) house; in Dublin the preponderance of casual and seasonal employment forced workers into low-rent, mainly tenement, accommodation. In 1911 one-third of Dublin city houses fell into the fourth-class category, much of it concentrated in the districts to the north of the Liffey and the Liberties. Life expectancy was higher in rural areas than in the major cities due to the prevalence of poor housing and disease. Public health legislation contributed to declining mortality rates from the 1870s, but the rate in Dublin fell only slowly and remained higher than that in other cities whether in Britain or Ireland.[15] In Belfast, levels of poverty and deprivation were higher amongst the Catholic population. Catholics made up over one-third of the city's population by 1861, but were more likely to be illiterate, to be living in poorer quality housing and to be working in manual, semi or unskilled employment than their Protestant counterparts. No other city could match Belfast and Dublin in size or economic importance. Cities, such as Cork and Limerick, experienced population decline as well as a decline in industrial employment, although they remained important regional centres. The number of men employed in industry in Cork, for example, fell from 8,000 to 4,000 in the period

13 Ó Gráda, *Ireland: A New Economic History*, pp. 241–2.
14 Royle, 'Industrialization, Urbanization and Urban Society', pp. 260, 263, 271. Daly cites the abnormal proportion of casual workers as the 'most important economic factor' in Dublin poverty: Mary E. Daly, *Dublin – The Deposed Capital: A Social and Economic History 1860–1914* (Cork: Cork University Press, 1984), p. 77.
15 Royle, 'Industrialization, Urbanization and Urban Society', p. 285. In 1880 the mortality rate in Dublin stood at 37.7 per 1,000, which was one of the highest rates in Europe. By 1905 it had fallen to 22.3 per thousand; all other cities recorded rates below 20 per 1,000: Carroll, *In the Fever King's Preserves*, p. 51.

1841–1901 while female employment fell from 3,500 to 3,200 leaving the city with one of the highest rates of urban unemployment in the country.[16]

Over the second half of the nineteenth century the diet of the labouring classes became more varied, but also more reliant on shop bought food, particularly bread. Analysis of a number of dietary surveys conducted over the course of the nineteenth and early twentieth century reveals the decline of a potato and milk diet, and the rise of one based on cereal products such as meal and bread, accompanied by small amounts of protein. Consumption patterns were subject to regional variations. Oatmeal was consumed more in the north and east, for example, while the decline in the consumption of potatoes was less marked in the west than in other areas. Continued reliance on the potato meant that the population in the west remained extremely vulnerable to food shortages following crop failures. In addition to charting changing consumption patterns, dietary surveys provide significant information about the household economies of the poor. The majority of families surveyed in 1859, for example, were living mainly on porridge made from either Indian meal or oatmeal together with potatoes and buttermilk. They generally used buttermilk, sour milk or skimmed milk rather than new milk, and had little butter in their diet. Foods such as bread were being used to vary the diet but were rarely everyday items. The poorest families very rarely ate meat or drank tea. These were treats. Families that had meat as a regular part of their diet were generally those of tradesmen living in towns with higher than average wages and/or smaller than average families. Where details of expenditure were given, families were spending between 70 and 90 per cent of their weekly income on food, although in some cases this included items such as whiskey and tobacco. Some families spent more than they earned, the difference being made up by remittances sent back by emigrants or by money earned by seasonal migration. With respect to one couple living with their four children in a rural part of County Kilkenny, it was noted that the man 'keeps a pig and hens; his wife sells apples etc. in the season, pays no rent; has a brother-in-law in America who sometimes sends a little help'.[17] Such a family could get by under normal circumstances but might be tipped into destitution by an unexpected event such as sickness or an accident.

A variety of factors contributed to the level of poverty experienced by the families surveyed. These included the number of children and

16 Royle, 'Industrialization, Urbanization and Urban Society', pp. 273–4, 281; and Maura Cronin, *Country, Class, or Craft?: The Politicisation of Nineteenth Century Cork* (Cork: Cork University Press, 1994), p. 17.

17 Report on the Subject of Workhouse Dietaries, and the Dietary of the Labouring Poor in Ireland, *Annual Report of the Commissioners for Administering the Laws for the Relief of the Poor in Ireland*, HC, 1860 [2654], p. 70.

particularly the number of young children; how many family members were contributing to the household income; and whether the family had to find money for rent and for items such as fuel. A number of rural families were described as foraging for fuel, but buying it when necessary. In all parts of the country women contributed to the family economy through paid work, taking in washing, raising hens and selling the eggs, weaving, knitting and sewing. Children also contributed; the older ones through paid work and the younger ones by collecting firewood. Where the wife was earning the family tended to be better off. Elizabeth S., for example, lived with her husband Thomas and three children in the rural part of South Dublin Union and was reported to earn two pounds a year from weaving 'which provides clothes etc.', Thomas earned fifteen shillings a week and the family regularly had meat and potatoes for dinner. The family of Patrick C., a labourer in Dublin city, only occasionally had meat. His wife Anne earned between one shilling and sixpence and two shillings and sixpence per week from sewing, which paid for repairs 'and occasionally gives bacon for dinner on Sundays'.[18] Other sources of income included turf-cutting, kelp-making and sea fishing.[19] In times of hardship, people resorted to strategies common to poor households throughout Europe, including pawning items, rent arrears, barter and credit.[20]

Consumption of Indian meal declined as living standards rose. Bread was increasingly shop bought if possible; baking bread was a sign of hardship. Although changing consumption patterns reflected rising living standards, the nutritional content of labourers' diets in the early twentieth century was poorer than it had been in the pre-Famine period. The average diet contained less protein, carbohydrate, calcium and iron, and had a lower calorific value. 'The retreat from the potato', Leslie Clarkson observes 'was not immediately good for health.'[21] This was particularly evident in the major cities where the poorest people had no access to land on which to grow food. Dietary information collected by Sir Charles Cameron in 1904

18 Report on the Subject of Workhouse Dietaries, p. 56.
19 Kelp-making involved the conversion of seaweed into ash, used the production of soap and glass.
20 Cameron noted that pawnbrokers provided a vital service to families whose incomes were intermittent and unreliable. It was only by regularly pawning small items that such people could get cash with which to buy food: Sir Charles A. Cameron, *How the Poor Live* (Dublin: John Falconer, 1904), pp. 5–6. For analyses of the 'economy of makeshifts' in England, see Steven King and Alannah Tompkins (eds), *The Poor in England, 1700–1850: An Economy of Makeshifts* (Manchester: Manchester University Press, 2003); and Samantha Williams, *Poverty, Gender and Life-Cycle under the English Poor Law 1760–1834* (Woodbridge: Boydell Press, 2011), pp. 131–59.
21 Leslie Clarkson, 'The Modernisation of the Irish Diet, 1740–1920' in John Davis (ed.), *Rural Change in Ireland* (Belfast: Institute of Irish Studies, 1999), p. 42.

showed that bread and tea had become the staple diet of the poor in Dublin. The poorest families had dry bread; the slightly better off were able to have butter. More meat and more potatoes were being consumed than in the 1850s but very few families regularly ate meat. Only those in constant employment were regularly able to include meat and fish in their diet. Out of the fifty-two families surveyed by Cameron, forty-five had some meat or fish in their diet even if only occasionally. The ones who did not were the larger families with the male head in very irregular employment. Cameron's inquiries revealed that thousands of families were surviving on weekly incomes of between ten and fifteen shillings. The highest rate of wages for labourers was twenty shillings and many were paid between fifteen and eighteen shillings. 'Even when they are sober and with small families', Cameron observed:

> they cannot enjoy much comfort on the higher rate of wages. When the labourer is of the inferior order, has precarious employment, earns at the most 15s. per week, and has a large family, it is easy to imagine his deplorable condition.

As an illustration he outlined the circumstances of a family living in Dame Court:

> His occupation is that of a tailor, but he can earn only 10s. a week. His rent is 2s. 6d. which leaves 7s. 6d. for food, fuel, light, clothes, bedding, etc. Their breakfast consists of dry bread and tea. They have only another meal, dinner and supper combined: it consists of dry bread and tea and herrings, occasionally porridge.[22]

Access to land in rural areas did not necessarily result in a better diet as home-grown produce was often sold for cash and replaced with cheaper often shop-bought alternatives. Evidence from the baseline reports, which were compiled in the early 1890s as an insight into conditions in the congested districts, shows that the most commonly mentioned foods were potatoes, bread, tea, milk or buttermilk, Indian meal and fish.[23] Poorer families turned to Indian meal when potatoes ran out in the months before the new harvest. Expenditure on food accounted for well over half of household expenditure in nearly all of the congested districts.[24] The diet was not in

---

22 Cameron, *How the Poor Live*, pp. 6–7. A larger survey of 1,254 Dublin families by the Local Government Board Medical Inspector, Thomas Stafford, in 1904 found the average income of heads of families to be 16s: Daly, *Dublin – The Deposed Capital*, p. 111.
23 Clarkson, 'The Modernisation of the Irish Diet', p. 42.
24 Ciara Breathnach, *The Congested Districts Board of Ireland, 1891–1923: Poverty and*

itself lacking in nutrition but the tendency to sell produce, such as eggs and butter, Ciara Breathnach maintains, had a negative impact of people's health, 'people clearly allowed their diet to suffer in order to engage in the increasing cash economy'. As in other parts of the country, the consumption of Indian meal in the congested districts declined over the period. Generally seen as a reflection of rising living standards, Breathnach suggests that this 'represents further engagement in the cash economy', which did not lead to enhanced lifestyles.[25] But this is to miss the point about living standards which reflect the economic rather than physical health of a society. People ate less Indian meal because they were able to afford to buy bread. This did not make them healthier, but it does reflect rising living standards.

Definitions of poverty are notoriously problematic depending on relative judgements of need and sufficiency. As Lynn Hollen Lees has noted, poverty is 'a relative concept definable only in comparison with a specific, locally relevant standard'.[26] Destitution was easier to define – lacking the necessaries of life – but often difficult to certify, as some relieving officers discovered to their cost. Defining poverty in Ireland was particularly problematic in the pre-Famine period since it was so extensive as to be almost universal. The Whately Commission explained the difficulties they had faced in undertaking an inquiry:

> about a population in which many of the ordinary distinctions of society are commonly merged in the same individual. To determine what measures might be requisite to ameliorate the condition of the poor classes in Ireland, required an investigation extending to almost the whole social and productive system; for the poorer classes in Ireland may be considered as comprehending nearly the whole population.

The commission believed that their report proved 'to painful certainty that there is in all parts of Ireland much and deep-seated distress'. This was rooted in the fact that there was insufficient employment for the size of the population. As a consequence it was:

> impossible for the able-bodied, in general, to provide against sickness or the temporary absence of employment, or against old age or the

---

Development in the West of Ireland (Dublin: Four Courts Press, 2005), p. 37. Stafford's survey of poor families in Dublin found the average share of income devoted to food to be 63%: Daly, *Dublin – The Deposed Capital*, p. 111.

25 Breathnach, *The Congested Districts Board*, p. 39.
26 Hollen Lees, *The Solidarities of Strangers*, pp. 13–14.

destitution of their widows and children in the contingent event of
their own premature decease.[27]

The total number facing distress on an annual basis, the commission
concluded numbered 2,385,000 (around 30 per cent of the total population).
This figure was disputed, however. George Nicholls, the architect of the
poor law system, calculated that provision needed to be made for just 1
per cent of the population, or 80,000 people, who were likely to require to
occasional relief. This figure was based on relief levels in southern England.
Since these counties had seen the highest levels of relief in Britain, they
could, Nicholls assumed, be taken as representing the maximum amount
required in Ireland, blithely ignoring the fact that social and economic
conditions in Ireland were totally different from those in southern England.
An alternative method of calculation by the Dublin statistician, William
Stanley, based on a 2 per cent rate of destitution in Dublin and 1 per cent in
rural areas, produced a slightly higher figure of 83,000.[28] The explanation
for such wildly different estimates can be found in their different premises.
The poor inquiry was attempting to estimate the total number at risk of
distress, while Nicholls was calculating the number of destitute who might
actually require relief. Nicholls' conservative estimate appeared justified in
the early years of the poor law system when the majority of Irish workhouses
remained significantly underutilised. However, the onset of the Famine was
to make his confident assumptions look like dangerous complacency, even
though he had explicitly stated that a workhouse system would not be able to
cope with famine conditions.

The introduction of the poor law and the bureaucratic apparatus that
went with it provided a new and, supposedly, more accurate means of
calculating levels of destitution and distress, as well as a new category of
poor, recipients of poor relief or paupers. Statistical returns obtained from
the poor law unions and published annually provided, according to the Chief
Commissioner, Alfred Power, one of 'the most reliable indications of the
material condition of the country and of the general state of the population'.[29]
Throughout the 1850s and 1860s, the Irish poor law commissioners regularly
cited the decline in the total number in receipt of relief to demonstrate the
improved state of the country. In their annual report for 1859 they noted the

27 First Report from His Majesty's Commissioners for Inquiring Into the Condition of the
    Poorer Classes in Ireland, HC, 1835 [369], pp. vi–vii.
28 Peter Gray, *The Making of the Irish Poor Law 1815–43* (Manchester: Manchester
    University Press, 2009), pp. 118, 165, 195.
29 Memorandum (1874) included in Power to Spencer, 3 February 1874, BL, Althorp
    Papers, Add MSS 76976/2.

steady decrease in pauperism and expenditure that had taken place since the Famine, observing that they could not:

> anticipate any further annual decrease of pauperism ... but may expect hereafter a decrease or increase of the numbers directly and solely dependent on the favourable or adverse character of the respective years which may be compared together.

Similarly, expenditure would now increase or decrease 'according to the favourable or adverse character of the year, and more particularly according to the high or low price of food'. In a memorandum produced the same year, Power identified further signs of economic progress. Prior to the Famine, pauperism had been most evident between June and August, before the new crop of potatoes became available; now it was in February, shortly before the spring work began. Numbers on relief generally declined from February until September or October, 'showing that the state of employment is the cause of the greater or less extent of pauperism and not the state of the potato crop as previously'.[30]

Annual returns of the number in receipt of relief provided a means of comparing the different parts of the United Kingdom. In 1860 the commissioners noted that comparisons had been made between rates of pauperism in different parts of the United Kingdom showing that around 4.5 per cent of the population of England and Wales was in receipt of relief compared to less than 1 per cent of the Irish population. At the same time, expenditure on poor relief was lower in Ireland at one shilling and sixpence per head of population, compared to six shillings per head in England and Wales. In relation to numbers relieved, however, expenditure was greater in Ireland being over nine pounds per recipient compared to seven pounds in England and five pounds in Scotland.[31] The commissioners attributed the difference to the different relief systems operating in the various countries. In Scotland 95 per cent of people were relieved outdoors and in England 86 per cent, whereas in Ireland it was only 3 per cent. Thus while the cost per person relieved was greater in Ireland, overall the system was more economical.

The commissioners then proceeded to summarise what they saw as the advantages of an indoor relief system, such as that operating in Ireland. Relief in workhouses provided:

---

30   Memorandum on the State of Pauperism, 29 December 1859, NLI, Larcom Papers, MS 7603.
31   Annual expenditure per head on the average daily number relieved.

everything requisite for the entire subsistence and relief of the inmate, excluding rigidly all other resources. It provides not only food, clothing, lodging, bedding, fuel and all other necessaries, but medical and surgical aid, medicine, medical comforts, and nursing for the sick; spiritual aid; and finally education for the young.

Indoor relief was sufficient, it was applied directly to its object and it was readily available, none of which were true for outdoor relief. Furthermore, it caused 'the least disturbance of the rights of property, and of the industrial energy of the working classes'. People were unlikely to give up outdoor relief voluntarily so the outdoor relief lists underwent little change over the course of the year: 'In Ireland, on the contrary, the changes are continual, through discharges occurring voluntarily on the part of the paupers, and through admissions freely granted to the applicant for relief.' The commissioners rejected the argument that insufficient relief was granted in Ireland, claiming that the relatively low level of relief reflected the lower rate of urbanisation, town populations being 'generally more liable to pauperism than rural populations' and the lower cost of living. While agricultural wages were relatively low, the costs of fuel and lodging were low also, so as to:

more than compensate for the difference in the daily wages. Finally, pauperism in Ireland is of recent growth and not hereditary, except among the mendicants; and thus the class of necessitous persons, which is created by the habit or the expectation of receiving out-door allowance on the contingency of a cessation or diminution of income, exists to a very small extent there. From these considerations we are led to believe that the number of persons needing relief in proportion to the whole population is less in Ireland than it is in Great Britain.[32]

As far as the commissioners were concerned, the higher rate of pauperism in England was a direct result of the lax poor law system. The English poor law, they believed, had created pauperism. In Ireland, by contrast, the poor law operated as it was intended to do; it relieved destitution. Thus the limited nature of the system, which critics saw as its main weakness, was for the commissioners its main strength.

Indoor relief was believed to rise and fall with the seasons and the condition of the country. The Local Government Board explained recent fluctuations in the numbers receiving relief in the early 1870s as a consequence of 'the character of the seasons'. Wet weather in 1872–1873 had damaged the potato

32 *Annual Report of the Commissioners for Administering the Laws for the Relief of the Poor in Ireland*, HC, 1860 [2546], pp. 6–9.

and turf harvests and this, coupled with an outbreak of fever, had resulted in an 'increased degree of distress and sickness in the population, which led to an increase of the number in the workhouses'. The following year had seen much better weather, and a very mild winter, leading to a reduction in the number in workhouses. In a memorandum compiled in 1874, Power declared confidently that the workhouse system of relief:

> as conducted in Ireland shows itself ready and prompt at all times to meet any increase in suffering arising from any cause in regard to the more indigent part of the population, and that amount of relief expands or contracts itself with perfect elasticity in response to the general condition of the people.

Outdoor relief, however, was of 'a totally different character'.[33] As the Local Government Board noted in their annual report for 1874, outdoor pauperism, in contrast to indoor, demonstrated 'a continuous but slow rate of increase' and was 'never referred to ... as an indication of the favourable or unfavourable condition of the country'. Unlike England where 'the popular or prevailing opinion is that out-door relief has been for a long time past in excess of what it ought to be', and 'active exertions' made to reduce its extent in Ireland, 'the popular opinion is that there has been too little out-door relief in comparison with in-door' and 'it is to the operation of this feeling at boards of guardians that the continuous increase is due'.[34] Power remained convinced that Ireland had much to teach England with regard to poor relief. As he explained to Lord Spencer in 1875, 'the moral to be drawn from the history of outdoor relief in Ireland appeared to be the necessity of providing a sufficiency of workhouse accommodation'. Without this, the populous towns of England would make only limited progress in the reduction of their outdoor relief expenditure.[35]

Outdoor relief in Ireland had started to rise in the 1860s and continued to do so throughout the 1870s. At the end of the 1870s, Ireland experienced a serious and prolonged agricultural crisis. The pressure of economic distress during these years was such that the government was forced to relax restrictions on outdoor relief to enable it to be given to the able-bodied and to landholders, who had previously been excluded.[36] Numbers receiving

---

33 Memorandum (1874) included in Power to Spencer, 3 February 1874, BL, Althorp Papers, Add MSS 76976/2.

34 *Annual Report of the Local Government Board for Ireland*, HC, 1874 [Cd. 967], pp. 12–13. The Local Government Board replaced the poor law commissioners as the central regulatory authority in 1872.

35 Power to Spencer, 24 December 1875, BL, Althorp Papers, Add MSS 76976/2.

36 For the government response to distress, see Virginia Crossman, '"With the experience

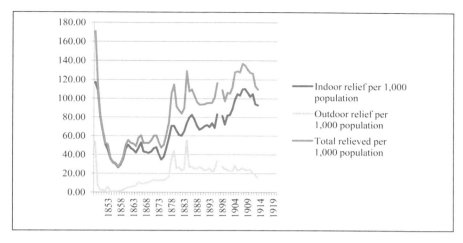

Figure 2.1   Rates of poor relief per 1,000 population 1850–1914.
Source: Annual Reports of the Commissioners for Administering
the Laws for the relief of the Poor in Ireland and the
Local Government Board for Ireland 1850–1914

both indoor and outdoor relief rose rapidly during this period. The overall
rate of pauperism (the total number in receipt of relief per thousand of the
population) more than doubled from 50.5 in 1877, to 115 in 1881. The level
of outdoor pauperism increased from thirteen per thousand to forty-four
(see Figure 2.1). Relaxation of the regulations governing outdoor relief was a
temporary measure. But in contrast to the situation after the Great Famine
when relief levels had dropped back to 'normal' after the crisis was over, this
did not happen after the crisis of 1879 to 1881. Levels of indoor and outdoor
relief did drop in the 1880s, but they remained significantly higher than they
had been before the crisis and they were to remain high right up until the
First World War. Indeed, levels of relief were climbing steadily in the final
decades of the nineteenth century and into the first decade of the twentieth,
before beginning to decline in the 1910s.

In contrast to England and Wales where poor law figures showed
declining levels of pauperism from the mid-nineteenth until the early
twentieth century, before rising again in the 1920s and 1930s, in Ireland
pauperism demonstrated a gradual rise over this period, before beginning
to decline in the second decade of the twentieth century. Not only was the

of 1846 and 1847 before them": The Politics of Emergency Relief 1879–84', in Peter
Gray, (ed.), *Victoria's Ireland? Irishness and Britishness, 1837–1901* (Dublin: Four Courts
Press, 2004), pp. 167–82; and Crossman, *Politics, Pauperism and Power*, pp. 106–16.

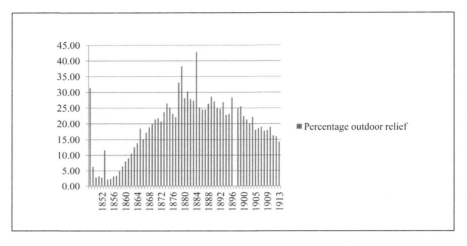

Figure 2.2   Outdoor relief as a percentage of total number relieved over the year.
Source: Annual Reports of the Commissioners for Administering
the Laws for the relief of the Poor in Ireland and the
Local Government Board for Ireland 1850–1914

general trend in pauperism in Ireland in the opposite direction from that
in England and Wales, but the relationship between indoor and outdoor
relief also appeared to be reversed. In England outdoor relief levels, which
fluctuated according to seasonal and yearly cycles, were more volatile than
indoor.[37] In Ireland, apart from the years of exceptional distress, numbers
on outdoor relief were more stable than those on indoor. Indoor relief
levels appeared more susceptible to short-term fluctuations, suggesting
that temporary distress was primarily relieved in the workhouse. Outside
the major cities, there was considerable spare capacity in the majority of
Irish workhouses, meaning that they could accommodate sudden influxes.
Moreover, as we shall see, those administering the system appear to have
regarded outdoor relief more as an allowance system for providing low-level,
long-term assistance than as a way of relieving temporary destitution. As a
proportion of total relief, outdoor relief had risen to 38 per cent of the total
by 1881. It dropped back to 28 per cent in 1882, but then remained at around
that level for the remainder of the century. It declined in the early twentieth

37   Keith Snell accounts for this by reference, first to constraints of space which imposed
     limits on workhouse accommodation, and second the nature of the workhouse
     population which contained more long-term categories of pauper such as the elderly
     and infirm: *Parish and Belonging: Community, Identity and Welfare in England and
     Wales 1700–1950* (Cambridge: Cambridge University Press, 2006), p. 219.

century but never fell below 14 per cent (see Figure 2.2). This appears very low in comparison to Britain where levels of outdoor relief never fell below 60 per cent of the total number of recipients and averaged 79 per cent over the period from 1840 to 1939.[38] However, it is important to appreciate that these figures are not directly comparable.

Confidence in the accuracy of total relief figures as a measure of economic prosperity began to falter in the 1870s. In his remarks about the level of pauperism in Ireland, Power referred to the total number in receipt of relief, and he continued to use these figures, explaining rising numbers in the 1870s, for example, by reference to the proportion of sickness prevailing in the population, as well as changes in economic circumstances. Around this time, however, there is a change in the way the poor law figures were presented in official commentary. Commenting on fluctuations in the numbers receiving relief in 1874, the Local Government Board cited the average daily number in workhouses, together with maximum and minimum numbers of workhouse inmates. From this period, official commentary on levels of relief tended to refer to the average daily number, not the total number in receipt of relief.[39] The reason for the change in practice was the belief that the total number conveyed a misleading impression. The numbers recorded as in receipt of indoor relief, a note in the annual report for 1894 explained, did 'not represent so many individual persons, inasmuch as the same person may be admitted to relief more than once in a year'. The average daily number, on the other hand, showed 'the average number of individual persons maintained in each workhouse each day throughout the year'.[40] This was closer to the figure provided by the English poor law commissioners for total numbers on relief, which was in fact an average based on the total number relieved on 1 January in the year under review and 1 July the preceding year. The English figures are generally thought seriously to under-represent the total number of individuals separately relieved, and are sometimes adjusted to take account of this.[41] However, the Irish authorities appear to have made the opposite assumption. They decided that the figures for the total number receiving relief overestimated the number of individual paupers. The average daily number, they felt, gave a more accurate impression of the number of individuals using the system. It is easy to see why the poor law authorities were more comfortable with the average daily

38 Snell, *Parish and Belonging*, pp. 219–20.
39 See for, example, the statistical appendices to the Vice-Regal Commission (1906) and the Poor Law Commission (1910).
40 *Annual Report of the Local Government Board for Ireland*, Appendix D, HC, 1894 [Cd. 7454], pp. 138–9.
41 Snell, *Parish and Belonging*, p. 217; and Karel Williams, *From Pauperism to Poverty* (London: Routledge, 1981), pp. 156–7.

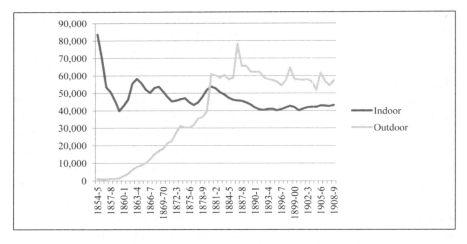

Figure 2.3   Average daily number in receipt of relief.
Source: Royal Commission on the Poor Laws and Relief of Distress. Minutes of
Evidence (with Appendices) relating Ireland, HC, 1910 [Cd. 5070], Table VI

number, since this showed an overall decline in the numbers accommodated in Irish workhouses (see Figure 2.3). They were less concerned about the rise in the average daily number receiving outdoor relief because that was not regarded as an indicator of the state of the country.[42]

Neither the total number in receipt of relief nor the average daily number should be taken as representing a 'real' total. The average daily number underestimates total usage, while the total number in receipt overestimates individual usage. Taken together, however, they do reveal significant trends and show the responsiveness of the system to economic circumstances. Relief figures peaked in 1881, 1886, 1898, 1907 and 1911. These were all years when Ireland was experiencing either an agricultural crisis or a crisis of employment, as in 1911. The rise in the overall rate of pauperism during the period from 1860 to 1912 is, however, a reflection of the way the system was operating, not the state of the country. More people were entering Irish workhouses in the late nineteenth and early twentieth century, but an increasing number of these were casual and short term. It is clear from an examination of workhouse admission registers that by the later decades of the nineteenth century, a significant proportion of admissions were people who stayed just one or two nights. These admissions skew the total relief

---

42   The annual returns include a figure for the average daily number in each workhouse from 1858. The average daily number on outdoor relief is available as a national figure only.

figures and inflate the yearly total giving the impression of large numbers of individual admissions when, in fact, on any particular day, many workhouses were half empty. From the 1880s, workhouse inmates increasingly fell into two distinct categories: casual paupers, many of whom were highly mobile and travelled around the country spending a night or two in the most convenient workhouse whenever necessary; and longer-term residents comprising the sick and infirm, children, single and lone mothers, and lunatics and imbeciles. While some people were making more, and more regular, use of workhouses, the total number of inmates on any particular day was considerably lower at the beginning of the twentieth century than had been the case in the early 1850s or 1860s.

The very low level of outdoor relief, which was the cause of such satisfaction to Power and his fellow commissioners in the 1850s and 1860s, is often seen as a defining characteristic of the Irish poor law system. In his discussion of outdoor relief in England and Wales under the new poor law, Keith Snell notes that outdoor relief in Ireland was 'miniscule compared to England and Wales'.[43] This was certainly the case in the 1850s. By the later decades of the nineteenth century, however, the contrast between England and Ireland was far less marked. Having risen gradually throughout the 1860s and 1870s, the numbers in receipt of outdoor relief surged during the crisis years of 1879–1881 to the point where the average daily number in receipt of outdoor relief exceeded the average number in receipt of indoor relief for the first time. From this time on, the daily average on outdoor relief remained consistently higher than the average number in workhouses. This seriously calls into question the idea that the Irish poor law remained an indoor system based on the institution of the workhouse. At around 60 per cent of relief granted, levels of outdoor relief were converging with those in England. This represents a fundamental change in the nature of the Irish relief system.

Expenditure figures provide another means of charting changes in relief provision. Official returns include two different figures for poor law expenditure, the total spent on relief of the poor and total union expenditure (see Figure 2.4). The total spent on poor relief included the amount expended on the salaries of officials and other administrative expenses. Total union expenditure encompassed the whole range of union activities and included amounts expended under the medical charities act, and the various sanitary and public health acts. As fresh legislation was passed extending the responsibilities of poor law boards, so new items of expenditure were added to union accounts, thus helping to explain the progressive rise in expenditure. Expenditure levels followed a similar trajectory to numbers in receipt of

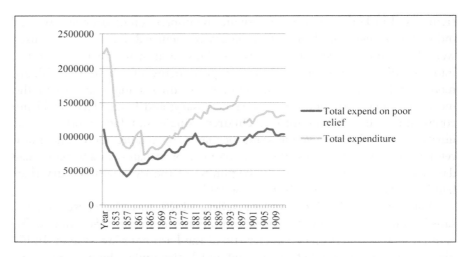

Figure 2.4   Total expenditure (in pounds) under the poor laws and on poor relief.
Source: Annual Reports of the Commissioners for Administering
the Laws for the relief of the Poor in Ireland and the
Local Government Board for Ireland 1850–1914

relief but with fewer fluctuations. After declining in the 1850s, expenditure increased steadily from the early 1860s. Expenditure on poor relief also rose but not as sharply. The very high numbers in receipt of relief during periods of exceptional distress were not reflected in expenditure levels because the cost of relief during these years was met in part by grants and loans from central government. Without such assistance many poor law boards would have been unable to cover their expenses. Local government reform in 1898 saw the transfer of some responsibilities from poor law boards to county and district councils. These included the administration of the Labourers Acts and the Sanitary Acts. As a result total expenditure levels dropped. This was an administrative rather than a real drop in expenditure; the expenses were still there, they were just being returned under different headings. Expenditure on poor relief continued to rise.

One of the defining characteristics of the poor law system was its intertwining of central and local responsibility. The central poor law authorities were responsible for maintaining the integrity of the system as a whole, while local poor law boards were responsible for the actual administration of relief. As a result, what was in theory a uniform system displayed in practice considerable local variation both within regions and between them. The nature and significance of such variations have begun to be explored for England, but the situation in Ireland remains much more opaque. Indeed, it is still widely assumed that the system in Ireland operated in much the same way across the country. Steven King has posited the existence of distinct welfare regimes in England under both the old and the new poor law. Under the old poor law he has identified contrasting welfare cultures in the north and west, as opposed to the south and east: the first relatively cost conscious and based on a rhetoric of self-reliance; and the second more flexible and generous. This division was maintained under the new poor law. By the beginning of the nineteenth century, he maintains, 'the rural counties and market towns of the south and west had put in place a wide definition of entitlement and the communal welfare system granted more substantial nominal allowances to more people than did communities in the north and west'. Speculating that England may have had 'several poor law systems and not one', he has tentatively identified eight separate welfare regions within England, 'in which generosity, entitlement and the sentiment of relief were different by order and degree'.[44]

Snell also regards the idea of a single poor law as anachronistic, observing that 'the new poor law was not a fixed entity, any more than it was standardised across regions'. One of the 'most striking aspects of nineteenth-century out-door relief', he notes, 'was its regional variety'. Mapping expenditure on outdoor relief reveals significant regional variations. Poor law unions in Wales and the southwest, as well as in parts of the northeast and south midlands, gave very high proportions of outdoor relief in contrast to those in the northwest and around London, which gave relatively little outdoor relief.[45] Historians have also commented on the difference between urban and rural areas under the poor law. Michael Rose observed that the new poor law 'operated under a different set of rules in many urban parishes as compared to their rural counterparts'.[46] Snell notes the relatively low levels of outdoor relief in urban unions, 'especially in and around London, some parts of the English midlands, and in south Lancashire'. While acknowledging that the relief policies of urban unions were 'often swayed by political and administrative attitudes towards the new poor law of the region in which they were situated', there was, he suggests:

a clear inverse relationship between urbanisation/population density and percentage of relief given as out-door relief – that is the most urban unions tended to make more use of the workhouse.[47]

44 Steven King, *Poverty and Welfare in England 1700–1850: A Regional Perspective* (Manchester: Manchester University Press, 2000), pp. 257, 266.
45 Snell, *Parish and Belonging*, pp. 212, 228–30.
46 'Introduction', in Michael E. Rose (ed.), *The Poor Law and the City: The English Poor Law and its Urban Context, 1834–1914* (Leicester: Leicester University Press, 1985), p. 7.
47 Snell, *Parish and Belonging*, pp 232–3.

There has long been awareness of the regional character of poor law administration in Ireland. The central poor law authorities produced maps showing the level of poor relief and expenditure in different unions in 1860 for example, and successive inquiries into the system highlighted local variations and differences.[48] The Poor Law Union and Lunacy Inquiry Commission which reported in 1879, produced statistical tables purporting to show an increase in pauperism in unions in which outdoor relief had been introduced, in contrast to a decline both in pauperism and expenditure in unions which had adhered to the indoor system.[49] Apparent anomalies in the geographical distribution of pauperism were noted in a statistical appendix produced by the royal commission on the poor laws in 1910. The comparatively high rate of pauperism in Leinster which had the highest valuation per head, compared with that in Connacht which had the lowest, was described as 'remarkable'.[50] Some senior officials sought to explain regional differences in essentialist terms. The chief characteristic of poor law administration in the north, H. A. Robinson remarked in his memoirs:

> was rigid economy. The members of local bodies were mostly business people with the Scottish instinct to get value for their money fully developed, and they kept the rates down and seldom fell foul of the auditor; while the southerners were characterized by a greater open-handedness and a more high-spirited contempt for the restrictions of English Acts of Parliament, and had to be more closely shepherded.[51]

While his explanation was overly determinist, Robinson's analysis of the character of welfare administration in the north and south was acute.

Geographical variations in levels of relief prompted Feingold to wonder whether discernible regional patterns existed and, if they did, whether they could be related to 'social or other conditions in those regions'.[52] Having attempted to correlate the membership and political radicalism of poor law boards with social factors, such as religion, relative poverty and landholding

---

48 *Annual Report of the Commissioners for Administering the Laws for the Relief of the Poor in Ireland*, HC, 1860 [2654], pp. 5. The maps are not reproduced in the online version.

49 *Poor Law Union and Lunacy Inquiry Commission (Ireland) Report and Evidence*, HC, 1878–9 [Cd. 2239], pp. 134–67.

50 Memorandum on Census of Paupers, March 31st 1906, *Royal Commission on the Poor Laws and Relief of Distress*, HC, 1910 [Cd. 5244], p. 13.

51 Rt Hon Sir Henry A. Robinson, *Memories: Wise and Otherwise* (New York: Dodd, Mead and Company, 1923), p. 132.

52 Feingold, *The Revolt of the Tenantry*, p. 193.

size, he concluded that religion was a factor in, but not a determinant of, the 'nationalization' of poor law boards and that there was no relationship between poverty or lack of economic development and either radicalism or conservatism. Thus he found that counties with a high proportion of Catholics in the population tended to be radical, while counties with a high proportion of Protestants tended to be conservative. He found that for radicalisation to take place the population needed to be more than 90 per cent Catholic. Radicalisation was most likely to occur in unions where there were large farmers and a high proportion of Catholics.[53]

Feingold attributed the conservative character of poor law boards in Ulster to the continued influence of the landed class, and the different attitude to government. In contrast to the three southern provinces where the proportion of total relief spent on outdoor relief rose significantly in the period from the late 1870s to 1890s, in Ulster the increase was much less marked. He believed that changes in relief practices were linked to the politicisation process, pointing out that the rise in the proportion of relief given as outdoor relief followed the same pattern as the rise in the percentage of board offices held by tenants. After 1879, he observed, 'something clearly happened in the relief-giving policies in Connaught and Munster', and to a lesser extent in Leinster. Moreover, having increased sharply, relief figures did not return to their pre-crisis level even after the crisis had passed.[54] Feingold was clearly correct in suggesting that something happened to relief-giving policies after 1879, but in order to understand the nature and magnitude of the change, it is necessary to look beyond the period 1875–1890, which formed the focus of Feingold's analysis.

Recent research on the operation of the poor law has explicitly adopted a regional approach. Low levels of relief in poor law unions in the west, D. S. Lucey maintains, need to be understood in relation to the local economy and the survival of a class of smallholders, who were less likely to resort to the workhouse 'to overcome short-term periods of distress'.[55] Georgina Laragy explains patterns of workhouse usage in the southeast with reference both to employment opportunities and 'the institutional and welfare landscapes of the different unions'. Relief figures, she suggests, should be seen as indicative of a union's 'ability to provide for the poor, rather than a measure of poverty itself'.[56] Whilst acknowledging the distinctive character of welfare administration in the north, Olwen Purdue argues that divisions within the

53 Feingold, *The Revolt of the Tenantry*, p. 211.
54 Feingold, *The Revolt of the Tenantry*, pp. 179–80.
55 Donnacha Seán Lucey, 'Poor Relief in the West of Ireland 1861–1911', in Crossman and Gray (eds), *Poverty and Welfare in Ireland*, p. 41.
56 Georgina Laragy, 'Poor Relief in the South of Ireland, 1850–1921', in Crossman and Gray (eds), *Poverty and Welfare in Ireland*, pp. 56, 60.

region were as important as those between the north and other parts of the country. She has identified a northeast/southwest divide. Unions in southern and western Ulster, she argues, were characterised by a more conservative outlook in contrast to the relatively liberal ethos evident in unions in the northeast. She has also highlighted the unique challenges facing workhouse managers in Belfast where annual admissions from the 1880s were generally in excess of 20,000.[57]

Too narrow a regional focus can, however, distort as well as illuminate. Purdue's analysis of outdoor relief in the north, for example, suggests that some unions in the north provided levels of outdoor relief that were consistently higher than the national average. This is not in fact the case. In the decades after 1880, no union in the north provided more than the national average in terms of numbers relieved. It is true that the percentage of relief given as outdoor relief was relatively high in unions such as Ballymena, but the total number relieved was still relatively low.[58] This highlights the importance of maintaining a broad national perspective whilst also paying attention to regional developments and the local character of relief. Understanding what was happening on a national level is essential if we are to appreciate the significance of local variations.

Mapping levels of expenditure on poor relief relative to population reveals clear regional patterns. There was a marked division in 1881 and 1901 between relatively low spending unions in the north and west of the country, and higher spending unions in the south and east (see Maps 2.1 and 2.2). Given that 1881 was a year of exceptional distress, we might expect to find the highest levels of expenditure along the western seaboard where distress was most severe. In fact, levels of expenditure in western unions remained relatively low in 1881. It would be a mistake therefore to use the rate of expenditure as a measure of poverty.[59] Other forms of spending on relief including grants and loans from central government as well as charitable spending would need to be included in order to obtain an accurate impression of the intensity of distress as measured by expenditure on relief. Expenditure levels overall tended to be higher in 1901 than they had been in

57 Olwen Purdue, 'Poor Relief in the North of Ireland, 1850–1921', in Crossman and Gray (eds), *Poverty and Welfare in Ireland 1838–1948* (Dublin: Irish Academic Press, 2011), pp. 23–36. The validity of a three-region approach is confirmed by Mel Cousins whose analysis of trends in relief and poor law valuation produced 'three clear groupings of unions': northern unions, peripheral western unions and southern unions. See, Mel Cousins, *Poor Relief in Ireland, 1851–1914* (Bern: Peter Lang, 2011), p. 44.

58 In 1891 the rate of outdoor relief per 1,000 population was 18.25 for Ballymena, compared to the national rate of 26.78. In 1901 the rate for Ballymena was 20.46 compared to the national rate of 24.85.

59 For a discussion of the use and interpretation of poor law expenditure figures for England, see King, *Poverty and Welfare in England*, pp. 79–91.

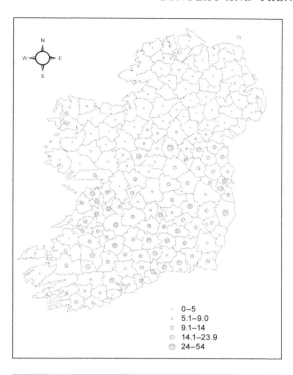

0–5
5.1–9.0
9.1–14
14.1–23.9
24–54

Map 2.1   Rate of expenditure poor relief 1881 (£ / 100 population).

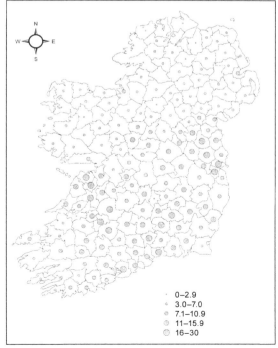

0–2.9
3.0–7.0
7.1–10.9
11–15.9
16–30

Map 2.2   Rate of expenditure poor relief 1901 (£ / 100 population).

1881, reflecting the general increase in expenditure on poor relief in the later decades of the nineteenth century. The northwest/southeast split, however, remained pronounced. The similarity between patterns of relative spending in 1881 and 1901 suggests that the figures reflect the relief culture of poor law unions rather than the extent of poverty, or the nature of the economy, within them. Higher spending unions were to be found along the southwest coast (categorised as congested districts from 1891) as well as in the more prosperous central and eastern areas, so the explanation cannot simply be that higher spending unions could afford to spend more; a wider range of causal factors was involved.

A similar pattern was evident with regard to numbers in receipt of indoor relief relative to the population (see Maps 2.3 and 2.4). Levels of relief increased overall, but once again the distribution was strikingly similar in 1861 and 1901, with unions on the eastern seaboard, together with those in the central southeastern portion of the country, providing significantly higher levels of relief than those in the north and west, and the far southwest. There is a closer correspondence in this case between the level of relief provided and socio-economic conditions; richer unions provided more relief. Since in 1861 the vast majority of people receiving poor relief received indoor relief, this suggests that contemporary critics of the poor law who argued that the system was failing to provide an adequate level of relief were indeed correct. Had poor law boards been relieving all those in need, the poorest unions would have been providing the most relief, the reverse of what was actually happening. By 1901 outdoor relief was provided on a far greater scale than had been the case in 1861, so that indoor relief now formed only part of relief provision. Mapping levels of outdoor relief highlights the major shift in practice that took place in the 1880s, outside the province of Ulster (see Maps 2.5 and 2.6). In 1861 very little outdoor relief was given. Unions that provided any significant amount of outdoor relief were small in number, and were clustered in the central southeast portion of the country. In 1901 patterns of relief across the country were very different. Levels of outdoor relief had increased across the country. Unions providing low levels of outdoor relief were now confined to Ulster and to the northwest of the province in particular.

How should we explain these trends? Conditions within the local economy clearly played a part. Hollen Lees observes that in England, 'relative desirability in the labor market appears to have shaped the allocations of aid to men and to women. Those needed were those aided.'[60] Irish unions that adopted outdoor relief in the 1860s all had relatively high average land valuations and contained substantial numbers of strong farmers dependent on paid labour.

60 Hollen Lees, *The Solidarities of Strangers*, p. 203.

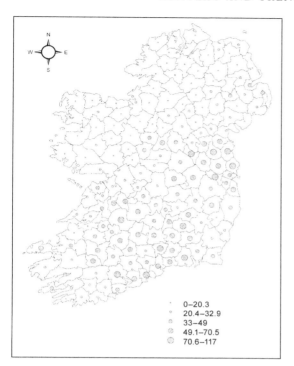

Map 2.3 Number of indoor relieved 1861 per 1000 population.

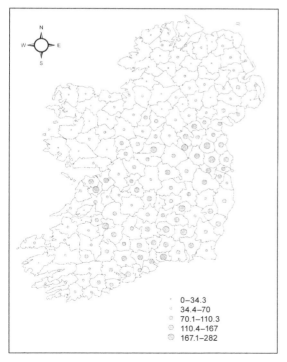

Map 2.4 Number of indoor relieved 1901 per 1000 population.

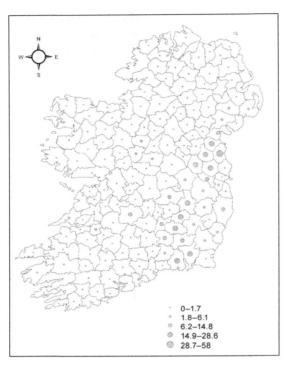

Map 2.5   Number of outdoor relieved 1861 per 1000 population.

0–1.7
1.8–6.1
6.2–14.8
14.9–28.6
28.7–58

Map 2.6   Number of outdoor relieved 1901 per 1000 population.

0–7.8
7.9–17.9
18–30.6
30.7–46.7
46.8–77.5

It seems reasonable to conclude, therefore, that the need to maintain a pool of available labour may have been one factor prompting poor law guardians to grant outdoor relief. Other factors may have been at work, however. The unions in question included a number, such as Dundalk, Drogheda, Wexford and New Ross, in which middle-class Catholics were beginning to have an influence as poor law guardians. Support for outdoor relief in these unions, therefore, is also likely to reflect the influence of the reform campaign led by Archbishop Cullen, which was pushing for a greater use of outdoor relief in order to keep the respectable poor out of the workhouse.

There appear to be a number of different trends taking place in relief practices. The southern provinces of Leinster and Munster saw significant increases in relief expenditure and numbers relieved over the second half of the nineteenth century. Ulster saw low levels of expenditure and relief throughout the post-Famine period. In Connacht by contrast, while levels of expenditure and indoor relief remained low, levels of outdoor relief rose significantly. In addition to regional variations, there were also notable intra-regional trends. Thus there were significant differences between predominantly rural unions and the major urban unions of Dublin (North and South) and Belfast. This was evident both in the relative amount of relief provided and in general trends over the period. Proportionate to population, Belfast provided lower than average levels of relief. The two Dublin unions (SDU and NDU) provided relief at levels (taking indoor and outdoor together) above the national average, but below that for neighbouring unions.[61] In contrast to the majority of unions throughout Ireland where the daily number of workhouse inmates declined from the 1880s, the average daily number in Belfast, SDU and NDU increased throughout the nineteenth century before declining in the second decade of the twentieth century (see Figure 2.5). Once again there are different ways of explaining this. The cities attracted migrants in search of greater economic opportunities, many of whom had little in the way of resources and thus little to fall back on if they got into difficulties. At the same time, the fact that many of those seeking relief in the cities were migrants meant that the relationship between applicants and the board of guardians was very different from that in rural unions where, with the exception of casuals, relief was largely restricted to local people who were either known to the guardians or recommended to them.

Feingold was clearly correct in linking the rise in outdoor relief in the 1880s and 1890s to the change in the composition of boards of guardians. The parts of the country affected by tenant radicalisation were also those

---

61 Cousins draws a distinction between northern cities where rates of relief were below average and southern cities were they were above average: *Poor Relief in Ireland*, pp. 50–1.

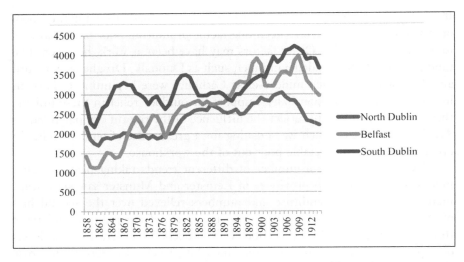

Figure 2.5   Average daily number in the workhouse in
Belfast, North Dublin and South Dublin Unions.
Source: Annual Reports of the Commissioners for Administering
the Laws for the relief of the Poor in Ireland and the
Local Government Board for Ireland 1850–1914

that adopted outdoor relief as a regular and integral element of their relief practices. Furthermore, unions that remained conservative in character, such as Mountmellick, Edenderry and Carlow, were often those that went against the general trend and provided lower than average levels of relief in the decades after the Land War. However, while politics was an important factor, socio-economic circumstances appear to have been equally important. Far western unions, such as Dingle and Glenties, were dominated by tenant guardians by 1886 but continued to provide low levels of both indoor and outdoor relief. Unions in Connacht were central to the process of board nationalisation and many did alter their relief practices by introducing outdoor relief, yet they continued to provide very low levels of relief overall. Here the real change in relief practices appears to have been linked to the provision of emergency relief. Feingold demonstrated that the sharpest increases in outdoor relief occurred during periods when emergency relief was provided: 1879–1881, 1883 and 1886.[62]

King has warned against positing a direct causal connection between economic conditions and relief practices in England, noting that at the macro-regional level 'attempts to relate socio-economic structures, poverty

62 Feingold, *The Revolt of the Tenantry*, p. 180.

type and welfare solutions meet with little success'. A more satisfactory explanatory framework, he suggests, may lie in the emergence of 'different welfare cultures on the part of both the poor and the poor law administrators'. Thus in contrast to what he sees as a culture of 'welfare dependency' in the south and east of England, a culture of self-reliance developed among poor people in the north and west, who consequently turned to the poor law only as a last resort.[63] Welfare cultures may offer a productive approach in the Irish context also. Rather than attempting to explain relief practices in terms of a political revolution or alternatively in relation to socio-economic conditions, the development of welfare cultures provides a means of understanding the interaction between different causal factors, whilst also allowing room for intra-regional variation. The spatial patterns noted above might then be interpreted as follows.

In the central southeastern portion of the country comprising most of Leinster and Munster, but excluding western and southwestern coastlines, there developed a welfare culture based on relatively high levels of relief and relatively easy access to relief. Indoor relief was available to almost all who applied for it and outdoor relief was provided to local people who met eligibility criteria primarily linked to ill-health and old age. In the north, and including the entire province of Ulster, there was a culture of limited and difficult to access relief. Here boards of guardians provided a minimal level of relief, and even indoor relief was more strictly regulated. There were variations within the province but compared to the rest of the country both relief and expenditure were low, and remained low throughout the period. In Connacht and along the southwest coastline there was a culture of low level but accessible relief. Indoor relief appears to have been readily available, although relatively few local people resorted to it. Outdoor relief became an increasingly important element within the local economy of the poor but primarily in the form of emergency relief. Outside periods of crisis, outdoor relief was provided at a very low level.

It is not the intention here to provide a detailed analysis of welfare cultures. Suffice it to say that a combination of factors (ideological, political, economic, social and cultural) gave rise not only to distinct patterns of relief provision, but also to distinct relief cultures that influenced both those applying for, and those administering, relief. In the north, for example, political and religious ideology appears to have promoted a culture of self-reliance amongst the poor and a minimalist relief culture. Maintaining this would not have been possible, however, without favourable economic conditions, in particular the availability of paid employment. The aim of this chapter has been to provide an explanatory context and framework. It is clear

63 King, *Poverty and Welfare in England*, pp. 266–8.

that the ways in which people utilised the relief system varied over time, and between regions. What remains to be seen is how these variations played out at the local level. To do this it is necessary to move from the general to the particular, and to examine the practical operation of the relief system.

3

Outdoor Relief

In Ireland, even more so than in England, the workhouse dominates popular awareness of the poor law. Despite recent research that has highlighted the importance of outdoor relief and its significance as a political issue,[1] the workhouse remains the element with which people are most familiar and which is believed to define the system. The reason for this, as Snell has noted in relation to England, is two-fold.[2] The workhouse generated a mass of archival material and it was the focus of extensive commentary and debate. Officials were required to keep detailed records relating to the management of the workhouse and its inmates, many of which have survived. For many unions we can see who was admitted to the workhouse and how long they stayed. We can discover how inmates were treated and how they behaved. Outdoor relief generated far fewer records and those that were produced have frequently been destroyed. It is difficult to establish who received relief and on what grounds, and even more difficult to follow claimants through the outdoor relief process. There was considerable drama and emotion attached to the workhouse as an institution. It provided the setting for stories of hardship and abuse, of sex, violence and disorder. The administration of outdoor relief was more prosaic, more mundane, and involved little that was dramatic or entertaining. Nevertheless, an understanding of how the outdoor relief system operated is essential to an understanding of the poor law system.

The poor law authorities associated outdoor relief with excessive expenditure, dependency and lax administration, based on subjective rather than objective assessment and personal feeling rather than rational need.[3]

---

1 Virginia Crossman, *Politics, Pauperism and Power Power in Late Nineteenth-Century Ireland* (Manchester: Manchester University Press, 2006), pp. 71–105; and Donnacha Seán Lucey, 'Power, Politics and Poor Relief During the Irish Land War, 1879–82', *Irish Historical Studies*, xxxvii (November 2011), pp. 584–98.

2 K. D. M. Snell, *Parish and Belonging: Community, Identity and Welfare in England and Wales 1700–1950* (Cambridge: Cambridge University Press, 2006), pp. 207–10.

3 For an analysis of debates over outdoor relief, see Virginia Crossman and Donnacha

The New Poor Law in England attempted to establish a system in which outdoor relief would be the exception rather than the rule. Under the Irish poor law of 1838 there was no outdoor relief. Offering only indoor relief, its architects hoped, would ensure that the system would be self-regulating and that costs would be manageable. The introduction of outdoor relief in 1847 represented a fundamental change, although it was not until later decades of the nineteenth century that the implications of this were to become fully apparent. Having been introduced against the wishes of a significant body of opinion in Ireland across the political spectrum, the experience of the Famine further polarised attitudes to the poor law. The manifest failures of the relief system during the Famine period, and the very high mortality rate within some workhouses, reinforced popular hostility and convinced many people that workhouses were to be avoided at all costs. Concentrating relief in workhouses was seen to have failed, particularly in remote parts of the country, such as the far south and far west. To many observers it was clear that the system needed modification. At the same time, the practical difficulties encountered by poor law guardians and officials in the administration of outdoor relief, fuelled fears that any expansion of the system would simply provide greater opportunities for abuse. As soon as it was practically possible, most boards of guardians reverted to pre-Famine practice. Eligible applicants were offered the workhouse and if that was unacceptable, they received nothing.

Workhouses came to symbolise the ugly face of British administration; alien, brutal, uniform, centralised and expensive, placing a burden on local taxpayers for which they received little direct benefit. Popular opposition to the poor law provides a barometer of attitudes to the British state, as critics attempted first to reform it and then to subvert it. In the view of Archbishop Cullen, the poor law highlighted the failure of British Government in Ireland. 'Reform, including greater Catholic involvement and a more overtly Catholic ethos in poor law administration, was necessary', he argued, 'both on the grounds of natural justice, since Catholics formed the bulk of the populace and thus a majority amongst the poor, and as a way of promoting better and more stable government.'[4] In the later part of the nineteenth century, Irish nationalists came to see the workhouse system as an element of a centralised state apparatus that was oppressing and impoverishing the Irish

---

Seán Lucey, '"One Huge Abuse": The Cork Board of Guardians and the Expansion of Outdoor Relief in Post-Famine Ireland', *English Historical Review*, cxxvi (December 2011), pp. 1408–29.

4   For an analysis of Cullen's views on the poor law and social welfare, see Virginia Crossman, '"Attending to the Wants of Poverty": Cullen, the Relief of Poverty and the Development of Social Welfare in Ireland', in D. Keogh and A. McDonnell (eds), *Cardinal Paul Cullen and His World* (Dublin: Four Courts Press, 2011), pp. 146–65.

people. Throughout the post-Famine period there were two major catalysts for changes to the system, political campaigns and economic crises. In the 1860s the campaign to reform the poor law coincided with economic distress in the far west. The perceived failure of the poor law to provide adequate relief in the distressed districts strengthened criticism of the system as too restrictive.[5] Severe economic distress also provided the backdrop to the land campaign. The pressure of near-Famine conditions in 1879–1881 forced many boards of guardians to abandon their opposition to outdoor relief. Outdoor relief now became an accepted, and acceptable, method of providing relief.[6]

The poor survival of records relating to outdoor relief, compared to those for indoor relief, may reflect not only the relative importance of the workhouse within popular and academic awareness, but also local sensitivities and a desire to protect recipients from public exposure. Publication of the names of applicants seeking relief was condemned by the *Kerry Sentinel* in February 1880, as 'an outrage on the feelings of the poor', which had 'acted as a deterrent to some parties in very great destitution, who otherwise would have applied for relief to the guardians'.[7] Many people appear to have regarded the posting-up of relief lists, which was a requirement under poor law regulations, as unwarranted and degrading. In 1906 the *Meath Chronicle* declared that the practice deserved:

the condemnation of all charitably disposed persons. It is adding to the load of sorrow and humiliation under which the afflicted creatures already groan – a needless cruelty directed against the poor for the crime of being destitute.[8]

Those receiving outdoor relief were perceived differently from those entering the workhouse and, it would appear, regarded with more compassion.

Debates over outdoor relief were highly politicised and tended to be framed in terms that pitted populist arguments in favour of outdoor relief against establishment statements of new poor law principles. In the 1880s and 1890s Irish nationalists sought election as poor law guardians and once

5 Virginia Crossman, '"Facts Notorious to the Whole Country": The Political Battle over Irish Poor Law Reform in the 1860s', *Transactions of the Royal Historical Society*, xx (2010), pp. 157–70.
6 See Virginia Crossman, '"With the Experience of 1846 and 1847 Before Them": The Politics of Emergency Relief 1879–84', in Peter Gray (ed.), *Victoria's Ireland? Irishness and Britishness, 1837–1901* (Dublin: Four Courts Press, 2004), pp. 167–82; and Crossman, *Politics, Pauperism and Power*, pp. 106–43.
7 *Kerry Sentinel*, 24 February 1880.
8 *Meath Chronicle*, 9 June 1906.

elected sought to utilise their powers, to advance the national movement. In a number of high-profile cases, nationalist-controlled boards of guardians sought to defy the central authorities by subverting poor law regulations, whether by setting aside accommodation for evicted tenants within the workhouse, as in New Ross; or by granting generous outdoor relief allowances to evicted tenants with the intention of putting pressure on the evicting landlord, as in Athy; or by granting large numbers of people outdoor relief in order to reserve the workhouse for the undeserving poor, as in Cork.[9] In all these cases, the board of guardians was eventually dissolved and replaced by paid, government-appointed, vice-guardians who reversed the policy. Attempts to rally popular support behind the deposed guardians by means of rates strikes proved unsuccessful, mainly because ratepayers tended to prioritise their own interests over those of the poor. As these episodes demonstrate, outdoor relief and poor law administration more generally became one element of the wider political struggle. Indeed, arguments over outdoor relief became conflated with arguments for and against Home Rule. However, while the political context is crucial for understanding the shift in relief policies that took place in this period, it is not the only, or the entire, explanation. In the cases mentioned above, there was a direct link with wider nationalist campaigns. In other unions political developments were an indirect rather than a direct influence, and relief practices were driven by other considerations. The following discussion shifts the focus away from political and ideological debates to the practical administration of outdoor relief, examining the nature of the relief system and how it operated.

The introduction of outdoor relief in 1847 necessitated the creation of a new position within poor law administration, that of relieving officer. Relieving officers were appointed by boards of guardians subject to the approval of the central authorities, who also determined the number required in each union. Relieving officers were required to be at least twenty-one years of age, able to read and write and keep accounts, not engaged in retail trade and able to provide financial security. Their duties were laid down in the General Order of 2 August 1847 regulating the administration of outdoor relief. They were to attend the regular meetings of the board of guardians, to keep a diary recording the execution of their duties and to keep records of all payments made. They were also required to be available at designated places, and times, for the purpose of dispensing relief and receiving applications. On receipt of an application the relieving officer was to inquire into the circumstances of the case:

9 Virginia Crossman, 'The New Ross Workhouse Riot of 1887: Nationalism, Class and the Irish Poor Laws', *Past and Present*, 179 (May 2003), pp. 135–58; Crossman, *Politics, Pauperism and Power*, pp. 87–99; and Crossman and Lucey, 'One Huge Abuse'.

by visiting the home of the applicant, and by making all necessary inquiries into the state of health, the ability to work, the condition, the family, and the previous earnings and other means of such applicant, and to report the results of such inquiries ... to the Board of Guardians at their next ordinary meeting.[10]

Instructions issued in November 1847 reminded relieving officers of the 'serious responsibilities' of the office and advised them to adhere closely to the rules prescribed.

Recognising that some boards of guardians were determined not to grant any outdoor relief, the commissioners advised relieving officers that lack of funds was 'no reason why you should relax in the performance of such of your duties as you can, under the circumstances mentioned, perform'. They should receive and investigate applications for relief and report their findings to the board of guardians. By such a course, they would not only 'avoid censure', but would have done 'everything within your province to remedy the defect of funds by showing, in the proper quarter, the necessity which may exist for providing them'. The commissioners then drew attention to the relieving officer's ability to provide provisional relief in any case of 'sudden and urgent necessity'. This could be done:

either by an order of admission to the workhouse ... or by affording such poor person immediate and temporary relief in food, lodging, medicine, or medical attendance, until the next ordinary meeting of the Board of Guardians ... On a judicious exercise of your powers under this section will depend in a great measure the success of your proceedings.

Relieving officers were warned against 'indiscriminately relieving all applicants', as likely to lead to 'overwhelming claims [and] much consequent embarrassment', but were also urged to be 'easily accessible, and keenly alive to the existence of actual suffering from destitution'. They were exhorted to exercise 'humanity, judgement, impartiality, and vigilant attention' to their duty, thereby ensuring that 'neither imposture will be successfully practiced by the applicants for relief, nor that the really destitute will fail to receive the relief which has been provided for them by law'.[11] Not surprisingly perhaps, very few relieving officers were able to live up to these ideals.

10 General Order, 2 August 1847: *First Annual Report of the Commissioners for Administering the Laws for Relief of the Poor in Ireland*, HC, 1847–1848 [963], pp. 74–5
11 Instructions to Relieving Officers, 10 November 1847: *Correspondence etc. Relative to Duties of Relieving Officers (Ireland)*, HC, 1867 [581], pp. 14–17.

Relieving officers' powers with regard to granting provisional relief appeared very extensive, but they were initially applied so narrowly that very little provisional relief was granted in the period prior to 1880. This was mainly because there appears to have been considerable uncertainty about the nature and purpose of provisional relief. In 1861 the Drogheda Board of Guardians wrote to the poor law commissioners to inquire whether they could authorise their relieving officer to afford provisional relief to able-bodied persons with large families, explaining that their inquiry related to fishermen who had been 'thrown idle by the severity of the weather'. The cases referred to sounded more like seasonal unemployment than sudden destitution, although the former could conceivably have led to the latter. In cases of sudden and urgent necessity, the commissioners cautioned, relief could only be provided as food, lodging, medicine or medical attendance. Cash payments, which the relieving officer appeared to have provided in this instance, were illegal and could be disallowed by the union auditor.[12] Relieving officers, the commissioners added, acted on their own responsibility. They did not need the authorisation of the board of the guardians to give provisional relief.[13]

Following the passage of the Poor Law Amendment Act in 1862, boards of guardians were advised that although the repeal of the quarter acre clause applied only to indoor relief, the provisional powers of relieving officers were applicable to people holding more than a quarter of an acre of land, as in all other cases.[14] Further clarification and instructions were issued in 1864, following the death of an elderly man who had been suffering from rheumatism and dropsy, but had been refused outdoor relief as he occupied more than a quarter of an acre of bog-garden. He had died 'after several months of severe privation', prompting the commissioners to issue a circular stressing that 'sudden and urgent necessity applies to all cases in which a necessity exists for action and the fact that distress had existed previously does not preclude the relieving officer from acting'.[15] The circumstances under which provisional relief could be granted became a matter of public controversy in 1867, when the Chairman of the Trim Board of Guardians, Samuel Winter, resigned in protest at official guidance provided to the board.

The issue arose in circumstances similar to those which had prompted the Drogheda Board of Guardians to consult the commissioners in 1861.

12 For the powers of auditors, see Crossman, *Politics, Pauperism and Power*, pp. 26–30.
13 *Dublin Evening Post*, 16 February 1861.
14 The quarter acre clause, which had been inserted into the 1847 Poor Relief Extension Act during the latter's passage through Parliament, rendered anyone in possession of more than a quarter of an acre of land ineligible for relief. It was repealed in 1862 with regard to indoor relief but remained in force with regard to outdoor relief.
15 Banks to Union Clerks, 15 June 1863; and Circular to Boards of Guardians, 3 October 1864: *Correspondence etc. Relative to Duties of Relieving Officers (Ireland)*, pp. 16–17, 19.

A number of labourers who were out of work due to the unusual severity of the weather had applied for relief and been given tickets for admission to the workhouse. The relieving officer had refused to grant outdoor relief saying that he had no authority to do so. The commissioners then intervened pointing out that the guardians could not interfere with the relieving officer in the granting of provisional relief. The Trim Board of Guardians had previously granted outdoor relief only to people who were physically unable to work. The able-bodied, the guardians had erroneously assumed, could not be relieved without a sealed order from the poor law commissioners. Echoing contemporary critiques of the pauperising effect of outdoor relief in England, Winter predicted that the effect of the commissioners' ruling would be to increase the financial burden on the ratepayers and 'pauperise the labouring population by causing many of them to rely more on the relief than to seek for employment', whilst encouraging employers to 'discharge their labourers when they have no urgent work to be done', knowing that 'they will be supported as destitute when suddenly thrown out of work'.[16]

The commissioners explained that they had obtained a legal opinion shortly after the passage of the 1847 Extension Act which stated that the power of relieving provisionally was unlimited. However, they sought to allay Winter's concerns observing that experience in other unions did not justify his apprehensions 'and that by the exercise on the part of the relieving officers of judgement and firmness in the discharge of their duties, the evil consequences predicted are not likely to occur'. Winter refused to reconsider his resignation, declaring that he had always assumed that one of the chief duties of poor law guardians was 'to exercise great watchfulness and careful supervision of outdoor relief to the able-bodied, which is well known to have been often greatly abused elsewhere, whereas such duty appears to be now entirely taken out of our hands'. If relieving officers were to give provisional relief to all able-bodied persons whenever they were out of employment, he saw no point in the guardians meeting:

The workhouse system we have always been told was intended principally as a test to prevent abuses arising from indiscriminate outdoor relief; but if this test is to be done away with, it would be much better to shut up the house altogether, discharge the officers, and put an end to all establishment charges, to allow the guardians to stay at home, and have the whole business carried on by the relieving officers and the auditor.[17]

16 Winter to Poor Law Commissioners, 7 May 1867: *Correspondence etc. Relative to Duties of Relieving Officers (Ireland)*, pp. 6–9.
17 Commissioners to Winter, 16 May 1867; Winter to Residing Chairman, 1 June 1867:

Given the reluctance of most relieving officers to grant any relief in this period, Winter's fears were clearly exaggerated. However, as the numbers in receipt of relief increased in later decades, so the role of the relieving officer became more important. By the early twentieth century, relieving officers were responsible for considerable sums of money, making them influential figures within their local communities.

A parliamentary return produced in May 1867 revealed that provisional relief to the able-bodied had been rising slowly but steadily over the previous ten years. In 1858 the total number of able-bodied people who had received provisional relief in the course of the administrative year was 436. By 1865, this figure had reached 2,235. The majority of unions, however, made nil returns so it is clear that there was a wide disparity in relief practices. Just how wide was evident from the return for the period from September 1866 to May 1867. During this period, a total of 4,489 able-bodied people had received provisional relief. This included 2,336 people in South Dublin Union who had been relieved, 'in consequence of the heavy snowstorm'. In North Dublin Union not a single person received provisional relief suggesting that it was either an extremely localised snowstorm or the relieving officers in the two unions applied a very different interpretation of sudden and urgent necessity.[18]

In their official guidance the commissioners sought to strike a balance between ensuring that relief was provided when it was needed, particularly when people were in extreme distress and preventing unnecessary or indiscriminate relief. In 1885, the Local Government Board received a query from a relieving officer in County Mayo asking whether he should dispense relief in accordance with the directions of the medical officer or the guardians. He was informed that having provided provisional relief, he could not give any further relief 'otherwise than by direction of the Board of Guardians', except in the case of a sick person whose circumstances or conditions had changed. In that case, 'you may entertain the applications for such further relief, and deal with the case again under the power you have to give provisional relief in cases of sudden and urgent necessity'. Faced with severe distress in Donegal in 1890, Local Government Inspector (LGI) William Micks suggested that relieving officers should be reminded:

that if there should be any change in the circumstances or condition

Correspondence etc. Relative to Duties of Relieving Officers (Ireland), 1867 (581), pp. 9–10, 12.

18 *Abstract of Return of the Number of Able-Bodied Persons who have Received Provisional Outdoor Relief in Cases of Sudden and Urgent Necessity ... from Relieving Officers in every Poor Law Union in Ireland ... from the Year 1858 to the Present Time*, HC, 1867 (427).

of an applicant (for the destitute are in as good a position as the sick), the relieving officer is not precluded from affording provisional relief.

He could not, he observed, 'imagine a case of imminent starvation in which a relieving officer would not be justified according to law and precedent in affording provisional relief'.[19]

A briefing note on provisional relief written in 1895 explained that the Local Government Board had 'always held' that boards of guardians had no authority to interfere with the powers conferred on the relieving officer, and that the latter could not be prevented 'from a ordering a continuance of the relief if it should again come before him as one of sudden and urgent necessity'. Since the relieving officer was responsible for ensuring 'that no person who applies to him for relief shall be allowed to suffer from severe privation, or to die from the want of the necessaries of life', the Local Government Board had ruled 'that in the person upon whom this grave responsibility rests shall also reside the power to determine what is or is not sudden and urgent necessity'.[20] When the Oldcastle Board of Guardians sought advice in 1900 concerning the case of a man suffering from an incurable malformation of the hand, who was in possession of more than a quarter of an acre of land but who was refusing to enter the workhouse, the board advised that, 'while every means should be adopted to persuade him to enter the workhouse, if he was in actual need the relieving officer was right to give him provisional relief'.[21]

There was little the Local Government Board could do, however, in the face of local intransigence. In May 1879, LGI John Roughan had reported that 'distress and want' prevailed to:

a pitiable extent among some of the artisans and labourers in Belfast. They have in very numerous instances been obliged to sell and pawn their furniture and even their bedding for the purpose of procuring sustenance and no-one can tell how they now find food or raiment.

Despite these conditions, no provisional outdoor relief had been given. 'It is difficult to understand', Roughan commented, 'how this could be so during a period of such widespread destitution. The relieving officers could afford no

19 Note by Micks, 13 November 1890, BL, Balfour Papers, Add MS 49817, folios 140, 147.
20 Provisional Relief, February 1895, Morley Papers, Bodleian Library, Oxford, Correspondence and Papers of John Morley as Chief Secretary for Ireland 1880–1895.
21 Local Government Board Precedent Book, Provisional Relief, Oldcastle/1900, PRONI, LGBD 2/1.

explanation on the subject.'[22] Belfast relieving officers persisted in interpreting their duties as narrowly as possible. Public protests over the refusal of outdoor relief to a sick woman in 1891, prompted the Local Government Board to suggest that the guardians remind their relieving officer of his powers of affording provisional relief and the fact that he would be 'held responsible for using his own discretion in cases of sudden and urgent necessity'. Investigation of the case revealed that the relieving officer had refused to act without a medical certificate, which the medical officer had refused to issue insisting the responsibility lay with the relieving officer. The guardians declined to intervene, resolving to remain 'neutral in respect of the matter'. Asked for an explanation of his conduct, Relieving Officer Samuel Mercer observed curtly that he had 'nothing to add'. Threat of censure from the Local Government Board, or the public, was of no concern. The board of guardians was his authority and he was clearly, and rightly, confident of their support.[23]

Although the total number in receipt of provisional relief was not included in annual returns, from 1863 national figures were provided for 'persons relieved provisionally, and not included in the foregoing columns'. These figures show that provisional relief increased significantly in 1881 and while it dropped back in the later 1880s, it began to rise again in the 1890s through the first decade of the twentieth century (see Figure 3.1). Since the total number relieved out of the workhouse was in decline from the mid-1880s it is likely that some of the people removed from regular outdoor relief lists by boards of guardians or refused regular relief, were granted provisional relief. That provisional relief was sometimes given inappropriately is evident from comments made by the Auditor of Tralee Union in 1900, drawing attention to 'the very large amount of provisional relief' given by the relieving officers of the Tralee district on their own responsibility. 'While in no way wishing to interfere with the responsibilities of the relieving officers as such', he pointed out that they were only empowered, 'to offer relief otherwise than by order of the guardians, in cases of urgency, and that urgency is scarcely likely to exist for the twenty-six weeks of a half year'. Noting that the vouchers for provisional relief were all accompanied by medical certificates, he observed that while it was open to the medical officers to recommend 'certain articles of food for patients', they could not order the granting of outdoor relief 'either in money or kind as the granting of such relief rests entirely with the guardians and in cases of urgency till the next ordinary meeting of the board with the relieving officer who must accept sole responsibility for his action'.[24]

22 Extracts from Dr Roughan's Report, 23 May 1879, Belfast Board of Guardians (Correspondence), PRONI, BG/7/BC/1.
23 Belfast Board of Guardians Minutes, 12 and 19 December 1891, PRONI, BG/7/A.
24 Tralee Board of Guardians Minutes, 12 June 1901, Kerry County Library, Tralee Board

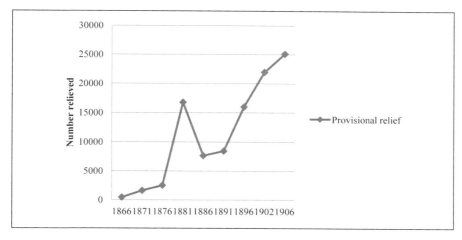

Figure 3.1   Number relieved provisionally 1866–1906.
Source: Classification of persons relieved out of the workhouse in unions
in Ireland during the year, Number of persons relieved provisionally,
and not included in the foregoing columns, Annual Reports of the
Commissioners for Administering the Laws for the relief of the Poor
in Ireland and the Local Government Board for Ireland 1850–1914

Medical certification became integral to the relief process. In 1881 the
Medical Officer of Tralee Union, Dr William Nolan, protested indignantly
on receiving a note signed by an elected Member of the Board, H. W.
Knight, directing him to authorise relief for 'such persons as I give you
orders to, as it will save you from visiting tickets'. The doctor protested that
the document was 'an extraordinary one, as I have learned for the first time
that the duties of relieving officer are added to those I discharge as medical
officer of the district, which I find are quite sufficient for my energies'.[25]
Concerned about the increase of outdoor relief in the North Dublin Union
in 1883, one guardian complained:

> that when a man came for outdoor relief the relieving officer simply
> asked him if any of his family were sick, and if so to go to the doctor
> and get a certificate so that if a child in the family were sick outdoor
> relief was given. The whole system was rotten.[26]

It remained the practice in many unions, however, to refer applicants for

---

of Guardians.
25 *Kerry Sentinel*, 10 August 1881.
26 *Irish Times*, 15 March 1883.

outdoor relief to the medical officer in the first instance. Writing to Mrs M. J. P. of Portartlington in July 1900, the clerk of the Mountmellick Board of Guardians explained that she could obtain an allowance 'in the way of outdoor relief provided that you are ill and procure a certificate to that effect from the Medical Officer of the district', assuring her that the guardians 'would be only too happy [to help] if it were within their power'. He added as a postscript that the medical certificate could be forwarded 'to Relieving Officer Mr Denis Molloy who can give you provisional relief pending a meeting of the Board of Guardians'.[27]

How relieving officers interpreted and performed their duties, the poor law commissioners had noted in 1847, would determine the character and efficacy of relief in their union. But it was disingenuous to suggest they could act independently of the board of guardians. As union officers, their actions were guided by the board and were largely dependent on the direction provided by guardians. In unions where guardians were strongly opposed to outdoor relief, relieving officers could find themselves in a very uncomfortable position. In 1875, for example, Members of the Ballycastle Board of Guardians were furious to discover that their relieving officer had provided provisional relief on the advice of the Medical Officer, Dr Cronin. The guardians were reported as saying that Cronin had 'no business' ordering relief and that the relieving officer 'should not have obeyed him'. RO Patrick Clarke explained that Dr Cronin had judged that 'the woman in the case was so ill that her life would be endangered if she was moved to the workhouse infirmary, the distance was so far'. Guardians were unmoved. 'We have set our faces against giving outdoor relief', Alexander M'Kennon, declared, 'for if once we begin that system we will be imposed upon.' When anyone was too ill to be taken to the workhouse, people in the locality could be relied on 'to give a little help'. The harassed relieving was less confident, observing that when he attempted to get help from local farmers the response was, 'What is the good of a poorhouse if we have to support the poor as well as paying to support the poorhouse.' If the guardians did not want him to grant any outdoor relief, they must, he warned, be prepared to protect him, 'in case that the commissioners should think differently from them'. He was also under pressure from the police. He explained the difficulty he faced when 'poor tramps come to me for a night's lodging – there is no place provided for them in Cushendall'. If he refused to pay for overnight accommodation they went to the police, 'and in one case the serjeant of police threatened to report me if I refused or neglected to provide a poor man with a bed'. Asked what he did in such cases, Clarke replied that he often paid for a bed out of

27 Clerk to Mrs M. J. Protzellor, 29 July (1900?), Mountmellick Board of Guardians Letter Book, Laois County Library, Mountmellick Board of Guardians.

his own pocket. The guardians refused to moderate their position, however. The relieving officer was warned that he must not give outdoor relief or he would be dismissed.[28]

Boards that began to grant outdoor relief in the 1860s appear to have done so because it was seen as both more humane and more economical. As the *Freeman's Journal* observed in March 1861, in the majority of cases of people, 'now immured in workhouses it would be found that relief more satisfactory to the recipients and less costly to the ratepayers could be given outside the workhouse than within its walls'.[29] In a letter to the *Daily Express* later that year, Joseph Harris, a member of the Drogheda Board of Guardians, argued that outdoor relief could 'benefit everyone'. Granting people small allowances, he maintained, encouraged them to 'make an exertion to bring themselves through ... but lock the poor man up in a poor house and he becomes useless to all society, and, losing caste, he becomes broken hearted, and dies in a short time'.[30] The classic arguments for and against outdoor relief were rehearsed at the Dundalk Board of Guardians in 1860–1861. In March 1860, Richard Byrne PLG proposed that outdoor relief should be given to 'well conducted poor widows having two or more children', arguing that the workhouse provided 'the worst possible nursery for children'. The measure would not be costly, he suggested, 'since the widows would be able to work and would, therefore, only need small allowances.' He regarded this, 'simply as a matter of justice and humanity, as a right which the Act of Parliament confers on widows and orphans, than whom there is no class more entitled to our sympathy and consideration'. Byrne's resolution was carried by thirteen votes to nine. The board remained divided on the issue, however, and the following year, ex officio guardian, W. M'Culloch, sought to reverse the decision. Giving outdoor relief to widows, he observed, discouraged them from working and was thus giving a 'premium to idleness and laziness'. His elected colleague, P. Callan, insisted that granting outdoor relief was cheaper than refusing it, since people who refused to enter the workhouse ended up begging. Their support was thus 'thrown on the poor struggling ratepayers, the humble farmers, and the shopkeepers'.[31]

Annual returns indicate that for the country as a whole by far the largest group, in terms of relief cases, comprised those permanently disabled

---

28 *Ballymoney Free Press*, 14 January 1875. Ballycastle Board of Guardians remained resolutely hostile to outdoor relief passing a resolution in April 1900, 'that we should not encourage outdoor relief and only give the same when the patient cannot be taken into the house': Ballycastle Board of Guardians Minutes, 28 April 1900, PRONI, BG/3/A.
29 *Freeman's Journal*, 3 March 1861.
30 *Daily Express*, 14 June 1861.
31 *Dublin Evening Post*, 1 March 1860; and *Packet*, 27 April 1861.

from work on account of age or disability.[32] Within this, group women outnumbered men by around two to one. In terms of total numbers relieved, however, the largest category comprised the temporarily disabled together with their dependents. The reason for this is that the permanently disabled tended to be elderly and thus had few if any dependents, while the temporarily disabled were often young adults with large numbers of dependents. A return of those in receipt of outdoor relief in the week ended 16 February 1861 shows that the 1,173 people receiving relief as permanently disabled had 319 dependents, while the 960 people receiving relief as temporarily disabled had 1,557 dependents.[33] The same return highlights the different approaches to outdoor relief adopted in different unions. Many boards of guardians granted no outdoor relief at all. Some, such as Dunshaughlin, Edenderry and Enniscorthy, granted relief in one category only, those temporarily disabled. It seems very unlikely that there were no eligible people in the other categories, so this appears to have been a policy decision. It is probable that in these cases outdoor relief was being used as a temporary expedient to enable working people with dependents, who found themselves in temporary difficulty, being forced to enter the workhouse. Where it appeared relief was likely to be more long term, applicants were offered indoor relief or nothing.

While many guardians remained hostile to outdoor relief, some were keen to extend their powers so that they could relieve a wider range of applicants.[34] In 1867 the Chair of the Kilmallock Board of Guardians, R. D. Bolton Massey, wrote to the chief secretary calling for a change in the law to allow boards of guardians to give outdoor relief to able-bodied poor during the winter months when labouring work was not available. 'Labour', he noted, 'ceased on 1 January, and many labourers suffered greatly from want during the two winter months.' They could not obtain outdoor relief without giving up their holdings, and this they were not willing to do. He claimed to have

---

32 Poor law officials were required to keep a record of the number of cases of outdoor relief (that is the number of people who applied for and were granted relief) and the number of persons in receipt of relief which included dependents. Nationally the number of persons was roughly double the number of cases.

33 Classified Return of Persons receiving Out-door Relief in the Week ended Saturday the 16th day of February 1861, *Report from the Select Committee Appointed to Inquire into the Administration of the Relief of the Poor in Ireland*, HC, 1861 (408), pp. 387–8.

34 North Dublin Union, for example, passed the following resolution in 1861: 'that it is the opinion of the Board that, with the exception of what may be done for orphans and deserted children, no alteration is required in the existing law regarding outdoor relief, as they feel that any enactment compelling boards of Guardians to impart outdoor relief contrary to their opinion, would be demoralising to the recipients and unjust and injurious to owners of property rateable for poor law purposes': NDU Board of Guardian Minutes, 1 May 1861, NAI, BG/78/A.

known cases in which a woman had entered the workhouse with her younger children, leaving her husband and older children outside, 'she stating that she never was married and that the children were illegitimate'. Where people were willing to go to these lengths, he suggested, the law clearly required some amendment. The Chief Secretary, Lord Naas, disagreed, arguing that 'very great objection would be made by the majority of ratepayers in Ireland' to giving boards of guardians:

> an unlimited power of affording outdoor relief to the able-bodied poor. The powers of the law given in respect to outdoor relief are already very large and until these powers have been exhausted I have reason to trust that Parliament would be indisposed to sanction so extensive an alteration of the law as that suggested.[35]

Nenagh Board of Guardians was another early adopter of outdoor relief and here too guardians appear to have been anxious to make provision for labourers and their families, who would otherwise be forced into the workhouse. Elected guardian, James O'Leary, declared in 1876 that he was in favour of the Nenagh guardians giving outdoor relief, 'instead of showing applicants into the infirmary. To thus force them into the house was unfair to the rural districts which would have to bear a portion of the burden of the Nenagh paupers.' His ex officio colleague, Henry Head, agreed saying that he considered that it was better 'to give these people a small share of outdoor relief, as their cost, if they come into the house, would after a certain amount of the rate on the Nenagh division, be extended over the entire union'.

The Chair, James Poe, reminded guardians that they had 'two duties to discharge, to look to the poor and to consider the ratepayers'.[36] By 1879, the amount expended on outdoor relief was alarming some members of the board who noted that neighbouring unions spent very little, in contrast to Nenagh. Outdoor relief, Poe observed:

> was not only impoverishing the union, but demoralising the people, for the applications were becoming indiscriminate, and the parties say they have as good a right to get outdoor relief as others who are in receipt of it.

Many guardians remained convinced, however, that it was an economical form of relief. It was, one observed, less expensive to the union 'than

---

35 Bolton Massey to Naas, 12 February 1867; and Naas to Bolton Massey, 28 February 1867: CSORP 1867/3118.
36 *Nenagh Guardian*, 12 February 1876.

bringing a whole lot of paupers into the house ... By getting some small share of relief here, with the aid they will receive from the neighbours, they will not come into the house.'[37]

The central arguments changed very little over the following decades. At a discussion on the Thurles Board of Guardians in the summer of 1900, D. McCarthy argued that forcing people into the workhouse was a 'false economy on the part of the guardians'. Ratepayers' interests were often cited:

> but I ask you will it be in their interests to refuse an application for 2s a week and compel this woman with her child to come into the house when it will cost 6s a week to support them ... Our first duty here is to relieve the poor.[38]

Guardians clung to the belief that outdoor relief was economical, despite clear evidence to the contrary. Poor law expenditure rose steadily throughout the period. Some boards acknowledged the problem of rising costs, but found it impossible to address it effectively. A committee of the Mountmellick Board of Guardians reported in September 1871, that 'the principal reason' for the increase in poor rates had arisen 'from the practice of giving outdoor relief which has increased within the last five years from £100 to £1,200 per annum causing at once for that item, a rate of about 3d in the pound on the valuation of the union', and recommending 'a general revision of outdoor relief with a view to a reduction'.[39] Relief expenditure in the union continued to increase, however.

Since the cost of outdoor relief fell on the electoral division in which the recipient resided, guardians from rural divisions often supported outdoor relief being given to people residing in urban divisions as a way of keeping people out of the workhouse and thus keeping down establishment charges, which fell on the union as a whole.[40] Following the 1898 Local Government Act, outdoor relief became a union charge so that from 1899 the cost was spread across the whole union. Whereas previously guardians had no reason to oppose an application for outdoor relief from another electoral division, since it would not directly impact on them or their neighbours, now all guardians had an interest in all applications. Prior to 1899, there was a general understanding that the guardians for the relevant division had the final say on whether or not relief was granted. After 1899 applications came

37 *Nenagh Guardian*, 3 May 1879.
38 *Nenagh Guardian*, 22 August 1900.
39 Mountmellick Board of Guardians Minutes, 23 September 1871, Laios County Library, Mountmellick Board of Guardians.
40 The residence qualification was increased from two years to four years in 1876: Poor Law Rating (Ireland) Act, 1876, 39 and 40 Vic., c. 50.

under scrutiny from the entire board. This helps to explain in drop in the numbers receiving outdoor relief in the first decade of the twentieth century. The local impact was evident at a meeting of the Cavan Board of Guardians in June 1899. An attempt to increase the allowance of Bridget R. from one shilling and sixpence to two shillings a week was voted down despite being supported by the local guardian, Philip Sheridan, the relieving officer and a local merchant, who recommended that Bridget should get extra help. She was said to have 'no means of support beyond the relief given her ... She is in delicate health and wants from nourishment.' Lamenting the refusal of the board to approve the increase, the Vice-Chair, A. McCarren, observed that it was 'very hard when the guardians of the division who knows the circumstances, and who represents the ratepayers of that district, speaks in favour of something extra being granted in such a case as this, that gentlemen who know nothing about it vote him down'.[41]

Annual totals for the different categories relieved out of the workhouse from 1852 to 1906 reveal a marked increase in all classes in the late 1870s and early 1880s, demonstrating that the rise in outdoor relief during this period was universal and not confined to a particular group (see Figure 3.2). In subsequent decades, however, the experience of different categories diverged. Most saw a decline in the numbers receiving relief after 1881. Those relieved on account of permanent disability, generally the elderly and infirm, continued to increase, with the number of women showing the steepest rise. It is clear, therefore, that the relatively high levels of outdoor relief in the later decades of the nineteenth century and early decades of the twentieth, were mainly due to the granting of allowances to the elderly, primarily women. Aggregate figures are useful for providing a means of comparing levels of relief granted, but they are a fairly crude indicator. More detailed information is needed if we are to come to a judgement about the nature of the relief system in operation. We need to know who was receiving relief, how much they received and how long the relief continued. Unfortunately this information is not generally available. Very few outdoor relief registers have survived for unions in the south of the country. Registers are available for many unions in the north but are less revealing than they might at first appear. Details of those admitted to relief are recorded, but not by how much they were relieved or, prior to 1899, for how long. People could be relieved for just a few days or weeks, or for months or years. If they were relieved on a long–term basis they remained on the relief list, so that the number of people entered in the register in any particular year may give little indication of the total number in receipt of relief that year.[42] The greatest discrepancies are

41 *Anglo-Celt*, 10 June 1899.
42 In the six-month period to September 1871, for example, a total of 257 people

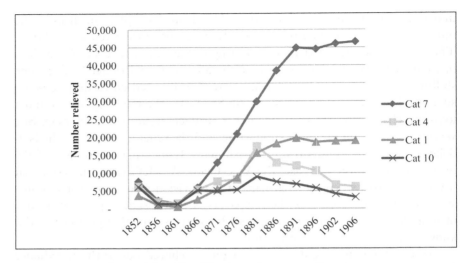

Figure 3.2   Classification of persons relieved out
of the workhouses in unions in Ireland
Category 1:   Adult males permanently disabled by old age or infirmity
Category 4:   Adult males relieved in cases of their own sickness or accident
Category 7:   Adult women permanently disabled by old age or infirmity
Category 10: Adult women relieved in cases of sickness or accident
Source: Annual Reports of the Commissioners for Administering the Laws for
the relief of the Poor in Ireland and the Local Government Board for Ireland

in those unions where outdoor relief was provided mainly as allowances for
the elderly. Once granted, these tended to continue for a number of years. In
other unions, where there was more short-term relief and more movement
on and off the relief lists, the difference between new and existing recipients
was less marked.

The potential for detailed comparative analysis is severely hampered
by the lack of outdoor relief records for unions outside Ulster. This is
particularly unfortunate given that outdoor relief was far more significant in
the three southern provinces than in the north, accounting for a substantial
majority of the daily total relieved in the decades after 1880. We can,
however, form some impressions from the material that has survived. This
suggests that the most significant differences between unions were in the

---

were recorded as being in receipt of outdoor relief in Ballymoney Union. Over the
same period forty-three people and forty dependents were entered in the outdoor
relief register. Half-yearly abstract of paupers relieved, September 1871, Ballymoney
Museum, Ballymoney Board of Guardians; and Ballymoney Outdoor Relief Register,
PRONI, BG5/EA/1.

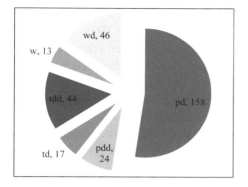 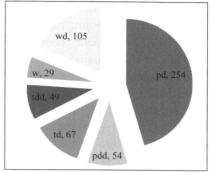

Figure 3.3   People relieved out of the workhouse by category.
Ballymoney 1875–76 (half year to March)
Source: Accounts of Paupers Relieved, 1875–76, Ballymoney
Museum, Ballymoney Board of Guardian Records
Nenagh 1876
Source: *Nenagh Guardian*, 12 Feb. 1876

w: widows   pd: permanently disabled
wd: widows' dependents   pdd: dependents of permanently disabled
td: temporarily disabled   tdd: dependents of temporarily disabled

categories of the temporarily disabled, and widows. More conservative
unions tended to restrict outdoor relief to those falling into the permanently
disabled category. Comparison of the different classes receiving outdoor
relief in Ballymoney and Nenagh in 1876, for example, reveals that the
Nenagh Guardians were relieving considerably more widows and people who
were temporarily disabled, together with their dependents, both numerically
and proportionately (see Figure 3.3).[43]

Analysis of annual relief returns and outdoor relief registers for five
poor law unions, four in the north (Antrim, Ballycastle, Ballymoney and
Enniskillen) and one in the southeast (Rathdown) highlights significant
differences in relief practices and in the type of people receiving relief.
Ballycastle and Enniskillen gave very little outdoor relief (see Table 3.1). The
only cases in which relief was granted were those where the applicant was
too ill or infirm to be moved to the workhouse. Ballymoney and Rathdown
both gave significant amounts of outdoor relief, but Rathdown was slower to
adopt this form of relief and the cohort relieved was different. Ballymoney
was unusual amongst northern unions in granting any outdoor relief prior

43 It is not clear exactly what period the Nenagh figures refer to but the format suggests
that the source may have been a six-monthly return. The Ballymoney figures refer to
the numbers relieved in the six months to March 1876.

to the 1880s. The board was providing a low level of relief from an early period, and the amount increased significantly in the late 1860s and 1870s. After 1880 the outdoor relief rate levelled off, and remained relatively stable throughout the remainder of the period. The level of outdoor relief granted in Ballymoney was higher than the average for the north, but below the national rate. Those entered on the Ballymoney registers in the early decades were a mixture of elderly and working-age adults. In 1870–1871, for example, people aged sixty-six and over made up 43 per cent of the total. In later decades the proportion of elderly recipients increased. In 1880–1881 they made up 59 per cent of entries and in 1891 66 per cent.[44] Women made up a slight majority of all entries and a more substantial majority of the elderly. Women accounted for 71 per cent of the elderly in 1870–1871 and 63 per cent in 1890–1891.[45] Very few children were relieved in their own right. Two were entered in 1865 and four in 1875, but none in any of the other years examined prior to 1901 and only nine after that date.

Table 3.1   Outdoor relief rate per 1,000 population in selected unions, Ireland, and regions of Ireland.

	1861	1871	1881	1891	1901	1911
Antrim	0	2.44	6.3	10.2	13.4	17.1
Ballycastle	0	0	0.1	0.8	6.2	5.7
Ballymoney	1	9.5	12.7	12.4	13.4	13
Enniskillen	0	0	3.4	0.7	3.5	6.4
Rathdown	0.2	0.7	92.1	15.2	23.4	43.1
Ireland	2.4	9.7	43.6	26.6	24.7	24.1
South-east	4.6	17.1	64.2	35.8	35.4	35.8
North	0.6	3.7	8.7	7.7	8.7	9

Source: Annual Reports of the Commissioners for Administering
the Laws for the relief of the Poor in Ireland and the
Local Government Board for Ireland 1850–1914

44 Thirty-eight of eighty-nine admissions in 1870–1871; forty-nine of eighty-three in 1880–1881; and forty-one of sixty-two in 1890–1891: Ballymoney BG Outdoor Relief Register. See below for a note on statistics and sources.
45 Twenty-seven of thirty-eight in 1870–1871; and twenty-six of forty-one in 1890–1891.

Compared to those in Ballymoney, the people entered in the outdoor relief registers for Rathdown Union were significantly younger. There were also more children, more single people and more people with dependent children. The Rathdown Board of Guardians was not an early adopter of outdoor relief. Very little relief was provided in the 1860s or early 1870s. This approach began to change during the mid-1870s and was to change radically in the early 1880s when the guardians provided outdoor relief to large numbers of people. The level of outdoor relief declined in subsequent decades and while it was higher than that in Ballymoney, it was generally considerably below the average for the southeast (see Table 3.1). In 1865 just seven people were entered on the outdoor relief register, two elderly people and five people in their thirties, who were presumably too sick to be moved to the workhouse. No dependents were recorded. By 1875 the picture had changed; 159 people were entered on the register. Of these, eighteen were boarded-out children (11 per cent). Most of the adults were of working age, with only 17 per cent aged sixty-six and over.[46] The average age of adults was forty-six, compared to fifty-eight in Ballymoney. Ten years later the number entered on the register had increased to 763. This was primarily due to an increase in the number of working-age adults and boarded-out children. The proportion of boarded-out children had increased to 24 per cent, while the elderly had declined just 11 per cent of adults registered.[47] The average age of adults was now forty-two, of whom 30 per cent had dependent children. Overall, 14 per cent of the Ballymoney adults entered in the sample years had dependent children compared to 34 per cent of the Rathdown entries. Given the profile of recipients and the number entered on the register each year, we can assume that the Rathdown Board of Guardians was granting mainly small allowances for relatively short periods, rather than longer-term relief, as in Ballymoney.

Even within the north there were significant variations. Some Ulster Boards adopted a deeply conservative approach to relief administration, characterised by minimal levels of outdoor relief. Others provided a low level of relief restricted to particular groups. The Antrim Board of Guardians, for example, restricted relief largely to the elderly and orphan or deserted children. These groups accounted for 67 per cent of those entered on the relief registers in the calendar years 1865, 1875, 1885 and 1895.[48] Relief practices in unions, such as Ballymoney were more liberal, but only in the

---

46 Twenty-four of 141: Rathdown BG Outdoor Relief Register, NAI, BG37/EA/1.
47 Boarded-out children were 186 out of 763 entries; 63 of 576 adults were aged over sixty-six.
48 Out of 172 entries, ninety-four were sixty-six or over; twenty were children. Women made up 55 per cent of entries. Of the Enniskillen cohort of seventy-four entries, 43 per cent were sixty-six or over; 70 per cent were women; 34 per cent were widowed: Antrim

context of the north. While the Ballymoney Guardians did provide some relief to people of working age, particularly in the 1860s and 1870s, in contrast to many northern unions, they appear to have used outdoor relief primarily as an allowance to support the elderly and, in particular, elderly women, over relatively long periods.

Despite coming under the control of elected guardians in the 1880s, Ballycastle Board of Guardians provided very little outdoor relief, with a profile closer to that of Enniskillen than Ballymoney.[49] In Ballycastle fewer people received relief than in Ballymoney, and those that were relieved were assisted for shorter periods. In 1900–1901 the average time a person remained on the relief list in Ballycastle was one year and four months, compared to three years and eight months in Ballymoney. Furthermore, six people were relieved for less than fourteen days in Ballycastle, the shortest period being two days. In Ballymoney, the shortest period of relief was sixteen days. The average age of adult recipients in Ballycastle was seventy. The only younger recipients were a small group of adult men (average age thirty-eight), all of whom had relatively large families. None had fewer than four children, and three had six. The average length of stay for this group was ten weeks. These men were presumably sick or injured, and either could not be moved or were relieved at home to save the expense of bringing the entire family into the workhouse.[50] Unusually, men outnumbered women among outdoor relief recipients in Ballycastle, accounting for 56 per cent of those entered in 1900–1901.[51]

Generally speaking, there was very little movement between the workhouse and the outdoor relief lists. Those who received outdoor relief appear to have been a different cohort from those who entered the workhouse, and there was very little overlap between them. The exceptions were people entering or leaving hospital. Eliza McM., for example, who was registered as a widowed housekeeper aged ninety-eight, received outdoor relief in Ballycastle between 15 May and 14 July 1901. On 16 July she was admitted to the workhouse as sick and died there on 30 April 1903. Mary McA., also a housekeeper, who was seventy-five years of age and single, made the reverse journey.

BG Outdoor Relief Register, PRONI, BG1/EA/1; and Enniskillen BG Outdoor Relief Register, PRONI, BG14/EA/1.

49 Ballycastle appears to be an exception amongst northeastern unions classified by Purdue as being 'liberal' in their relief practices: Olwen Purdue, 'Poor Relief in the North of Ireland Ireland 1850–1921', in V. Crossman and P. Gray (eds), *Poverty and Welfare in Ireland 1838–1948*, (Dublin: Irish Academic Press, 2011), pp. 24, 27.

50 They included three labourers, one dealer, a housekeeper and a miner. Ballycastle BG Outdoor Relief Register, 1900–1901, PRONI, BG3/EA/1; and Ballymoney Outdoor Relief Register, 1900–1901, BG/5/EA/2.

51 Twenty-eight of fifty entries: Ballycastle BG Outdoor Relief Register, 1900–1901.

Having been treated in the workhouse hospital from 9 to 20 July 1901, she was entered on the outdoor relief list on 16 November 1901, where she was registered as a servant. She was still receiving relief when she died on 8 February 1902. Even the very elderly could not assume that relief would continue indefinitely. In Ballycastle and Ballymoney, elderly people were discharged from the relief list after a number of years. They do not appear to have died or to have entered the workhouse, but may have been admitted to another institution or been taken in by relatives. The introduction of old-age pensions in 1908 had a marked impact on relief lists.[52] Far fewer elderly people were entered on the Ballymoney registers in 1910–1911, than had been the case in 1900–1901. The majority of people were now under sixty, and two-thirds of working-age adults had dependent children. It would also appear that many elderly people had their outdoor relief discontinued when they became eligible for a pension. Of fifteen people on the register aged between sixty-five and sixty-nine, ten were discharged in their early seventies.

Discussion of individual cases indicates the highly localised nature of the decision-making process. Guardians made personal recommendations and could veto applications if they thought them to be unworthy. Local landlords and clergymen frequently wrote in support of applications and ratepayers became involved through memorials, letters to the board of guardians, and information provided to guardians and relieving officers. Successful applicants generally needed to be known to at least one guardian, to have a good local reputation and to have made some effort to support themselves. The exceptions to this were urgent medical cases. In 1901 the Roscrea Board of Guardians considered an application for outdoor relief from Ellen R., who had three young children and whose husband had been committed to a lunatic asylum. She was reported to be 'entirely destitute'. Despite being informed by the clerk that the woman was not in fact eligible for outdoor relief, the Chair, Edward Keeshan, supported the application on the grounds that, if they did not give her relief, she would be forced to enter the workhouse, 'Given a little assistance with her own industry she would be able to maintain herself outside.' Rodolphus Meagher agreed. She was, he noted, 'a most respectable woman ... if they attempted to carry out the letter of the law in the administration of the poor law acts it might be as well for them to stay at home. If the guardians attempted such a task it would be as

<hr>

52 For a detailed analysis, see Mel Cousins, *Poor Relief in Ireland 1851–1914* (Bern: Peter Lang, 2011), pp. 252–7; and T. W. Guinnane, 'The Poor Law and Pensions in Ireland', *Journal of Interdisciplinary History*, 1993, 24 (2): 271–91. For an account of the introduction of the old age pension, see Cormac Ó Gráda, '"The Greatest Blessing of All": The Old Age Pension in Ireland', *Past and Present*, 175 (2002), pp. 124–61.

good for the poor that no such system existed.' The board granted Ellen an allowance of four shillings a week.[53]

Character and reputation were very important. Asked about the character of one applicant in 1876, Nenagh Relieving Officer, John Kennedy, replied that 'he never knew him to drink a drop of liquor; he sold his dresser the other day to buy food'.[54] Discussing the case of an elderly man who had applied for an increase in his allowance in 1907, the Chair of the Tuam Board of Guardians commented that he had 'no objection to granting relief to deserving cases, but he had a great objection to giving it to persons who would go into the public house and drink it again'.[55] A few years later the Tuam Guardians were warned by the Vincent de Paul Society that they were 'rather encouraging those people in their habits by giving them relief', after two elderly women had been 'fined twice for drunkenness on receipt of outdoor relief'. It was, the chair observed, 'outrageous to think that this is the way ratepayers' money is spent'. Since both women were over seventy years of age, however, and it was winter it was decided not to strike them off the list, but to revisit their cases after Christmas.[56]

It was often assumed that disreputable people were ineligible to receive outdoor relief. Having refused an application from a woman with an illegitimate child, despite the fact that the mother was confined to bed with spine disease and the child too young to be removed to the workhouse, the Ballymoney Board of Guardians wrote to the poor law commissioners to ascertain whether 'this is one of those cases which would come within the powers of relieving officers to relieve provisionally'.[57] Ten years later, Ballymoney Guardian, Joseph Dunlop, consulted the Local Government Board regarding another single mother, Ellen Q., who had applied for outdoor relief. She was suffering from a serious disease of the knee joint and was 'a fit subject for removal but is too sick to be removed'. The guardians, Dunlop explained, were anxious to grant relief, but thought they could not do so 'owing to the fact that the woman had an illegitimate child some years ago'. The relieving officer had provided provisional relief in kind, 'but we want it in the form of cash'. On being assured that Ellen could legally be relieved the guardians ordered a payment of three shillings a week.[58] Thurles Board of Guardians appears to have operated under a similar misapprehension regarding the eligibility of unmarried mothers. In August 1900 it was reported that a 'heated discussion' had taken place regarding the case

53 *Nenagh Guardian*, 3 July 1901.
54 *Nenagh Guardian*, 12 February 1876.
55 *Southern Star*, 21 December 1907.
56 *Connacht Tribune*, 17 December 1910.
57 Ballymoney Board of Guardians Minutes, 22 May 1871, PRONI, BG/5/A.
58 Ballymoney BG Minutes, 17 January 1881; and *Ballymoney Free Press*, 20 January 1881.

of Margaret S., 'The Local Government Board wrote stating that a woman with an illegitimate child was entitled to outdoor relief, and eventually on a division, it was granted by a majority.'[59]

The way in which people framed applications for relief suggest that they were well aware of prevailing attitudes to eligibility. A letter sent to the Ballymoney Board of Guardians in 1873 requesting outdoor relief stated that:

The ratepayers of the district are agreeable that I should get it. I paid rates for twenty-five years on a large farm. I now have a small house to live in, and the people are kind to me, so that a small trifle from you would enable me to eke out an existence, and cost much less to the ratepayers of the division than if I was in the [work]house. Under these circumstances I trust you will be so very kind as to grant my request.

Despite presenting as a hard-working, respectable and respected member of the community and stressing the modest nature of his needs, and the saving it would represent, the applicant was refused outdoor relief and offered admission to the workhouse. Some years later, Mrs C., a widow, applied to the board in person explaining that her husband had died leaving her with three young children, one an infant. She had two sons able to work at breaking stones but they could not support the family, 'If she could get a little money to tide over the hardships of the next few weeks until she could get employment in the Balnamore Mills, she would be content.' The guardians granted her two shillings a week for a fortnight. After that, she was warned, the relief would cease.[60] Applicants often stressed the limited nature of their claim. Margret R., who had been receiving treatment in Lismore Workhouse Hospital, wrote to the board of guardians in July 1883, requesting 'one week's outdoor relief as I have a bad leg and [am] unable to work as I want to get back to my children as they are without a father. If you grant this request I will never trouble you again.' She was granted three shillings.[61] The Mountmellick Board of Guardians received a letter in 1916 from Mrs Annie R., of Maryborough applying for 'some assistance for her two step sisters whom she has on her hands for the past year and nine months'. She explained that she had been 'instructed to make this appeal through the Clergy'. Her husband was 'earning a little every week ... he works hard and constant', but was finding it 'very hard to meet his wants as everything is very dear'. The board decided that they could not

59 *Nenagh Guardian*, 29 August 1900.
60 *Ballymoney Free Press*, 6 November 1873 and 29 January 1880.
61 Lismore Board of Guardians Correspondence, Waterford County Archives, BG/LISM/83 (1).

grant outdoor relief in this case, but ordered their relieving officer to make inquiries into the case and report to the next meeting.[62] It is probably no accident that out of these four applications, it was the requests for temporary aid that were successful, while those for longer-term assistance were refused. All the appeals shared a number of common elements, however, including the stress on hard work and personal responsibility.

While the elderly were normally regarded as having a strong claim to assistance, their entitlement could be called into question if they had adult children living in the locality. A 'respectable looking woman' from the Latteragh Electoral Division appeared before the Nenagh Guardians in 1881, and on the recommendation of the local guardian, Patrick Kennedy, was granted an allowance of one shilling and sixpence per week. The relieving officer stated that the woman had two sons, 'both of whom refused to support her'. When Chairman Poe observed that it was hard on the ratepayers 'supporting such a class of people', the applicant responded that 'one of her sons was a carpenter by trade, and the other had quite enough to do to support his own family'.[63] In 1906, the union auditor imposed a surcharge in a similar case pointing out that 'contrary to what the guardians seem to think, children are liable to support their aged parents'.[64] Reporting on the case of Elizabeth B. in June 1911, Tralee Relieving Officer, Thomas Shanahan, noted that some of the people of the district were:

> against granting relief as they want to have her family support her. I know the son and he is not fit to support himself. I am sure the poor woman is very badly off and would require something to support her in the line of outdoor relief. She was getting the Old Age Pension but it was stopped as her age was not fully 70 on the census.

It was unanimously decided that she get two shillings and sixpence per week.[65] As this suggests, local people resented relief going to anyone they believed capable of supporting themselves. The Tralee Board of Guardians received a number of anonymous letters in 1911 making allegations about individual claimants, including a patient in the union hospital who was stated to own a public house in Castleisland, 'and has yearly rent of £18 or £20 of it'.[66] The board had a policy of not acting on anonymous allegations, but the fact that the letters were sent says much about local attitudes.

62 Mountmellick BG Minutes, 14 October 1916.
63 *Nenagh Guardian*, 29 October 1881.
64 *Nenagh Guardian*, 21 November 1906.
65 Tralee BG Minutes, 26 August 1911.
66 *Nenagh Guardian*, 29 July 1911; see also 10 May and 17 June 1911.

By the early twentieth century, there appears to have been a strong sense of entitlement amongst claimants. People became more assertive when applying for relief, and were more likely to complain if they were refused or did not receive what had been granted. In 1901 Margaret B. complained to the Local Government Board that she was not being supplied with milk for her three children, despite this having been ordered by the doctor:

> I appealed to the relieving officer Mr O'Sullivan to get the milk that was ordered by the doctor but he says that we are getting 3 shillings relief and that we would get no more. I am getting this 3 shillings for over two years and ... when sickness comes to the house of course we want extra relief.

Margaret had no doubt about her entitlement to additional help. In his response, Tralee Relieving Officer, Jeremiah O'Sullivan, explained that in addition to Margaret's weekly allowance he had afforded her:

> provisional relief in the shape of milk to the value of two shillings weekly as I found her children were suffering from whooping cough which I discontinued as soon as they got well. I visited this woman's family regularly and provisionally supplied the children while unwell with milk and oatmeal as recommended by the medical officer to the value of three shillings which I discontinued after one week as I found the children convalescent and consider the three shillings a week outdoor relief allowed to them by the Board now sufficient for their maintenance.

This explanation was considered satisfactory.[67]

People were only eligible for relief if they were destitute. Enforcing this rule could be problematic, however. Many poor people relied on small amounts received from a variety of different sources. In 1869, for example, Nenagh Guardian, Robert Gabbett, was reported to have 'interceded on behalf of a worthy poor couple in his district, aged eighty years, who were partly kept alive by the kindness of some of the neighbours. The Board accordingly acceded by adding a trifle to the allowance of the old pair.'[68] Charity cases were often difficult to assess since they were, almost by definition, 'deserving', but at the same time could not, strictly speaking, be regarded as destitute if they were in receipt of aid. Boards of guardians in the north appear to have been stricter in their interpretation of poor law

---

67 *Nenagh Guardian*, 12 and 26 June 1901.
68 *Nenagh Guardian*, 6 November 1869.

regulations in such cases than those in the south. When the Clogher Board of Guardians sought advice regarding an application from a local widow, whose children, 'of whom she has care, receive £8 a year (in total) from the Presbyterian Orphan Society', the Local Government Board responded tartly that 'a person in receipt of £8 a year could scarcely be considered destitute'.[69] Responding to a similar inquiry from the Banbridge Board of Guardians in 1901, the Local Government Board reiterated that the only ground for relief was destitution, 'The object of the poor law is not the improvement of the condition of the person in poor circumstances, but the immediate relief of actual destitution.'[70]

The dangers of applying an overly literal interpretation of destitution were highlighted in Mountmellick in 1901, in what the local paper described as 'a very pitiable case'. Mrs D. and her family had been receiving outdoor relief as her husband was blind and suffering from dropsy, but had been forced to sell everything they had, including their bed, when the relieving officer failed to make any payments for six months. They took legal action against the relieving officer and he finally paid some of the money that was owing to them. Mrs D. was then informed that, because of the money they had received from the relieving officer, their weekly allowance had been stopped. The case was brought before the board by a member of the Ladies Visiting Committee, Mrs Beale, who was the superior of the local convent. The chair expressed sympathy for the family but explained that it would be illegal to resume their allowance as they were not destitute. They could reapply for relief when the money they had received had been exhausted. Mrs Beale claimed to have got into 'bad odour' in the town over the case and had been criticised for interfering. Anyone complaining about the relieving officer, she noted, had been struck off the relief list, 'It was said they had pigs or were getting money from private charity.' This was clearly unjust she felt, 'How anyone can go in to the background of private charity she could not see, there is scarcely anyone getting outdoor relief, who is not supported also by private charity.' The following week it was reported that all of the money had been spent paying off debts, providing Mrs D. and her family with a bed and other items, and paying the rent, and that the couple were now 'quite destitute'. Their allowance of three shillings a week was then resumed.[71]

Outdoor relief could take a number of different forms. Provisional relief

---

69 Clogher Board of Guardians Minutes, 20 and 27 October 1877, PRONI, BG/9/A. The Ballymoney Board of Guardians refused outdoor relief to a widow, Mrs M'C., in 1912 on the grounds that she was in receipt of relief from the Orphan Society in connection with her church: Ballymoney BG Minutes, 7 March 1912.
70 LGB Precedent Book, 39060/01 Banbridge, PRONI, LGBD 2/1.
71 *Nationalist and Leinster Times*, 9 and 16 February 1901.

could only be granted as food, medicine or lodgings, but ordinary relief could be given in cash or kind. In April 1871 it was reported to the NDU Board of Guardians that beef, wine, meal and cash had been supplied to Emily R., 3 Stirrup Lane, who had been recommended outdoor relief by Dr Speedy until she was fit to be removed to hospital.[72] In many southern unions, relief was often given in form of cash allowances; in the north it was more likely to be given as food or medicine. In January 1875, for example, Enniskillen Relieving Officer, Richard Maguire, reported that he had administered provisional outdoor relief in food, to the value of three shillings and two pence, to a woman living in Henry Street who was destitute and dying of cancer. She had been certified as unfit for removal by the medical officer. The board decided to continue the relief to a value of five shillings a week for four weeks.[73] However, in the case of William M. of Stragolen who had applied for outdoor relief for himself, his wife and three children, 'his wife being in bad health', the relieving officer reported that while the family appeared to have 'small means of support', the woman was judged to be in a fit state to be moved and he had, therefore, offered to send an ambulance car to remove the family to the workhouse. When they refused to go, he 'declined to give them any further relief'.[74] Maguire's receipt and expenditure book shows that relief was almost always paid in kind.

As the system expanded in the 1870s and 1880s, more attention was paid to its practical operation and regulation. In 1880, the Local Government Board advised boards of guardians that it was:

> very important that each relieving officer should be directed to attend at stated times in different parts of his district for the purpose of receiving applications for relief, and of enquiring into the circum-stances and requirements of the poor, and that his diary should be carefully examined every week with the view of ascertaining whether he discharges the duty in accordance with the instructions.[75]

The circular met with a mixed reception. Some boards of guardians

---

72 NDU BG Minutes, 5 April 1871.
73 A number of other cases involved elderly people who were deemed unfit for removal, together with a young woman 'recently confined': Enniskillen Board of Guardians Minutes, 5 January, 9 and 20 February and 11 May 1875, PRONI, BG/14/A. The Enniskillen Board of Guardians did not normally grant outdoor relief. The only cases granted were those in which the person could not be removed to the workhouse for medical reasons. Because it was so unusual, when relief was granted it was generally noted in the minutes.
74 Enniskillen BG Minutes, 20 February 1875.
75 *Tralee Chronicle*, 3 March 1880.

simply noted it; others were openly sceptical. Discussing the matter at a meeting of the Ballymoney Board of Guardians, William Hunter observed that if the relieving officer went about 'looking for cases to relieve we will be inundated with applications for outdoor relief', while Thomas M'Elderry complained that if the board was obliged 'to carry out these instructions the relieving officer's duties will be materially increased' and they would have to increase his salary. Concluding that people knew how to apply for relief if they wanted it, the guardians agreed to defer any further discussion of the matter.[76]

Where problems arose it was often because boards of guardians failed either to appoint suitable candidates or to ensure that those appointed attended to their duties. In a report on relief arrangements in Westport Union in the spring of 1880, LGI H. A. Robinson observed that he could not 'consider Relieving Officer [John] Moran an efficient or intelligent man'. Noting that Relieving Officer, John Fitzpatrick, also held the offices of municipal rate collector and town sergeant of Westport, the Local Government Board observed that although they believed that Fitzpatrick had 'hitherto discharged his duties with efficiency', all his energies were likely to be required over the coming months and they questioned 'whether his time should not be devoted exclusively to his duties as relieving officer'. They further suggested that an additional relieving officer should be appointed temporarily to take charge of the Islandeady dispensary district. The guardians replied that they would appoint:

a separate relieving officer for Islandeady dispensary district as soon as the applications for relief increase sufficiently which has not been the case up to the present. Relieving Officer Fitzpatrick attends regularly at the dispensaries on the public days but there has been no increase in his duties up to the present and the guardians allow car hire when he has to go a distance.

With regard to Moran, they were unwilling to recommend his immediate dismissal owing to 'the difficulty which at present exists in finding a more efficient and suitable person to act as relieving officer for Clare Island Electoral Division', but undertook to consult with the owner of Clare Island, who was a member of the board, in order to 'ascertain what course is best that they should recommend the Local Government Board'.[77] The reluctance to act unless forced to do so by circumstances, or the Local Government Board, was typical of many boards of guardians in the southwest.

76 *Ballymoney Free Press*, 4 March 1880.
77 Westport Board of Guardians Minutes, 18 March 1880, NLI, MS 12654.

Despite the requirement for relieving officers to be available in order to receive applications, the refusal to grant relief in many unions prior to 1880, discouraged even those in direst need from applying. Reporting on the state of Ballyvaughan Union in 1880, LGI Richard Bourke expressed serious concern about the condition of the poor which was 'daily becoming more distressing'. He attributed this to a continued absence of employment and 'the withholding of outdoor relief by the Board of Guardians from those classes to whom they possess the legal authority of affording it'. The disinclination of the guardians to grant relief 'is so well understood by the poor that applications for the purpose have ceased, and on that account the limited number of people in receipt of that form of relief affords no criterion of the real condition of the poor'.[78] Distress in Tralee, Bourke reported a few days later was 'fast assuming such proportions that I believe the guardians will soon find themselves obliged to relax the hard and fast rules they have made with regard to the administration of relief'. There was no outdoor relief and no admission to the workhouse 'without the severest scrutiny', making 'the union of Tralee one in which the people have learnt that the poor law of Ireland is not designed for any other purpose but for the relief of absolute destitution'.[79] For this to change, a shift in attitude was required not only on boards of guardians but also amongst applicants.

When the central authorities issued a revised version of the general regulations in 1882, the duties of relieving officers had been significantly expanded. In addition to their other duties they were now required 'to visit all persons in receipt of outdoor relief whose relief is made necessary by temporary sickness at least once in each week, and all other persons in receipt of outdoor relief at least once in each month', and to make a report to the board of guardians. They were to dispense weekly allowances, 'as far as possible, at the home of the applicant, and in no case to be paid at a house licensed for the sale of intoxicating drinks'.[80] With more people in receipt of relief, the regulations regarding visiting became increasingly difficult to adhere to. When the Cork Board of Guardians instructed their relieving officers to make monthly visits to all recipients in 1908, in an attempt to prevent further expansion of the relief lists, RO Patrick Ryan protested that

---

78 Report of R. Bourke, 17 January 1880, NAI, CSORP 1880/4115. For an analysis of response to distress in 1879–1882, see Crossman, '"With the experience of 1846 and 1847 before them": The Politics of Emergency Relief 1879–84', and Lucey, 'Power, Politics and Poor Relief During the Irish Land War'.

79 Extract from Mr Bourke's Report, 22 January 1880, NAI, CSORP 1880/2456.

80 General Order … for Regulating the Meetings and Proceedings of Boards of Guardians in Ireland and the Appointment and Duties of Union Officers, 18 December 1882: and Thomas A. Mooney, *Compendium of the Irish Poor Law* (Dublin: Alex, Thom and Co., 1887), pp. 274–6.

'the law with reference to visiting outdoor relief cases once every month was passed at a time when there were few cases, but the number had greatly increased, and it would be impossible to visit them'.[81] Relieving officers frequently cited the size of their lists in mitigation for poor performance. During a discussion of the administration of outdoor relief on the NDU Board in 1913, one relieving officer observed that in his district the distribution of relief amounted to over £200 a year and that the keeping of accounts and related work 'forces me to go at top speed all the time'.[82]

Common complaints against relieving offices concerned misappropriated funds and unpaid allowances.[83] Anne D. of Clonterry, Mountmellick, complained in 1871, for example, that RO Frederick Elliott had withheld part of her weekly allowance of two shillings and sixpence. Insisting that the charge was 'entirely unfounded', Elliott explained that when Anne's application was granted:

I directed her to attend every Monday morning at my residence for payment which is scarcely a quarter of a mile from where she lives. For a length of time she attended punctually but latterly she has not, which is the cause of the present complaint. On the week alluded to in her charge she did not attend until Thursday when she came to my house. I found I had only one shilling in change which I declined giving her, telling her I would send for change, but she insisted on receiving the shilling saying it would do for the present.

He claimed that he had made up the amount owing over the subsequent two weeks. The poor law commissioners concluded that there had been no 'wilful fraud', but deplored the 'want of proper system' and noted that the 'abusive epithets' said to have been used by Elliott, 'were unjustified'. He was 'called before the board and severely reprimanded'.[84] Even where there was clear evidence of malpractice, boards of guardians often proved extremely reluctant to take action against their officers. The Nenagh Board of Guardians refused to dismiss their Relieving Officer, Michael Haugh, despite the recommendations of an official inquiry. His misconduct was not held to be serious and was attributed to overwork. This attitude incensed LGI C. H. O'Connor who urged the guardians to reconsider:

We are all clamouring for Home Rule, and when we get Home Rule we

81 *Irish Independent*, 17 July 1908.
82 *Irish Times*, 23 January 1913.
83 See, for example, *Freeman's Journal*, 15 February 1878.
84 Mountmellick BG Minutes, 21 October and 11 November 1871.

are unable to make use of the opportunities we get. The thing is put before you quite clearly that this officer is not discharging his duties properly, and still you want to keep him on ... Surely to goodness the guardians should have some sense of responsibility.[85]

There were other complaints concerning the manner in which allowances were paid. In 1906 the Local Government Board sought an explanation regarding allegations that RO William Greene of Westport Union had been leaving bread in place of money. The fact that Greene's son was a baker made the arrangement particularly suspicious. Greene denied the allegations explaining that one woman, Sabrina G., had asked him 'to leave the shilling relief with her friend John G. who lives on the public road while Sabrina G. herself lives nearby a mile up in the mountain', although he admitted that he had been sending the money with his son, 'who goes that way'. In future, he would leave 'the one shilling at another neighbour's house which will be more convenient to the old woman if you desire me to do so'. This explanation was considered 'very satisfactory', yet it was clear from Greene's evidence that he rarely visited the homes of pensioners. Stating that he left the relief due to one elderly man to be collected by his relatives when they came to market every Thursday, he added that had been speaking to the man, 'not 12 months ago'. Regulations required monthly visits to all recipients. In his defence, Greene declared that this was the 'first time in twenty years that I have heard any complaint about the way I give relief'.[86] Complaints against Daniel Ryan, a relieving officer of the Mountmellick Union, elicited a similar response. Accused of running accounts with local grocers and paying people monthly rather than weekly, Ryan stated:

in extenuation of my breach of the rules in paying these people by arrangements with Messrs Austin and Sheeran, who are both respectable grocers; that the outdoor relief was paid in like manner by my predecessors and had been done so for a considerable number of years; that I was requested by the poor people themselves to follow the same system and that I was never warned by your Board.

He promised 'never to deviate by a hair's breadth' in future. Ryan's account was corroborated by his clients, one of whom wrote to the board of guardians requesting that he continue to leave her relief with a neighbour, 'as she could not attend at the time the Relieving Officer paid his visit, owing

---

85 *Nenagh Guardian*, 28 September 1907.
86 Westport BG Minutes, 12 April and 3 May 1906, NLI, MS 12690.

to her being at work'. No one appeared to question why someone who was working was also in receipt of relief.[87]

One of the reasons that the central authorities sought to discourage outdoor relief was that they regarded Ireland as being too poor to support an outdoor system such as that operating in England. The only feasible system would be an 'economical' one and this, Power argued in 1865, would be 'especially dangerous' for the poor. Small weekly allowances would encourage people to remain in their own homes, rather than enter the workhouse 'and as the allowance is insufficient for food alone, it is clear that in respect of lodging and clothing and fuel they would be permitted to starve themselves, although on the relieving officer's book'. There was little doubt, he asserted, that 'those small outdoor allowances go to subsidize the ranks of mendicancy'.[88] These concerns proved to be justified. Information on the sums granted, limited though it is, indicates that the normal payment for an individual was between one and two shillings a week. Families generally received more. According to Susanne Day, a member of the Cork Board of Guardians in the 1910s, some boards had definite rules as to the amounts granted, with a set amount for each adult and each child, 'more often the amount to be given is left entirely to the discretion of the Guardians present'. Relief, she maintained, had become 'little more than a dole grudgingly bestowed on the unfortunate'.[89] Since outdoor relief was often insufficient to support the recipient, it became a supplement used either to support irregular or inadequate earnings, or as an addition to charitable aid.[90]

In 1870, RO Daniel Gilligan of the NDU reported to the board on a case which demonstrates not only the precarious financial state of many outdoor recipients, but also the potential benefits of workhouse relief in certain circumstances. John K., who was seventy-four years old, had been admitted to the workhouse on 15 December:

He states that he came from Strokestown, County Roscommon, that he was three weeks on the road and that the persons in the different lodging houses where he stopped told him to go on to Dublin and that he would be taken into the NDU workhouse there. He states he had 18d per week as outdoor relief which paid for tobacco and lodging and that he begged for his food. He complains of Mr Flynn [RO of Strokestown Union] who he says took him off the outdoor relief list

---

87 Mountmellick BG Minutes, 30 September and 5 November 1910.
88 Power to Larcom, 7 January 1865, NLI, Larcom Papers, MS 7781.
89 Susanne Day, 'The Crime Called Out-Door Relief', *Irish Review* (1912), pp. 72–3.
90 This was also the case in England and Wales. See Snell, *Parish and Belonging*, pp. 290–1, 301–2.

and that he was thinking of complaining to the [poor law] commissioners but he would now be satisfied to stay here for the rest of his
life.[91]

The following year a woman appeared before the Thurles Board of
Guardians to complain that she was only receiving one shilling and sixpence
a week, when others were getting two shillings. They were 'able, strong
women who are begging every day. Most of the women also have sons and
daughters earning for them, and some of them have husbands. I have no
person to give me anything, and I am not able to go further than the town to
beg.'[92] Here again relief comprised just one element of the woman's income.
In many unions, allowances of one or two shillings a week appear to have
become the norm. In his half-yearly report for 1895, the Auditor of Youghal
Board of Guardians, Courtney Croker, drew the attention of the guardians to
'the large number of persons who receive 1s per week. If such persons were
really destitute', he observed, 'such a grant would be wholly inadequate, but
they are not destitute and therefore the grant of so small a sum only has a
demoralising effect on the recipient and unduly increases the burden on the
rate-payers.'[93]

In Belfast, where outdoor relief was a kept to an absolute minimum, one
of the few categories to be regarded as eligible to receive relief were blind
workers. In May 1879 it was noted that there were 2,169 people receiving
relief in the workhouse and:

> forty-seven cases on outdoor relief, thirty-seven of whom are working
> for small wages in institutions where wicker work and basket making
> is carried on, and this relief is given to supplement their earnings. The
> remaining ten are cases of ordinary outdoor relief such as midwifery
> and casuals.[94]

When David P. applied for outdoor relief in 1883, it was stated that he
was employed in the workshop for the industrious blind in Howard Street,
but that 'trade was in a dull state owing to gaol work of the same kind being
sold at a lower price'. David was seen as a deserving case. 'Of all classes
none deserved their help so much as the blind', John Reid PLG declared,

91 NDU BG Minutes, 21 December 1870.
92 *Nenagh Guardian*, 1871.
93 Youghal Board of Guardians Minutes, 25 January 1896, Cork City and County
   Archives, BG/163/A.
94 LGB to Belfast Board of Guardians, 26 May 1879, PRONI, BG/7/BC/1. This helps to
   explain the number of people in the Belfast outdoor relief registers whose occupation
   was listed as basket-maker, brush-maker or willow-stripper.

'especially when they were trying to support themselves.' It was decided to grant an allowance of two shillings and sixpence a week for three months. The following year it was reported that a number of blind people:

> both male and female, who are at present employed in the workshops for the blind, appeared before the Board and solicited supplemental relief. Sums varying from 2s to 7s 6d per week were granted according to the exigencies of the case. Some of the poor blind people had large families depending on them.

Relief in aid of wages was officially discouraged. Outdoor relief, the Local Government Board advised the Clonmel Guardians in 1896, should not be granted to the following classes: doubtful destitution; intemperance; applicants who were unable to take care of themselves; applicants living in insanitary dwellings; or where relief was in aid of wages.[95] It is clear however, that this guidance was widely disregarded.

Relieving officers witnessed the consequences of low payments. In November 1890, Relieving Officer, David Cronin of Kilmallock Union, reported that a Ballincreena woman who was in receipt of two shillings a week outdoor relief had 'no proper bed or bedding and all about her filthy'. Her son had 'threatened to leave her to the care of the Relieving Officer if her allowance of outdoor relief was not increased'. Cronin sent for transport to take her to the workhouse, but she refused to go. Another elderly woman, who was living alone in a house in Ballincreena, was reported to be 'very feeble and dependent on her neighbours to bring her whatever she requires'. The relieving officer stated that he considered it dangerous to have this old woman living alone and requested the guardians consider the case. No action was taken, however.[96] Cronin was not alone in his concerns. Questioned by the Vice Regal Commission in 1905, many relieving officers criticised the practice of giving small doles of money to the aged and infirm poor. This was acknowledged to be popular but it acted as 'an inducement to people of this class to live outside in uncomfortable houses on a starvation allowance'. As Thomas Lydon, Relieving Officer for Clifden Union, County Galway, explained, people applying for outdoor relief were 'satisfied with almost any trifle the guardians would give before they would be compelled to break up their little homes and enter the workhouse of which they have a horror'. Another suggested that old people with no family to look after them should

---

95   LGB Precedent Book, Clonmel, 3403/96, PRONI, LGBD 2/1.
96   Kilmallock Board of Guardians Minutes, 13 November 1890, Limerick County Library, BG/106/A.

be compelled to enter the workhouse rather than live alone 'in hovels in the country'.[97]

Outdoor relief was popular with poor law guardians and ratepayers in Ireland, as in other parts of the United Kingdom, because it was perceived to be economical, it went direct to the applicant and guardians could exercise a wide degree of discretion in awarding it. As a former guardian explained in a letter to *Meath Chronicle* in 1906, outdoor relief was 'the medium through which the rates reach the poor without being eaten into by officials [and] contractors'. Its distribution was 'a very tangible advantage to the ratepayers, as without it the poor people should resort to indoor relief in the house and there they would be chargeable on the rates, double or treble the amount of the outdoor relief'.[98] Amongst the settled poor, there was a growing sense of entitlement with regard to outdoor relief and a growing understanding of how to obtain it. People knew how to utilise the system and how to frame their claims to assistance. For the system to work effectually there needed to be adequate numbers and effective supervision of relieving officers. This was rarely the case. Most relieving officers had far more cases on their books than they could effectively supervise. Investigations were generally made into initial applications, but once an allowance was granted little was done to monitor the recipient or their situation. If the average relieving officer rarely recommended the withdrawal of money, Day remarked caustically, this was due 'not so much to the immaculate virtue of the poor, as to the multifariousness of his duties, which allow little time for supervision, and also to the want of interest taken by the Board as such'.[99]

For the poor, there were advantages to an outdoor system. They could remain in their own homes and they could capitalise on local reputation and good will. However, the low rate of allowances condemned many vulnerable people, particularly the elderly, to live a hand-to-mouth existence. The Vice-Regal Commission found that outdoor relief was:

often, and we think we may say generally, given to persons who, though poor, are by no means destitute of resources and means of livelihood ... Instead of being the sole support of the destitute, it has become merely an item in the receipts of the poor person ... This is not at all what was intended by the Poor-law, but the system seems to be popular, and it appears to have taken root.[100]

97 Replies received from Relieving Officers as to administration of outdoor relief, *Poor Law Reform Commission (Ireland)*, HC, 1906 [Cd. 3203], pp. 490–98.
98 *Meath Chronicle*, 9 June 1906.
99 Day, 'The Crime Called Out-door Relief', p. 74.
100 Report of the Vice-Regal Commission on Poor Law Reform in Ireland, HC, 1906 [Cd. 3202], p. 66.

Those that lacked social capital, however, were largely excluded from the system, unless they presented an urgent medical case. The 'morally dubious' together with those without local connections were forced into the workhouse, making that institution even less attractive to the settled poor.[101]

Boards of guardians that adopted outdoor relief in the 1860s and 1870s appear to have done so primarily for economic reasons. They hoped to reduce the burden of poor rates and to maintain a supply of labour by ensuring that local labourers were available to work, and not be shut up in the workhouse. However, guardians were also influenced by the campaign to reform the poor law, believing that it was inhumane and unjust to force respectable working people into the workhouse at times of personal or economic crisis. The adoption of outdoor relief as a general system after 1880 was a response to, and a consequence of, the economic crisis of 1879–1881. The widespread use of outdoor relief to relieve the able-bodied during the crisis removed the psychological barrier that had existed in many guardians' minds. The land campaign acted as a catalyst for this process, but its impact was far wider than the areas controlled by the Land League and affected boards of guardians across the political spectrum. But while high levels of outdoor relief cannot be explained in purely political terms and were not confined to boards of guardians controlled by nationalists, in one sense the move to an outdoor system was a profoundly political development. It represented a rejection of one of the fundamental principles of the poor law; a challenge to the centrality of the workhouse and the workhouse test. The result was a relief system governed by a strong sense of localism and 'belonging'; the impact evident in the distribution of both outdoor and indoor relief. Except for overnight accommodation, the workhouse became largely restricted to the local, settled poor. The consequences of this for the institution, and its inmates, are discussed in the following chapters.

---

101 Awarding the 'deserving' outdoor relief, Snell argues made the workhouse 'a place of moral scrutiny': *Parish and Belonging*, p. 298.

4

The Workhouse

The workhouse was central to the Irish poor law system. Any move to convert vacant workhouse buildings to other uses, Chief Commissioner Power insisted in 1859, would send out a very unfortunate message with regard to the poor law system as a whole. It should be remembered 'above all things', he observed, 'that the whole poor law of an Irish union is concentrated in its workhouse; that the administration of relief in the union is good or bad according to the good or bad state of management of the workhouse', and that state depended 'on the strict enforcement of classification and the continued appropriation of the several parts of the building to the uses for which they were originally designed'. Power accepted that change was inevitable, but was confident that no change which was likely to be made 'need be regarded with apprehension so long as the workhouses are left intact'.[1] As he anticipated, the poor law system underwent fundamental revision in the succeeding decades yet workhouses remained intact and essential to relief administration. The physical edifice of the workhouse marked the site of relief, a manifestation of government concern for the destitute. The organisation of its interior imposed a semblance of order on lives disrupted by poverty and distress. This chapter adopts a split-screen approach to the workhouse. It provides an analysis of trends in occupation and usage, and an exploration of the institutional life of the workhouse, tracing the relief process from admission to discharge. Finally, it focuses on the experience of families within the workhouse, family separation being generally regarded as one of the cruellest aspects of the workhouse system.

Workhouses were a significant architectural feature in the Irish landscape. Generally built to accommodate between 500 and 900 people, they were positioned wherever possible on sloping sites that provided natural drainage. The 'first intimation of approach to any town or district of consideration' was thus 'the appearance on rising ground of the Tudor gables and lattice

---

1 Power to Larcom, 25 July 1859, NAI, Official Papers, OP 1859/44.

windows of the Union Workhouse'.[2] An English visitor to Ireland in the early 1880s, William Hall, described Killarney Workhouse as typical of Irish workhouses in being 'an imposing edifice, splendidly situated on high ground, with an air of neatness and finish on the outside'.[3] Others reported less favourable impressions. One commentator referred to workhouses as 'gloomy, ugly buildings generally found on the outskirts of a village or town', while the workhouse reformer, Laura Stephens, observed that a visitor would have no difficulty in recognising the workhouse 'for the great gloomy pile of grey stone buildings, surrounded with high walls is unmissable'.[4] The prison-like appearance of Irish workhouses struck many observers. Touring Ireland in 1850, Englishman, Archibald Stark, found the entrance to the Cork Workhouse to be 'through a gate of great size and not very promising aspect. A stranger would be apt to take it for the outer door of a prison.'[5] When visiting Manorhamilton Workhouse in the early 1880s, the Canadian journalist, Margaret McDougall, described how 'every door was unlocked to admit us and carefully locked behind us, conveying an idea of very prison-like administration'. In terms that echoed accounts from the period of the Great Famine, she went on to reflect that she could not 'imagine the feeling of any human being when the big door clashes on them, the key turns, and they find themselves an inmate of the workhouse at Manorhamilton. I do not wonder that the creatures starving outside preferred to suffer rather than go in.'[6]

Equally contrasting viewpoints were evident in regard to descriptions of workhouse interiors. On entering Cork Workhouse, Stark had found its outward appearance to be deceptive. Inside he had been pleasantly surprised to find hundreds of:

> able-bodied persons, sufficiently fed, warmly clothed and engaged in an agreeable occupation, who, if they had not this institution to fly to ... would be perishing in the streets, living by plunder, or languishing in jails. Happy, quite happy they may not be; but they are far from being miserable, or their looks belie the fact.[7]

2 'Begin at the Beginning', *Irish Quarterly Review*, 8 (1859), p. 1081.
3 W. H. B. Hall, *Gleanings in Ireland after the Land Acts* (Edward Stanford: London, 1883), p. 24.
4 Laura Stephens, 'An Irish Workhouse', *The New Ireland Review*, 13 (May 1900), p. 129.
5 Archibald G. Stark, *The South of Ireland in 1850; The Journal of a Tour in Leinster and Munster* (Dublin: James Duffy, 1850), p. 100.
6 [Margaret Dixon McDougall], *The Letters of Norah on Her Tour Through Ireland, Being a Series of Letters to the Montreal 'Witness' as a Special Correspondent to Ireland* (Montreal: Public Subscription, 1882), p. 103.
7 Stark, *The South of Ireland*, p. 102.

The favourable impression created by Killarney Workhouse, however, was not continued within. The contractors, Hall observed, seemed to have considered 'that the chief part of their work was done when they had erected imposing shells of buildings; for within, ceiling and plastering have been totally omitted'.[8] Having investigated the state of Belfast workhouse in 1885, a reporter from the *Belfast Newsletter* provided a glowing account of the sleeping quarters which he described as 'a long, clean dormitory, full of clean beds, and altogether a place pervaded by an air of snug comfort'. He claimed to have seen room after room 'bright, clean, well ventilated, warm, in which thousands of persons, some stricken down with disease and others who had succumbed to biting poverty, were sleeping'.[9] The maverick Catholic priest, John Barry, on the other hand, who spent time as an inmate in Clonmel, Limerick and Thurles Workhouses, recalled bitterly how each night:

the able-bodied are driven into, and at seven o'clock locked up in, a large barn where numbers are, like so many hogs, huddled together on straw mattresses thrown down on the bare floor without the necessary addition of straw pillows even. There a man well reared may have for an immediate neighbour another man who tries to act the fool by dinning nonsense into his ear and who poisons the air that all must inhale by imitating the habits of a hog.[10]

The contrast between these accounts is not simply between different workhouses, but in different ways of seeing. Descriptions of workhouses were strongly coloured by ideology and assumptions; one person's prison was another person's refuge. It is important, therefore, to treat such descriptions as impressions, not exact representations.

The majority of Irish workhouses were purpose-built to standard designs in a cruciform arrangement. Figure 4.1 shows a bird's-eye view of a medium-sized workhouse. The small building at the front contained the boardroom, where the board of guardians met, office space, probationary wards, baths, toilets and refractory rooms. The main building contained schoolrooms, dayrooms, nursery, workrooms, stores, the master's rooms and sleeping accommodation for the inmates. The one-storey building behind the main building housed the kitchen, laundry and store rooms, together with the dining room and chapel. The building at the back was the infirmary and

---

8 Hall, *Gleanings in Ireland*, p. 24.
9 *Belfast Newsletter*, 9 March 1885.
10 Rev. John Barry, *Personal Experiences in Clonmel Workhouse* (Clonmel, 1887). For Barry's life, see Martin O'Dwyer, 'Fr. John Barry – The Pauper Priest 1841–1920', *Boherlahan-Dualla Historical Journal* (2000), pp. 67–72.

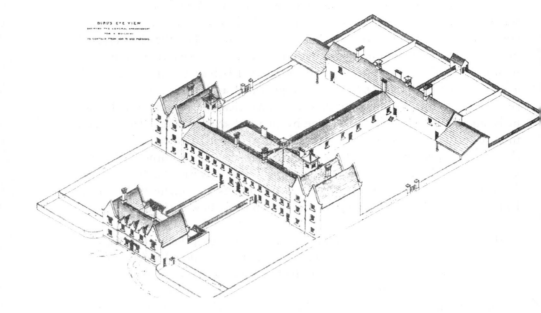

Figure 4.1   Birdseye view of an Irish workhouse.
Source: *Fifth Annual Report of the Poor Law.*
Commissioners, HC, 1839 [239], following p. 90.

the small block at the far back contained the mortuary. Interiors were very simple, which was one of the main reasons why Irish workhouses were constructed at a comparatively low cost. Walls and ceilings were not plastered and floors were made up of a mixture of clay and lime. Initially, dormitories were rarely provided with bedsteads. Instead mats made from straw were laid side by side on wooden platforms. These were gradually replaced by beds in later decades.

Within the workhouse, inmates were divided into five classes according to age and health. These were aged and infirm men; able-bodied males over the age of fifteen; aged and infirm women; able-bodied women over the age of fifteen; and children. The architects of the New English Poor Law had envisaged separate accommodation for each class, but this was not considered practicable in Ireland. Adoption of a simpler classification system had advantages in terms of organisation and design, and made workhouses cheaper to build. The aged and infirm were recognised as a separate category with regard to diet, for example, but not accommodation. However, this was to prove problematic in the long term since buildings were often difficult to adapt to meet changing demands and priorities. In the 1860s, for example, complaints about the lack of dedicated space for religious services prompted many boards of guardians in the southern provinces to cause part of the dining hall to be sectioned off for this purpose. Recommending this arrangement to the Nenagh Guardians in 1861, PLI Richard Bourke observed that it had been widely adopted in other unions in the region, with the exception of Thurles, where the part of the boys' school room was used.[11]

Declining numbers of able-bodied inmates allowed for some degree of flexibility in the allocation of space. Infirmary buildings were generally small and by the later decades of the nineteenth century were often in need of enlargement, but as the infirmary block was usually separate from the rest of workhouse expanding into the accommodation wards was rarely straight-forward. Having been informed by the master in January 1878 that the infirmary was full and that the medical officer had 'requested that another part of the building be used for overflow', a committee of the Clogher Board of Guardians recommended making 'use of the unused dormitories attached to the old men's ward'. The Local Government Board urged the guardians to adopt this suggestion, recommending that 'similar arrangements be made on the female side for women if necessary'. This was approved and the master directed to purchase a stove and have it placed in the dormitories.[12] The Tralee Board of Guardians considered converting the sewing room into an infirm ward in 1901, but decided against it when the master reported that 'some of the infirm female inmates have taken their discharge and a few have been admitted to hospital'. There was 'consequently ... no necessity for converting the sewing room into an infirm ward at present'.[13]

Excess numbers in the sick and infirm wards was a particular problem in city workhouses. In July 1880, LGI Frederick McCabe reported that Belfast Workhouse was seriously congested, a situation made worse by the initial design of the buildings. The blocks of buildings which constituted the main body of the house, and some of the adjacent blocks, he noted:

are lofty, and have been built in such close proximity to each other, that there is not sufficient air-space between them, and sunlight is too much excluded. These defects are now irremediable, but their

11 *Nenagh Guardian*, 7 September 1861.
12 Clogher BG Minutes, 19 and 26 January 1878.
13 Tralee BG Minutes, 13 November 1901.

existence renders it very important that the buildings should not be overcrowded with inmates.[14]

Despite a limitation order fixing the total number that could be accommodated in Belfast Workhouse at 2,502, the number in the workhouse in November 1881 exceeded 2,600. Referring to the problem of overcrowding, an official inquiry anticipated that ongoing work on the construction of separate accommodation for lunatics, would 'relieve the infirmaries and afford ample space for the sick, adult and children', while the 'erection of a number of permanent shed buildings' would accommodate 'excess in other departments'. Nevertheless, it was acknowledged that the day room accommodation for the healthy classes of both sexes was inadequate and that there was a need for additional space to effect a separation between 'the aged and the young who currently use the same day rooms ... The probationary wards also require extension, the present sleeping accommodation being quite insufficient.'

Lack of space remained a serious issue in Belfast. In January 1901, the master warned the board of guardians that the situation in the infirm wards was becoming serious and was affecting classification and discipline. Every available space had now been utilised for the infirm class:

but owing to overcrowding and the congestion thus created it has been found useless to attempt the adoption of any system of classified employment for these inmates or indeed to properly classify them for dormitory purposes and as the congestion is increasing and is likely to do so for some months it has become imperative that something should be done and at once.

Shifting people around caused its own problems. Any 'redistribution of the inmates throughout the establishment', the master noted, 'is surrounded with great difficulties as regards classification, dining, laundry and sanitary arrangements'. As a temporary solution and until the new buildings contemplated by the board were erected, he proposed moving over two hundred male infirmary patients out of the wards known as Corry's Buildings. These could then be 'devoted to the use of the aged and infirm men for which purpose it was erected'. Later that year further measures were found necessary to accommodate the high level of admissions. The master reported that vacant wards in the male probationary department had been 'taken over for male convalescents and the vacant rooms in the main building (lately

14   Report of Dr McCabe on the State of the Belfast Workhouse, 2 July 1880, NAI, CSORP 1881/6139.

occupied by the assistant master) have been taken for the accommodation of some of the nurses'.[15]

In England, the physical separation of different classes of inmate, which was originally conceived as a means of deterrence and discipline, later facilitated the introduction of different disciplinary regimes, as well as specialist provision for the sick, lunatics and children.[16] Similar developments were evident in Ireland, but they were sporadic rather than general. The North Dublin Union, for example, established a separate children's department in Cabra in the 1870s under the management of the Daughters of Charity, which later developed into specialist institution for the mentally handicapped.[17] In Belfast, separate accommodation was planned for epileptics in the 1890s in the form of a detached cottage in the workhouse grounds. In many unions, however, boards of guardians struggled to provide for the growing number of elderly and infirm in buildings designed to accommodate mainly able-bodied inmates.

Analysis of data from indoor relief registers reveals changing modes of workhouse usage over the post-Famine period. Of the workhouses studied, there are two broad distinctions that need to be made, first between workhouses in the north and those in the three southern provinces; and second between city workhouses and provincial workhouses. Workhouses in the south saw the average length of stay (excluding stays of under a week and over 1,000 days) decrease while the proportion of people making very short stays increased (see Table 4.1). The proportion staying for extended periods (defined as more than 180 days) also decreased. In Kinsale, for example, the average length of stay declined from three months in 1870–1871, to two months in 1900–1901. The proportion of long stays in Thurles declined from 9 per cent of admissions in 1870–1871, to 2 per cent in 1900–1901, while the proportion of one-night stays increased from less than 40 per cent of admissions in the 1870s, to more than 70 per cent in the 1889–1890 and 1900–1901. The pattern in NDU was different in that while the average length of stay once again decreased, the workhouse saw a consistently higher proportion of admissions staying for long periods and a much smaller proportion staying for one night, than was evident in provincial workhouses.

15 Belfast BG Minutes, 3 September 1901.
16 M. A. Crowther, *The Workhouse System System 1834–1929: The History of an English Social Institution* (London: Batsford, 1981); Felix Driver, *Power and Pauperism: The Workhouse System 1834–1884* (Cambridge: Cambridge University Press, 1993), p. 72; Lynn *Hollen Lees, The Solidarities of Strangers: The English Poor Laws and the People, 1700–1948* (Cambridge, CUP, 1998), pp. 280–1; and Karel Williams, *From Pauperism to Poverty* (London: Routledge, 1981), p. 119;
17 Joseph Robins, *From Reflection to Integration: A Centenary of Service by the Daughters of Charity to Persons with a Mental Handicap* (Dublin: Gill and Macmillan, 1992).

Table 4.1　Average length of stay in workhouses.

Average Length of Stay In months (excluding less than 6 days and more than 1000 days)

Year	1851	1861	1864	1871	1878	1879	1881	1889	1891	1901	1911
Union											
Ballycastle		3.4		2.2		2.8				4.2	2.9
Ballymoney	4.7	4.2		3			4		2.8	4	2.7
Belfast			2.2		1.9					2	
Clogher				2.2					2.9		3.5
Cork	1.7			2.8						2.5	2.1
Glenties		5								1.3	
Kinsale				3.1			2.5		2.5	2.1	
NDU	4.1	3.7		3.2			2.8		3.4	2.6	1.2
Thurles				2.8		2.7		2.2		2.1	2

Percentage one night stays

Year	1851	1861	1864	1871	1878	1879	1881	1889	1891	1901	1911
Ballycastle		0.9		26.3		42.4				38.3	63.3
Ballymoney	0.3	21.3		55.6			61.6		71.9	77.8	84.5
Belfast			6		6.9					5	
Clogher				40.8					73.1		88.4
Cork	8.6			15.2						29.7	18.4
Glenties		0.5								41	
Kinsale				19.9			43		55	60.9	
NDU	4.9	4.3		5.5			10.2		8.4	44.6	9.2
Thurles				38.7		29.7		76.8		72.5	44.8

Percentage 1000+ days

Year	1851	1861	1864	1871	1878	1879	1881	1889	1891	1901	1911
Ballycastle		2.2		2.2		0.5				1.6	0.2
Ballymoney	6.8	3.5		0.5			1.1		1.1	1	0.1
Belfast			0.6		0.3					0.6	
Clogher				0					0.9		0
Cork	0.1			1.7						0.6	0.3
Glenties		5.5								1.6	
Kinsale				0			0.3		0.6	0	
NDU	4	3.2		1.5			1		2.3	1.5	1.8
Thurles				1.1		0.8		0.2		0.2	0

Percentage 180+ days

Year	1851	1861	1864	1871	1878	1879	1881	1889	1891	1901	1911
Ballycastle											
Ballymoney		11		3.9					3	3.7	
Belfast			7.5		5					5	
Clogher											
Cork	6.3			10.5						5.6	3.8
Glenties											
Kinsale				8.5			5		4	1.7	
NDU	19.7			17.6					18.5		10
Thurles				8.7		9.7		2.5		1.9	2.9

Source: Indoor Relief Registers

There was, therefore, a significant shift in the way people used workhouses in the later decades of the nineteenth century. Far more people were entering provincial workhouses for very short periods, while fewer were making extended stays. The latter development was linked to the increased availability of outdoor relief and the growing willingness to support the elderly and infirm in their own homes. In NDU, people who stayed overnight made up only a small percentage of those entering the workhouse, while the number of people who required longer-term assistance remained significant. The different pattern of short-stay usage in Dublin appears to be linked to the presence of the Night Asylum on Bow Street which provided shelter (but no food of any kind) to the homeless poor. Established in 1838, the asylum accommodated on average one hundred men and seventy women. It did not accept women with young children who were directed either to the workhouse or to St Joseph's Night Refuge for Women and Children in Cork Street which was run by the Sisters of Mercy.[18] In the north of the country, where outdoor relief was provided at much lower levels than in the southern provinces, patterns of workhouse usage were different. Here the average length of stay remained more stable, and was higher than in workhouses in the south. There was, however, a similar increase in the proportion of overnight stays in provincial workhouses in the north as in the

18 'Report on Inadequate Provision for "Destitute Wayfarers, and Wanderers" termed "Casual Paupers" through Want of Casual Wards in Workhouses in Dublin', *Reports of Charity Organisation Committee of the Statistical and Social Inquiry Society as to Houseless Poor* (Dublin: Edward Ponsonby, 1876); and George D. Williams, *Dublin Charities: Being a Handbook of Dublin Philanthropic Organisations and Charities* (Dublin: John Falconer, 1902), pp. 157–8.

Table 4.2   Profile of one night stays
(as percentage of admissions).

Union	1871 children	women	men
Ballycastle	16	25	59
Clogher	13	19	68
Cork	59	11	30
Kinsale	15	18	67
NDU	22	35	43
Thurles	24	24	52
	1891 children	women	men
Ballycastle			
Clogher	10	13	76
Cork			
Kinsale	13	12	75
NDU	32	41	27
Thurles	20	21	59
	1901 children	women	men
Ballycastle	13	15	72
Clogher			
Cork	19	20	61
Kinsale	16	23	62
NDU			
Thurles	20	21	59

south. One-night stays increased from less than 1 per cent of admissions in Ballycastle in 1860–1861 to 63 per cent in 1910–1911, and in Ballymoney from 30 per cent to 85 per cent over the same period. In Belfast, as in Dublin, the proportion of one-night stays was smaller than in provincial workhouses and remained relatively stable.

Women and children made up the bulk of the inmate population in English workhouses in the mid-nineteenth century, as they had done in the eighteenth century. Research on pre-Famine Irish workhouses suggests that they contained more women than men and roughly equal numbers of sick and able-bodied. In the post-Famine period, the proportion of children and able-bodied women declined, while the proportion of able-bodied men remained roughly stable at around 5 per cent of the total population in the decades from 1870.[19] It is important to note, however, that the gender balance varied according to age, and length of stay. In many unions, men outnumbered women amongst older inmates.[20] As we have seen, elderly women were more likely to be granted outdoor relief and may also have been better able to look after themselves in old age. Generally speaking, workhouse inmates who remained for six months or more were more likely to be female than male, while those making overnight stays were more likely to be male than female (see Table 4.2). Where women predominated among the long-stay cohort, this group included working-age women with children together with elderly women. Where men predominated they were mainly elderly. In provincial workhouses, men comprised a substantial majority of one-night stays averaging 68 per cent in Thurles and 77 per cent in Kinsale, for example, reflecting the high number of single, adult men amongst the itinerant poor.

All destitute persons were eligible to receive relief in the workhouse. Under the general regulations issued in 1849, admission was by written or printed order of the board of guardians (following a personal application to the board); by a written or printed order signed by a relieving officer of the union (following a personal application to the relieving officer); or by a recommendation signed by a warden. Wardens were appointed by the board of guardians. It was also possible to apply directly to the master or, in his absence, the matron of the workhouse in a case of 'sudden and urgent necessity'.[21] Individual guardians had no authority to issue admission tickets, although their recommendations were usually acted upon by the master. A NDU relieving officer stated in 1909 that guardians frequently 'gave notes to persons which they presented to the Master, and demanded admission to the house'.[22] Any admission order or ticket had to be used within three days of it being issued. Admission, other than by order of the board of guardians, was provisional and required the person admitted to be brought before the board at their next meeting to 'decide on the propriety of the pauper's continuing in the workhouse or otherwise'.[23] In most cases, people applying to the board

---

19 Classified return of the number of inmates in workhouses on the first Saturday of January, *Annual Report of the Local Government Board for Ireland*, HC, 1900 [Cd. 338], p. xviii.

20 Cormac Ó Gráda found that in the pre-Famine period older inmates of both NDU and Midleton were more likely to be men than women: *Ireland: A New Economic History 1780–1939* (Oxford: Oxford University Press, 1994), pp. 100–103.

21 General Order for regulating the Management of Workhouses and the Duties of the Workhouse Officers, 5 February 1849, in Thomas A. Mooney, *Compendium of the Irish Poor Law* (Dublin: Alex, Thom and Co., 1887), pp. 283–4.

22 *Irish Independent*, 7 January 1909.

23 Article 3, General Order for Regulating the Management of Workhouses, in Mooney, *Compendium of the Irish Poor Law*, pp. 283–4.

were examined and questioned. However, some boards appear to have avoided direct interaction with applicants simply requiring them to be present while their case was decided. In his account of workhouse life, Barry claimed that the Thurles Guardians 'never allow an applicant to appear before them'. Having applied for admission to Thurles Workhouse in October 1889, Barry was admitted provisionally on a ticket from the relieving officer. At the end of a week, he recalled, the 'guardians assembled and without hearing a single word on my side of the question, they discharged me'.[24] It was for the board of guardians to determine whether or not an applicant should receive relief and whether it should be continued. How they reached that decision was up to them.

Once admitted to the workhouse, the pauper's name and religion was entered in the admission register and they were sent to the probationary ward, where they remained until being examined by the medical officer of the workhouse. If the medical officer decided that they were 'labouring under any disease of body or mind', they were sent to the sick ward or to a ward 'appropriated to the reception of such cases'. Most workhouses had separate accommodation for fever cases and some had separate wards for lunatics, idiots and epileptics. If judged not to be sick, they were sent to that part of the workhouse 'assigned to the class to which he may belong'. Before leaving the probationary ward, the rules directed that the pauper was to be 'thoroughly cleansed' and clothed in workhouse dress. This was made out of coarse material and generally comprised frieze suits for men, knickerbocker suits for boys and plain dresses for the women and girls. The women also wore black bibs or aprons, and flannel petticoats.[25] The clothes the pauper was wearing when admitted were removed, cleaned and put into storage for when they left. Paupers were searched on admission and prohibited articles removed; these included money, food, alcohol and tobacco.[26] How long the admission process took and how rigorously the regulations were enforced, varied considerably depending on the individual officers, the number of people being admitted and the time of day. Admission to a large city workhouse could take hours. How people experienced the admission process depended on the physical environment, the manner in which they were treated and the weather. Common complaints included rude or harsh treatment and being kept waiting for hours in the rain or cold.[27]

24 Rev. John Barry, *Life in an Irish Workhouse* (Thurles, 1890), p. 42.
25 Interviews with John Marrinan, Michael Hanrahan and Michael Morris: National Folklore Collection, MS 1436, 1391, 1221.
26 Articles 4–8, General Order for Regulating the Management of Workhouses, *Compendium of the Irish Poor Law*, p. 284.
27 In September 1881, for example, a complaint was made concerning the admission of Eliza M. to the NDU Workhouse. Relieving Officer, Blakemore, stated that he had

Entry to the workhouse was designed to operate as a test of destitution, the intention being to ensure that only people who were in dire need would apply for and accept relief. However, relieving officers and boards of guardians were still expected to satisfy themselves that applicants were destitute and it was not unknown, although it was unusual, for people to be refused entry. Some boards and some workhouse officials appear to have been stricter than others in assessing applicants. When people were refused admission to the workhouse, it was generally because they were young and healthy, and therefore able to support themselves or where someone else could be regarded as legally responsible for their upkeep. In December 1873, the Enniscorthy Board of Guardians refused admission to Mary R. who was described as being aged around twenty-three years of age, able-bodied and well dressed. She was said to have left a good situation where she had fair wages and good board without just cause. The board not only refused Mary admission, but passed a resolution directing 'that any woman who comes before the guardians under such circumstances, be refused admission'. This prompted a swift rebuke from the Local Government Board reminding them that they had no power to make such an order 'and that the case of each applicant for relief must be decided on its own merits'.[28] The NDU Board of Guardians rejected an application for relief from Daniel M. in July 1881. On being asked for an explanation, the board explained that he was 'refused by the admission board as appearing a strong man, and that work was very plentiful'. He had 'never applied since'. Later that year the Nenagh Guardians refused to readmit a young man who had left the workhouse in order to enlist in the army. When he returned to the workhouse having been rejected by the army, he was refused admission on the grounds that 'he could find plenty of work outside'.[29]

A married woman could be refused entry if the guardians believed the woman's husband was willing to support her. Bridget C.'s application was turned down by the Enniskillen Board of Guardians in July 1875. Her husband had emigrated and left money for her to follow, but she did not want to go and had applied for admission to the workhouse. The guardians refused and advised her to join her husband.[30] Alice C. applied to the Tralee Board of Guardians in March 1878. Her husband was a baker, but she claimed he would not support her and she 'threw her life on the guardians'. Being informed by the relieving officer that there was a

---

'received her application the usual way and told her to appear at the admission board on the following Monday'. He emphatically denied the statement 'as to his being rude or harsh to her in any way'. NDU BG Minutes, 14 September 1881.

28 *Enniscorthy News*, 27 December 1873 and 3 January 1874.
29 NDU BG Minutes, 31 August 1881; and *Nenagh Guardian*, 29 October 1881.
30 Enniskillen BG Minutes, 6 July 1875.

'misunderstanding between herself and her husband', the guardians refused admission. When Johanna D. was denied admission to Tralee Workhouse a few years later, she complained to the Local Government Board claiming that her husband had deserted her. The guardians strongly defended their decision stating that the husband had been prosecuted for desertion, but had been 'discharged on his representing that he was perfectly ready to support his wife but that she had refused to live with him'. Furthermore, since the husband resided in Listowel Union, 'this Board considers that the Listowel Guardians are those who should take any action to be taken in the matter'.[31]

Boards of guardians struggled with the concept of entitlement. Asked for guidance in 1844 on what constituted destitution 'and whether a strong able-bodied pauper who can obtain a situation as a servant but dislikes to enter it, or being in it refuses to retain it, is entitled on application to be admitted into the workhouse', the poor law commissioners had explained that it was impossible to give any precise definition of destitution which would be universally applicable. This was why the legislature provided 'that the relief to be afforded should be at the discretion of the Guardians; each case should be determined on its own merits'. Destitution, they suggested, 'consists of an inability to procure the necessaries of life, and that a person able to procure them by entering service, but who refuses to do so from choice is not, therefore, destitute in that sense and should not be relieved in the workhouse', but recommended that the applicant should have a chance to appear before the board and make a statement 'as it would be imprudent of the guardians to decide on an ex parte case'.[32] When the Tralee Guardians directed their relieving officer in 1901, 'not to give tickets of admission to able-bodied inmates who can live out of the workhouse', they were reminded by the Local Government Board that 'it is within the Relieving Officer's discretion to issue tickets of admissions to the workhouse to any person whom he may consider destitute'.[33] Most relieving officers, however, preferred following orders to acting on their own discretion, whatever the Local Government Board might say.

Applicants who did not 'belong' to the union were regarded with suspicion.[34] Despite having no legal right to refuse relief in such cases, boards

31   *Tralee Chronicle*, 22 March 1878 and 7 May 1881.
32   Local Government Board Precedent Book, Destitution, Coleraine 25060/44: PRONI, LGBD 2/1.
33   Tralee BG Minutes, 9 January 1901.
34   For an extended detailed discussion of 'belonging' in England and Wales, see K. D. M. Snell *Parish and Belonging: Community, Identity and Welfare in England and Wales 1700–1950* (Cambridge: Cambridge University Press, 2006). In England entitlement was linked to legal settlement acquired by birth, marriage or residence.

often attempted to send people back to their place of origin or at least to persuade them to return. In 1899, the Cavan Board of Guardians discussed the case of an elderly man who had been in the workhouse for a fortnight when it was discovered that he 'belonged' to the neighbouring union of Clones. The Chairman of the Board, Samuel Sanderson, told the master not to put the man out, 'but to ask him to leave saying this was the wish of the board'.[35] When Mary M. appeared before the Tralee Board of Guardians in July 1871, she explained that after staying a fortnight in the Listowel Workhouse with her four children, 'the Relieving Officer, John Riordan, who had given her a provisional ticket, told her on the board day that she should leave the house and go to her own union, and discharged her without bringing her before the Board'.[36] The poor law authorities frequently had to write to boards of guardians reminding them that that they could not refuse someone simply because they did not reside in the union. In November 1878 it was reported that a woman named Maryanne M. was admitted to Nenagh Workhouse having been discharged from Thurles, 'the guardians refusing to allow her to become a burden on the rates, as she belonged to the Nenagh Union'. She complained to the Local Government Board, who sought an explanation from the Thurles guardians. They replied that the woman was not a subject for hospital treatment and 'was discharged as she belonged to the Nenagh Union'. They were informed that 'having become destitute in the Thurles Union [she] was relievable there, and the Guardians were not legally entitled to remove her on the ground that she did not belong to their union'. Such rulings appear to have made little impression however. In March 1901, the Nenagh guardians ordered that Mary C. of Tipperary and Bridget R. of Roscrea be sent back to their own unions after the master reported that there were women in the house who belonged to other unions and asked the board to make some order in the matter.[37]

What constituted 'sudden and urgent necessity' was another issue that gave rise to confusion and complaint. In October 1870 the NDU Guardians complained to the poor law commissioners with regard to the case of Teresa W., who had been refused admission to the South Dublin Union workhouse. Teresa was twenty-two years of age and 'unable from blindness to find her way'. After waiting nearly three hours to be admitted she had been turned away from SDU workhouse 'at half past eight in the evening instead of being provisionally admitted pending the report of a relieving officer as would have been the case in this union'. She then applied to the NDU, where she was admitted and a complaint made to the poor law commissioners. Following

35 *Anglo-Celt*, 10 June 1899.
36 Tralee BG Minutes, 11 July 1871.
37 *Nenagh Guardian*, 23 November 1878 and 20 March 1901

an official investigation the commissioners ruled that, although the relieving officer's conduct, 'in causing the woman to wait for an hour and quarter while he went out on his private affairs, instead of deciding the case when it first came before him' was open to censure, 'the only circumstances in favour of admitting her at once as an urgent case was her defective sight, but beyond this there was nothing whatever to indicate urgent destitution' and thus no reason for the relieving officer to exercise his power of affording provisional relief in cases of sudden and urgent necessity. Indeed, the commissioners went on to conclude that the fact of her having become chargeable to the NDU, was not 'attributable to any default on the part of any officer of the SDU, but to the fact of her having gone from the union in which she had been resident to another union for the purpose of seeking relief', a proceeding which was 'a direct violation of the provisions of the Irish Vagrant Act'. This view was strongly rejected by the NDU Guardians, however, who remained convinced that Teresa had been very badly treated.[38]

Those applying for relief paid little heed to poor law regulations. Most were unaware of the regulations or did not understand them, but some were intent on circumventing them. In 1885 it was discovered that two men had gained admission to Kinsale Workhouse using forged notes of admission. 'Caution should be observed', the master noted in his journal, 'to prevent persons obtaining the forms of admission supplied to the relieving officers.'[39] Rather than apply to a relieving officer for relief, many people simply turned up at the workhouse gate. The response they received depended on the character of the officers in charge and the circumstances of the case. Admitting all comers was likely to result in censure from the board of guardians, but turning people away could lead to a master being censured for failing in his duty to relieve the destitute. As the Master of Belfast Workhouse remarked in 1883, if 'any person lay down and died at the gate during the night the result would be very serious for him, as the Board would not likely exonerate him from responsibility'.[40] Striking an appropriate balance was no easy task. Concerned about rising maintenance costs in 1905, the NDU Guardians instructed the master to use more discretion as to daily admissions and only admit urgent cases. If he did this, one guardian observed, 'there would be more room for the decent inmates'.[41]

Workhouse gates were locked at 9 p.m. After this time, anyone seeking admittance had to apply to the porter. He then notified the master, who was

---

38 NDU BG Minutes, 28 October 1870. For a similar case, involving Christopher F., who was refused admission in NDU, admitted to SDU and subsequently transferred to NDU, see NDU BG Minutes, 30 November and 7 December 1870.
39 Master's Journal, Kinsale BG, CCCA, BG/108/F1, 24 September 1885.
40 *Belfast Newsletter*, 14 June 1883.
41 *Irish Independent*, 19 January 1905.

meant to come and assess the applicant to see whether they qualified for provisional admittance as an urgent case. This process could take some time causing people to wait for long periods outside the workhouse. It was not unusual for people refused admittance to wait overnight at the workhouse gate and apply again the following day. People allowed out on day passes who returned after 9 p.m. could also find themselves locked out and forced to wait until morning for readmittance. This was a particular problem where women and children were concerned. Refusing them admission opened officials to charges of inhumanity, but admitting them at any hour undermined order and discipline within the house. The problems were compounded when alcohol was involved. In December 1881, the Master of Enniscorthy Workhouse complained to the board of guardians about the behaviour of a group of female tramps who arrived at the workhouse 'under the influence of drink' and were 'most disorderly'. The women had been in and out of the workhouse all week and he was annoyed at the relieving officer for giving them admission tickets, observing that 'as these parties have money to procure whiskey, I submit that they do not come under the law of destitution to entitle them to receive tickets of admission ... particularly when they are under the influence of drink'. The relieving officer, however, insisted that the women had 'presented all the appearance of destitution ... and were not then under the influence of drink', a claim that the master contested.[42] In April 1884, the Master of Kinsale Workhouse reported that he had been obliged to have charges brought against three young women who had left the house on Saturday, were readmitted on Sunday, left again on Monday and appeared at the front gate on Tuesday night drunk and disorderly, and demanding admission, 'After much trouble and a scene of great disorder they were removed by the police and remanded ... at Douglas Petty Sessions.' People could get very irate if refused. The following month the Kinsale Master reported that his clerk had been assaulted by a woman named Ellen H., who had been part of a large crowd that had gathered at the front gate on Friday night demanding entry. She was given over to the police and sentenced to one month's imprisonment.[43]

City workhouses received large numbers of applicants. This put considerable pressure on workhouse officials, particularly at night. In October 1878 a dispute occurred between officials of the Cork Workhouse and the local police concerning disorderly scenes outside the workhouse. The Master of the Workhouse, Richard Steele, had requested that extra police patrols should be introduced in the vicinity of the workhouse to prevent disorder. The local constabulary inspector, however, objected to the constabulary being

42 Enniscorthy BG Minutes, 3 December 1881; and *The People*, 10 December 1881.
43 Master's Journal, Kinsale BG, 10 April and 1 May 1884.

'employed in remedying the effects produced by workhouse officials'. He stated that he had been informed by the constable at Blackrock that destitute people regularly applied at the gate for admission, but were refused after 10 p.m. They often complained of this and of having received rough treatment from the porter, 'and naturally feel annoyed at not being admitted which I have no doubt is the cause of the disorder complained of ... If these poor people were treated civilly I have no doubt there would not be such complaints.' Asked to report on the matter, LGI McCabe explained that some delays were unavoidable. Cork Workhouse consisted of several blocks of buildings, with large open spaces in between. The buildings were 'so extensive that it takes from two to three hours to walk quickly through the different wards'. It took 'from half an hour to an hour for a message to go from the porter's lodge and to return with the master's order, and it may take even longer if the master happens to be in some of the remote wards at the time'. Whereas the police sympathised with the poor and blamed workhouse officials for mistreating them, McCabe sympathised with officials and blamed the poor for acting irresponsibly. It was common practice, he observed, for inmates to take their discharge in the morning, 'pass the day in Cork, and return at night (sometimes under the influence of drink) demanding readmission'. Furthermore, although such persons might be 'roughs and prostitutes', the master could not 'refuse such readmission except at this own peril, even if the applicants present themselves drunk at the gate. At the best he has a most difficult and thankless task to discharge requiring exceptional patience and forbearance.' The master, McCabe insisted, was an exemplary officer, whose benevolence was 'perfectly well known in Cork'. In this case, the conduct of workhouse officials survived scrutiny. In Belfast, similar complaints in 1880 were to lead to the resignation of the master.

In 1877, following reports of destitute people congregating at the workhouse gate, the Belfast Board of Guardians had directed that women with children applying at night should be treated as urgent cases and admitted at once. The chairman expressed the hope 'that no child will be left exposed at the gate', but made clear his frustration at the behaviour of 'these inhuman mothers' in taking their children out of the workhouse 'and dragging them through the streets of Belfast half clothed and hungry until they think fit in the middle of the night to come back with them again'. With respect to 'able-bodied men and women who voluntarily and habitually ... persist in discharging themselves in the morning and returning after midnight seeking readmission', he proposed that 'we should not consider them urgent cases and they should not be admitted unless in the usual way'.[44] The Master, J. B. Whitla, appears to have followed the spirit rather than the

44 Belfast BG Minutes, 13 November and 11 December 1877.

letter of these remarks. During the course of an official inquiry, it emerged that on the night of 1 October 1880 he had refused to admit a couple and their two young children, and had abused a local resident who had attempted to intercede on their behalf. Whiltla maintained that he had seen:

> nothing sudden or urgent in the case. The woman was fairly dressed, the man able-bodied. I saw one child at the woman's foot, but I observed no infant in arms then. It was a fine night, mild for the season, and not raining ... The woman was very impertinent, and abusive in her language, and I came to the conclusion that she was a regular tramp, and not a fit person for the exercise of my provisional power.

He claimed to have forgotten the guardians' order to admit women with children. The inquiry concluded that while Whitla's general management of the workhouse was satisfactory:

> he fails in many essential requisites; in sympathy to the poor, in a thorough knowledge of all this duties of his office, and in general language and demeanour towards those with whom he is brought into official relation, as well as in exact performance of the orders of the Board, whose servant he is.[45]

Whilta was forced to resign, but admission remained a controversial issue. Two years later a similar incident gave rise to an inquiry into the conduct of his successor, George Macniece, in a case that reveals the pitfalls facing inexperienced applicants.

Sub-Constable, John Duke, informed the inquiry that on the night of 27 June 1883, he had found a woman with two children at the gate of the workhouse. Observing that she was respectable in appearance, he had questioned her as to the circumstances under which she was seeking admission. She had said that her husband was a bank clerk, and had been away for three months, 'during which time he had not given her any support'. When the constable returned, the woman was still at the gate, and was crying. On making further inquiry, 'he came to the conclusion the woman was very destitute, and that she was unable to go away with the children'. Duke attempted to get her admitted, but was informed by the master that he had refused her admittance earlier and he refused to admit her now.

---

45 *Copies of the Minutes of Evidence taken at the recent Inquiry held at the Belfast Workhouse by Inspectors Bourke and Brodie, together with their Report thereon, and Final decision of the Local Government Board* (1 February 1881), HC, 1881 (123), pp. 1–34.

Speaking to the woman 'in a very insulting tone', he had told her to go home to her husband. Duke then went to the relieving officer, who agreed to give the woman 'a line' and she was admitted shortly after one in the morning. A local resident, Hugh Williamson, who lived next to the workhouse gate, confirmed the constable's account adding that he had observed 'when the woman got up from the ground, that she was not the usual class of person to seek admission to the house ... the woman appeared to be respectable'. The master 'did not use any bad language to the woman, but he spoke in loud and angry tones, such as he [the witness] would not use to a dog'. Fifteen months experience of the neighbourhood, Williamson stated, had convinced him that the noise from the gate often arose 'from the taunting remarks made by the porters to persons seeking admission'.

When Ellen M. came to give evidence, she admitted that she had lied about her husband; she was unmarried. The father of her children had been supporting her but had stopped sending her money. She had initially supported herself by 'parting with her clothes' and had then been 'advised to come to the workhouse in order that the guardians might take proceedings against the father of my children'. The mistake Ellen made was trying to maintain an appearance of respectability. While this made her an object of sympathy in the eyes of the constable and Williamson, it made her look suspicious to the master who assumed that she was not destitute and had simply quarrelled with her husband. When she had applied a second time, later the same night, he explained that he had thought it was 'perverseness on the part of the woman not to go home ... The children appeared to be comfortable, and the night was fine, and the woman was strong and healthy.' Had she said that the father of her children was not her husband and that he was refusing to support her, he would have admitted her.[46]

As these cases demonstrate, workhouses operated according to unwritten as well as written rules.[47] These determined whether someone was admitted, how they were treated once admitted and how long they were allowed to stay. Some groups automatically qualified for assistance, were allowed to make repeat visits and to stay for relatively long periods. The elderly and infirm, orphan and deserted children, and people who were seriously ill or had an obvious disability that prevented them working, had little difficult gaining admission to a workhouse or being allowed to stay for weeks or months at a time. Women with young children were rarely refused admission unless they were married and their husband was known to be living locally. However,

---

46 *Belfast Newsletter*, 15 August 1882.
47 A similar point is made by David Green in his analysis of indoor relief in London; *Pauper Capital: London and the Poor Law, 1790–1870* (Farnham: Ashgate, 2010), pp. 158–9.

they had to be careful about the reason they gave for needing relief. It was necessary to present as deserted, even if this was not strictly true. Marriage breakdown was not an adequate reason and was likely to prompt a refusal. Unmarried mothers would generally be admitted without question, but might be accommodated separately.[48] Much depended on local knowledge, on how people looked and how they behaved when in the workhouse. As Ellen discovered, it was unwise to look too respectable.

Able-bodied adults were judged according to a number of criteria: first whether they were destitute, that is lacking the means to pay for food and/or lodgings; and second whether they were local. Even though there was no law of settlement, local residence increasingly became an essential qualification for staying any length of time in a workhouse. If an applicant was local and could provide a convincing explanation of why they were destitute, they might be allowed to stay for periods of weeks or even months. If they were not from the locality and had not been living locally prior to their applying, they would not usually be allowed to stay for more than a few days, unless they were sick or their spouse was sick. Margaret H., for example, entered Thurles Workhouse on 13 August 1871 with her husband John, a painter, who had sore feet. Both were described as tramps. She stayed until 11 September. He stayed until 12 September. They were the only people described as tramps who stayed in the workhouse that year for more than three days.[49]

Stays of around one month were common in many workhouses, suggesting that a month operated as some kind of limit. Winifred G., for example, stayed in Thurles Workhouse in 1871 from 10 April until 9 May. She was thirty-two years old, single and a servant, with no apparent medical issues. Similarly Thomas F., a fifty-year-old widow of no occupation, stayed from 25 April until 24 May. Both were charged to the union indicating that they were not local residents.[50] It is difficult to tell whether people were asked to leave after a month or whether they were not admitted unless they agreed to remain at least a month. The Belfast Board of Guardians, adopted a policy of requiring women 'to remain a month without quitting', in order 'to check the practice of frequent running in and out of females, and especially women with children'. But there is also evidence of people being asked to leave Belfast Workhouse after a certain period of time. James M. told the Belfast

---

48 For further discussion of single mothers, see below.
49 Thurles BG Indoor Relief Registers, Tipperary Local Studies Library, Thurles, 1870–1871.
50 Thurles BG Indoor Relief Registers, 1870–1871.

inquiry in 1881 that a week after being admitted with his family he was told that 'our time was up, and we must go'.[51]

Being young, male and able-bodied made it particularly difficult to remain any length of time. Michael R., a nineteen-year-old Catholic labourer, entered NDU Workhouse from an address on Mary's Lane on 31 December 1910 and stayed a little over two weeks. He was readmitted on 28 January from the Night Asylum and remained for nine days. He returned a few days after being discharged giving an address in Cumberland Street and stayed for a month departing on 13 March. He was readmitted on 23 March, when he was recorded as a 'cab case' having been found by the police sleeping rough in a hallway on Church Street and was discharged five days later. He entered once in April, when he remained for four days and then stayed for a month from 1 May until 1 June. He was back within a week and stayed for six days. When he was readmitted on 17 June, a note was made in the register to discharge him in seven days, although he was not in fact discharged until 21 July. On these last two occasions he was listed as having no address.[52] Despite being both destitute and homeless, Michael was still identified as someone to be discharged. In such cases, homelessness helped to establish destitution but did not confer any entitlement beyond provisional admission.

People who went in and out of the workhouse on a regular basis were represented as abusing the system. This was a particular issue in cities where guardians and others regularly complained about people using the workhouse as a lodging house. In 1883, Belfast Board Member, Thomas Gaffikin, reported his surprise on discovering:

> the number of able-bodied young fellows who came into the house at night, got supper, went to work at half past seven in the morning, were called in to breakfast at a quarter to nine and left the house at ten. They thus got a couple of meals at the expense of the ratepayers.[53]

In Dublin, the location of the Night Asylum reduced the number of people seeking overnight accommodation in NDU Workhouse. Since the asylum did not have accommodation for young children, however, officials experienced similar problems with regard to late-night applications from women with children as their colleagues in other city workhouses. Following

---

51 Belfast BG Minutes, 18 February 1879; *Copies of the Minutes of Evidence taken at the Recent Inquiry*, 1881, p. 17.
52 NDU BG Indoor Relief Registers 1910–1911, NAI, BG/78/G.
53 *Belfast Newsletter*, June 1883. In a wide-ranging critique of the Belfast Workhouse published in 1879, Magistrate R. L. Hamilton had complained that the workhouse was 'more like a lodging-house to many of the inmates than anything else': *Northern Whig*, 12 February 1879.

the death of an infant in 1889, the master explained that he had refused the mother admission as she had been going in and out on a regular basis. If he admitted people indiscriminately, he observed, they would have 'half Dublin at the gates'.[54] In November 1900, RO David Fagan informed guardians that having refused to admit a woman and child who had applied to him between eleven and twelve at night, he had the woman charged with 'exposing her child at that late hour'. She had been sentenced to one month's imprisonment with hard labour. Although the guardians resolved to adopt the relieving officer's suggestion that 'a notice be printed and posted up as a warning to others', a proposal to hand over to the police 'any women seeking admission to the workhouse after the hour of 9 pm and bringing young children with them for prosecution for cruelty and neglect', does not appear to have been adopted, and it is doubtful whether either the Local Government Board, or the police, would have agreed to such a directive.[55]

Examples of multiple repeat admissions are not hard to find. Mary G., for example, entered NDU Workhouse twelve times in 1870–1871, generally from the Night Asylum. Described as a servant and a dealer, and in her thirties, she rarely stayed more than a few days although she did make three slightly longer stays of between eight and eighteen days over the winter months. It would appear that this was a regular way of life for her since she can also be found in the workhouse register for 1880–1881. She entered nineteen times that year, always from the Night Asylum, making stays of between two and seven days. Her longest stay was from 29 August until 10 September.[56] Joseph S., a forty-year-old single labourer entered Belfast Workhouse nine times in the months of January, April, July and October 1901, from an address in Chadally Street, staying for between one and four days on each occasion.[57] Joseph appears to have been making the most of the restricted resources available to him.

Complaints from guardians and officials notwithstanding, multiple repeat admissions were in fact relatively rare, making up a small proportion of all workhouse admissions. The vast majority of people entering workhouses throughout Ireland in the course of the administrative year either left and did not return within the year or remained in the workhouse. It is important to note however, that any numerical count is likely to underestimate the real number of repeat visits since it fails to take account of the number of people who were readmitted under a different name. In some cases details may have been misheard or wrongly entered in the register, in others people may

54 *Freeman's Journal*, 29 August 1889.
55 NDU BG Minutes, 16 November 1900.
56 NDU BG Indoor Relief Registers, 1870–1871, 1880–1881.
57 Belfast BG Indoor Relief Registers 1900–1901, PRONI, BG/7/G.

have deliberately given false information in order to mislead officials. This is likely to have been a particular problem in larger workhouses where officials would have been unable to remember people easily. In addition to his nine admissions to Belfast in 1900–1901, Joseph S. also appears to have entered twice as James and once as John. As James, he stayed for three weeks from 27 October to 19 November 1900. His use of a different name on this occasion may have assisted him to remain in the workhouse for longer. He was not registered as having any ailment or disability, except on one occasion in October when he stayed four days and was noted as having a chest complaint.

Comparing the proportion of repeat admissions in different workhouses is problematic given the difficulty of accurate identification, but a numerical count of repeat entries reveals some intriguing variations. Taking an average across the period, the proportion of admissions that were admitted at least twice within the administrative year, ranged from around 9 or 10 per cent in Ballymoney and Thurles; to 14 or 15 per cent in Kinsale and NDU. It is not surprising to find a higher level of repeat admissions in city workhouses, since the pressure on such workhouses was much greater and it would have been more difficult for officials to keep a check on individual admissions.[58] It is likely that the relatively low level of repeats in provincial workhouses, such as Ballymoney and Thurles, reflects the relief culture of the union. Officials here actively discouraged people from returning. Officials in Kinsale, on the other hand, tolerated higher levels of repeat visits. This may have been partly due to poor record keeping, but it would appear that officials adopted a more lenient approach.

Kinsale Workhouse recorded the highest number of individual visits of any of the workhouses studied. John N. was admitted thirteen times in 1870–1871. He was forty-three and described on some occasions as a labourer and on others as a fisherman. He generally stayed for one or two days, with a number of longer stays over the winter months. During the summer he was unwell. He was admitted with an itch in June 1871 and as sick in July. He remained a regular visitor to Kinsale Workhouse and appears to have no fixed residence since he was always chargeable to the union. In 1880–1881 he was admitted twenty-one times. He generally stayed no more than two days, but again spent the winter months in the workhouse being admitted on 23 September 1880 and not leaving until 17 February 1881. He then re-entered on 20 February and stayed until 15 June. He was described at one point as an ex-soldier. In 1890–1891, James, now in his sixties, was admitted twenty-five times generally remaining a few days and once again staying in the workhouse

---

58 Belfast also appears to have had a relatively high level of repeat admissions. In January 1878, 5.5 per cent of admissions were repeats: Belfast BG Indoor Relief Registers, PRONI, BG/7/G, 1878.

for much of the winter.[59] He was mostly described as able-bodied, but twice as infirm. John was clearly well known to workhouse officials and was able to come and go as he pleased. This suggests that he was well behaved while in the workhouse, making himself useful and keeping out of trouble. Those who complained about 'ins and outs' assumed that these people were abusing the system, rarely acknowledging going in and out was a strategy that allowed people to make full use of the workhouse whilst also accessing other forms of support, such as casual employment and charitable aid.

The popular image of the workhouse is of a prison-like institution that was difficult to leave. Inmates' movements were certainly restricted. They were locked into the wards at night, were restricted to certain parts of the workhouse during the day and required permission to leave. It was not uncommon for inmates to abscond. In October 1865, for example, the Westport Board of Guardians 'cautioned Frank C., age sixty, for scaling the boundary wall to visit his daughter'. The following month Frank absconded again, this time 'taking with him the union clothes'. The police were notified and on 23 November guardians were informed that he had been 'sentenced to a week's imprisonment for absconding from the workhouse and deserting his wife and children. He exchanged the union shoes for a worn-out pair of socks going to gaol.' Young boys were often tempted to break out, particularly in the summer months, though they generally returned. In August 1866, seven schoolboys scaled the walls of Westport Workhouse 'and went to the races and returned at 5.30 o'clock'.[60] In August 1871, the Master of Tralee Workhouse reported that 'three of the school boys scaled the walls yesterday and were caught stealing apples from a poor man who has an orchard convenient to the house'. Some months later another boy 'scaled the walls ... and went to town where he spent the day'. When adults absconded, alcohol was often involved. In November 1871, the master informed guardians that two men had 'scaled the walls on the evening of the 31st ultimo. They were arrested by the night watch for drunkenness and brought before the magistrates who sent them to jail for a week.'[61]

While some inmates resorted to breaking out of the workhouse, others resisted efforts to make them leave. The position of able-bodied inmates was kept under regular review in all workhouses. Fourteen able-bodied men were brought before the Kilmallock Board of Guardians on 23 March 1871, for example, and informed that if they were still in the workhouse the following week they would be discharged.[62] In the spring of 1866, the

59 Kinsale BG Indoor Relief Registers, CCCA, BG/108/G.
60 Westport BG Minutes, 19 October, 23 November 1865 and 9 August 1866.
61 Tralee BG Minutes, 1 August, 7 November 1871 and 2 January 1872.
62 Kilmallock BG Minutes, 23 March 1871. The NDU Board of Guardians passed a

Mountmellick Board of Guardians had adopted a particularly hard-line approach to able-bodied inmates. Believing there to be work available locally, the board decided to discharge all able-bodied adults, irrespective of their circumstances or whether they had children. Following complaints from the Catholic workhouse chaplain and some of the discharged paupers, the poor law commissioners wrote to the guardians querying the policy. It did not appear, they noted:

> that any offer of employment has been made in any instance and the position of persons sent out of the workhouse without lodging whilst in search of work may be one of hardship and possible suffering. In the case of women with children, this observation applies with greater force.

The commissioners advised the guardians to reconsider, observing that the 'only effectual mode of excluding the idle from the workhouse is the enforcement of a severe labour test which shall render their residence there less attractive than a life of labour outside'.[63] The guardians were unrepentant, however, insisting that offers of employment had been made. This did not satisfy the commissioners who reminded the guardians that they needed to be sure that any employment offered would provide, not only for the individual pauper, but for any dependents they might have 'otherwise the Guardians might incur a serious responsibility' by discharging them.[64] The commissioners believed that no able-bodied pauper would want to stay in a well-regulated workhouse any longer than was absolutely necessary and so would not need to be discharged. It was better, they believed, to let the pauper make the decision, since it absolved the authorities from any responsibility in the matter. The Mountmellick guardians, however, appear to have taken the view that they would be spared the burden of maintaining a well-regulated workhouse, if there were fewer paupers in it to manage.

Those discharged from the workhouse in this instance clearly felt aggrieved at their treatment, a good indication that it was seen as unusually harsh. Some complained directly to the poor law commissioners, some to the Catholic chaplain who wrote to the commissioners on their behalf. Others took more direct action. One young woman was summoned before the magistrates at petty sessions 'for refusing to put on her clothes or leave the

---

resolution in May 1881 directing the master 'to bring before the admission board every Monday any persons in the house whom he may think fit to discharge', the final decision to be made by the admission board: NDU BG Minutes, 18 May 1881.

63 Mountmellick BG Minutes, 26 May 1866.
64 Mountmellick BG Minutes, 2 June 1866.

workhouse after the board ordered her discharge'.[65] The guardians, however, persisted with their policy. The following week they refused to readmit one of the discharged families, arguing that the man, Joseph H., had been offered employment by a member of the board, J. G. Adair. Adair explained that Joseph was a healthy young man of about thirty-five years of age and:

> was almost the only able-bodied pauper in the workhouse, and as I knew the great want of labour in the district he was discharged on my motion. I provided ... work for him as a stonebreaker at a rate of wages by which other men in his employment earn 9s per month, stone breaking being the only employment almost at which an unskilled man can earn wages.

Joseph had rejected the offer, however, telling Adair that he 'could not and would not work, that he was a gentleman's servant and that the guardians were bound to provide a place as such for him'. Adair queried whether relief should be given 'to such a person' under these circumstances. The final decision on individual relief cases, the poor law commissioners stated firmly, rested with the guardians 'who must decide according to their judgement upon the facts before them'.[66] That their policy could prove counter-productive became clear the following month when two single mothers who had been discharged from the workhouse deserted their children, leaving the union responsible for their upkeep.[67]

Mountmellick was abnormal in the rigour of its discharge policy but at least two other boards consulted the Local Government Board about forcibly removing inmates. They were informed that while boards of guardians possessed the power to order a person to be compulsorily removed from the workhouse if they did not consider them a fit subject for relief, care should be taken 'not to use more force than necessary to effect the removal'. The Local Government Board clearly regarded such a step as a sign of poor management observing that it would rarely be necessary:

> where the workhouse is well managed and where each inmate is kept fully employed according to his capacity ... If the discipline be carried out the workhouse will cease to be attractive to able-bodied persons who are capable of earning a maintenance for themselves but who are too idly-disposed to do so.[68]

---

65 Mountmellick BG Minutes, 9 June 1866.
66 Mountmellick BG Minutes, 23 and 30 June 1866.
67 Mountmellick BG Minutes, 14 July 1866.
68 LGB Precedent book, Workhouse, Shillelagh 17780/74; and Millstreet 23912/96.

Official rhetoric always placed greater emphasis on discouraging shirkers than making adequate provision for the needy.

As their name indicated, workhouses were envisaged as sites of industry and labour. Work was regarded essentially as a means of instilling discipline into the pauper population, but it was also required to render the workhouse unattractive to its occupants. It could not therefore be profitable work. In order to be profitable, the political economist, W. Neilson Hancock, noted in 1851, 'industrial activity within workhouses would require first-class workers who would require inducements in order to maintain productivity'. This was contrary to the principle of workhouse relief.[69] During the late 1840s and 1850s, the amount and variety of work being carried out in Irish workhouses was extensive. This can be divided into three main types of activity: agricultural; domestic; and industrial. Most of the domestic work of the institution, such as cooking, washing and cleaning, was undertaken by inmates, as were the nursing duties, although these were gradually taken over by salaried staff from the 1880s.[70] Inmates also undertook tasks, such as pumping water and chopping wood. Many unions engaged in food production. Some, such as Enniscorthy, had a workhouse farm under professional management. Most simply grew vegetables either within the workhouse grounds or nearby. Many of the larger workhouses also had substantial industrial departments engaged in a range of activities including spinning, weaving, wool and linen processing, knitting, embroidery, sprigging, tailoring, shoe and clog making, net-making and mat-making.[71]

Goods produced were usually consumed within the workhouse but surpluses were sold. Archibald Stark was impressed to discover that the sewing room of Cork Workhouse made a profit of £130 per quarter in 1850.[72] Stark was not alone in seeing the adoption of an organised industrial system as a way of reducing establishment costs and thus the burden of poor rates. In 1851, the Thurles Board of Guardians proposed the introduction of an incentive scheme 'to induce the paupers to work cheerfully and steadily', thereby enabling articles made in the workhouse to be sold for a profit. They suggested that 'a preference should be given in selection for emigration; also some little addition should be made in their diet and clothing'. To their surprise, the poor law commissioners vetoed the plan arguing that it would 'derange the discipline of the workhouse' and 'interfere with its utility as a

---

69 W. Neilson Hancock, 'Should Boards of Guardians endeavour to make Pauper Labour self-supporting', *Transactions of the Dublin Statistical Society*, 2 (1851), p. 6.

70 See below, pp. 147–9.

71 *Abstract of Return from each of the Poor Law Unions in England, Wales and Ireland, showing what kinds of employment are carried on the workhouses, or on land attached*, HC, 1852–1853 (513), pp. 43–62.

72 Stark, *The South of Ireland*, p. 109.

test of destitution'. Inmates who were not selected for encouragement and reward, would be 'led to decline their proper share in the labour of the establishment', while those who were selected would be 'induced to remain in the workhouse instead of seeking the means of support by independent industry'. This made no sense to the guardians. Surely it was better, they argued, to induce the paupers:

> by premiums rather than penalties, to labour for their own support, and to maintain the workhouse, with its officers as a self-supporting institution, capable, if permitted to be properly managed, of defraying its own liabilities ... The principle that every institution should if possible support itself is so self-evident, so based on common sense, it should require no argument to assert it.[73]

But this was to misunderstand the principle of workhouse relief. The workhouse, as George Nicholls had explained in 1836, was merely 'a medium of relief; and in order that the destitute only may partake of it, the relief is administered in such a way, and on such conditions, that none but the destitute will accept it'.[74]

The main reason why industrial activity declined in Irish workhouses in the decades after 1850, however, was due not to strict adherence to poor law principles on the part of boards of guardians, but to the decline in the number of able-bodied inmates. In Thurles Workhouse, for example, the proportion of able-bodied inmates (men and women) declined from 40 per cent of the total in 1861, to 2 per cent in 1891.[75] Furthermore, able-bodied people who did enter generally made short stays. It was unusual to find able-bodied people staying in Thurles Workhouse for more than a few days, unless they were sick or injured, or had young children. In workhouses across the country, it was often difficult to find enough able-bodied people to perform the regular work of the house. In 1866, the Medical Officer of the Mountmellick Workhouse, Dr Joseph Clarke, informed the board of guardians that he had been:

> put to some inconvenience in consequence of my inability to procure amongst the inmates of this house a suitable person to undertake the duties of wardsman over the male department of the Fever Hospital.

73 *Copies of all Correspondence between the Thurles Board of Guardians and the Poor Law Commissioners ... relative to the Employment of the Inmates in Remunerative Labour*, HC, 1851 (292), p. 3. See also *Hansard 3rd series*, cxv, 231, 20 March 1851.
74 Sir George Nicholls, *A History of the Irish Poor Law* (London: John Murray, 1856), p. 198
75 Thurles BG Minutes 1860–1861, 1890–1891.

The only person I could prevail on (a man over 70 years of age) I was obliged to discharge for neglect and general incompetence. The duties are now discharged by an old woman.

Given the 'increasing objection' on the part of inmates to work in the Fever Hospital, Clarke recommended the appointment of a paid wards man. After pressure from the poor law commissioners, the board of guardians eventually advertised the post at a salary of eight pounds per annum with rations.[76]

As the potential to engage in industrial activities declined and the emphasis on work as a deterrent grew, the nature of work performed in workhouses assumed a largely penal character. Tasks, such as stone breaking and oakum picking, were required of able-bodied inmates in many workhouses, particularly those which admitted large numbers of night lodgers. Some workhouses, however, had neither the staff nor facilities to require inmates to perform a task of work, beyond routine domestic chores. NDU Workhouse, for example, had no facilities and no desire to introduce them. Opposing a proposal to introduce stone breaking as a means of discouraging casual admissions in the summer of 1882, the chairman observed that:

in the first place they would be obliged to erect premises for a work yard, and in the second place they would have to provide a person to keep supervision over them. Under the circumstances it appeared to him they would get very little value if they made these people work.

Having been assured by the master that 'the present rush of casuals was owing to the temporary closing of the Night Asylum and that that institution would be opened in about a fortnight', the guardians decided there was no need for further action.[77]

Where industrial departments survived, they increasingly concentrated on providing training for the young. A return of the nature and extent of industrial employment and instruction in Belfast Workhouse in 1880, for example, shows that this consisted of forty-eight boys receiving instruction in agriculture, tailoring or shoe-making; twenty boys being trained to perform in a band; and 106 girls receiving training in domestic skills including needlework, knitting and making clothes.[78] For some inmates work was seen

---

76 Mountmellick BG Minutes, 9 and 30 June 1866. Similar problems were noted in English workhouses: Crowther, *The Workhouse System*, pp. 196–201.

77 *Dublin Evening Mail*, 14 June 1882, cited in Georgina Laragy, 'Poor Relief in the South of Ireland, 1850–1921', in V. Crossman and P. Gray (eds), *Poverty and Welfare in Ireland 1838–1948* (Dublin: Irish Academic Press, 2011), p. 61.

78 Nature and Extent of Industrial Employment and Instruction, *Belfast Workhouse:*

as therapeutic. Reports on the lunatic department of Belfast Workhouse in the 1890s stressed the importance of giving lunatics and epileptics something to do and suggested that they be taught a trade or occupation, chopping wood being suggested as one possibility. The resident medical officer was doubtful. While he agreed that 'some congenial employment' would be beneficial, he confessed he would worry about placing 'Scottish wood choppers in the hands of our Irish lunatics.'[79]

Just as there was a contradiction in the attitudes of the central authorities to work – it was to be reformative and yet at the same time repellent – so there was a contradiction in their attitude to families. The family was regarded as a unit in relation to the granting of relief; thus a successful application for outdoor relief automatically included dependents, while acceptance of workhouse relief required the entire family to enter the workhouse. Once inside, however, the family was split up. The separation of families within the workhouse, which was one of the most hated aspects of the institution, was widely regarded as unnatural and inhumane. Critics of the poor law made frequent reference to the detrimental effect of the workhouse on families and family life. One of 'the greatest means of preserving morality', Archbishop Cullen maintained, was 'the operation of the family tie upon the individuals of a family, and that is altogether destroyed in the workhouse'.[80] Speaking in New York in January 1880, C. S. Parnell described the Irish poor law system as 'the most fiendish and ingenious system of all those that we have received from England for the purpose of slowly torturing our country to death'. The ties of family, he noted were broken up 'and the wretched inmates of the workhouse from the day they enter it, are consigned to what is for many of them but a living death'.[81]

Descriptions of workhouse life continue to highlight family separation as one of the most negative aspects of the institution. Workhouse populations, however, contained very few families.[82] By far the most common way to enter a workhouse was alone, not as part of a family group. Out of a sample of 1,214 admissions to Cork Workhouse between 23 January and 23 August 1851, for example, 5 per cent were members of family groups comprising a married couple with children, compared to 25 per cent in single-parent

Copy of Dr McCabe's Recent Report on the State of Belfast Workhouse, HC, 1880 (359), p. 5.

79 *Belfast Newsletter*, 4 May 1892.

80 *Report from the Select Committee Appointed to Inquire into the Administration of the Relief of the Poor in Ireland*, HC, 1861 [408], Q3969.

81 *Freeman's Journal*, 17 January 1880.

82 This was also the case in England and in pre-Famine Ireland: Anthony Brundage, *The English Poor Laws 1700–1930* (London: Palgrave, 2002), pp. 122–3; and Ó Gráda, *Ireland: A New Economic History*, p. 99.

family groups and 65 per cent who entered on their own, or apparently on their own.[83] It would appear that some of these created their own support networks. Thus Patrick M., aged fifteen, who was described as being 'in rags' and with no shirt, was admitted on 11 December 1850 together with ten other children of around the same age. All had the same address, Coal Quay, and were described in the same way and all left together the following day.[84] We have no more information on this group of children but they appear to have created their own 'family'.

Married couples with children formed only a small minority of workhouse admissions. Furthermore, contrary to popular belief, families that did enter the workhouse were relatively small in size.[85] The majority contained one or two children. Very few contained four or more. The reason for this is not that the poor had small families, but that older children were able to work. They could thus support themselves or be left with relatives without being a burden on them. Where there were older children, therefore, they were often left outside. Family dissolution was a survival strategy. Couples frequently split up, and split their children up. One partner might enter the workhouse with all, or some, of their children, while the other remained outside or was admitted at a later date. Other families entered the workhouse together, but left separately. John and Sarah B., for example, a Catholic couple in their early forties, were admitted to Belfast Workhouse on 9 January 1901, together with their two children, a son aged twelve and daughter aged four. All four were discharged on 17 January and readmitted two days later. On 31 January, John and Sarah left the workhouse with their son. Their daughter remained in the workhouse until 22 February. In April, Sarah entered the workhouse with the children and stayed for ten days. The family spent three days in the workhouse in early July. John returned on 14 July together with his daughter. He left alone on 18 July, but returned the following day. Sarah, who was now pregnant, was admitted on 21 July together with their son. All four were discharged on 23 July. John was described either as a labourer or as having no occupation; while Sarah was variously noted to be a mill worker, a weaver and a char, or to have no occupation. They entered the workhouse from a variety of different addresses in the city including Short Strand, Samuel Street, North

---

83 In total, fifty-five admissions can be identified as members of a two-parent family; forty-one entered as a family unit, the remaining fifteen were cases in which one parent entered with children, the other parent being in the workhouse already: Cork BG Indoor Relief Registers, CCCA, BG/69/G, 1850–1851.

84 The proportion of two-parent families among admissions to Cork remained at around 4 per cent throughout the period under examination.

85 John O'Connor states that 'whole families entered the workhouse together and ... they were invariably large': *The Workhouses of Ireland: The Fate of Ireland's Poor* (Dublin: Anvil Books, 1995), p. 95.

Dock Street and Gardiner's Court.[86] For this family, both the workhouse and temporary separation were integral to their survival strategy.

City workhouses admitted very few couples with children and those that did enter generally stayed no more than a few days, unless one or more members of the family had health problems. John W., a thirty-two-year-old Protestant tailor, for example, was admitted to NDU Workhouse on 12 August 1861 from an address in Church Street. He was noted to be suffering from burns. His wife, Bridget, who was twenty-three and a servant, was admitted a few days later together with their four-year-old son, Edward. The couple's other child was admitted some months later. All four remained in the workhouse until 28 April 1862, suggesting that the family left together.[87] Separate entry by family members was particularly evident in NDU in 1870–1871. In total, twenty two-parent families were admitted during the year, but only nine entered the workhouse as a family group. In the remaining eleven cases both parents entered the workhouse during the period, but not together. In some cases entry was for medical treatment, but in others it appears to have been a temporary respite. Maria T., for example, entered with her four children on 20 February 1871. She was discharged the following day 'by leave of the chairman', leaving the children in the workhouse. James T., who was a baker, was admitted on 23 February and was discharged with the children two days later. In addition to ill-health, old age appears to have been a contributory factor in a number of cases. Patrick and Margaret S., for example, were admitted to the workhouse with their two children aged ten and seven on 11 January 1871, staying for a week. Patrick was seventy-four and was described as a labourer. Margaret was forty. The family returned in February and stayed twelve days. They were readmitted in early March and remained until 26 April, when they were all discharged. However, Margaret and the children were readmitted the same day and stayed until 1 July, while Patrick remained outside. The family always gave the same address in Mary's Lane.[88]

The proportion of two-parent family groups in the NDU Workhouse declined in subsequent decades. In 1910–1911, twenty-five families were admitted comprising less than 2 per cent of total admissions, as compared to 8 per cent in 1850–1851, and 4 per cent in 1860–1861.[89] Parents continued

---

86 Belfast BG Indoor Relief Registers, BG/7/G, 1900–1901.
87 Family groups accounted for 155 of 4,112 admissions in 1860–1861 (4 per cent). Nearly all of the families contained at least one member requiring medical treatment: NDU BG Indoor Relief Registers, NAI, BG/78/G, 1860–1861.
88 NDU BG Indoor Relief Registers, 1870–1871.
89 The twenty-five families accounted for 110 admissions out of a total of 7,491 (1.5 per cent). In eleven cases the family left after one or two nights. Two families stayed for a week: NDU BG Indoor Relief Registers, 1910–1911.

to leave their children in the workhouse on occasion, either with or without the permission of the authorities. Where permission was given, it was generally the mother who remained in the workhouse. Thus John F., who had entered with his wife Mary and two-year-old daughter on 25 July 1911, was discharged on 8 August, his wife and daughter remaining until 19 August. Thomas R., who was admitted with his wife and two children on 16 November, was permitted to leave on 28 January. His wife and children remained until the end of February, the children being treated in hospital. In other cases the parents absconded. Richard D., who was in his twenties and described as a dairy boy, was admitted with his wife Anne and two young children in July 1911. Anne left the workhouse on 14 November 1911 on a temporary pass, but failed to return. Richard remained until 8 June 1912, when he too left on a temporary pass and did not return. The children remained in the workhouse until 26 January 1913.[90] It is not clear into whose care they were discharged.

Provincial workhouses admitted proportionately more family groups than did city workhouses, but increasingly these were casual, overnight admissions. In 1870–1871, twelve two-parent families were admitted to Thurles Workhouse, for example, comprising 8 per cent of admissions. Eight of the twelve families stayed one night and one for a week. The remaining three families stayed between three weeks and five months.[91] In later decades it was rare to find family groups staying in Thurles for more than one night, unless there were health problems. In 1889, for example, around 13 per cent of admissions appear to be members of a two-parent family, but in only two cases did the family stay for more than two days and in both cases the father was noted as being sick.[92] It would appear, therefore, that while Thurles Workhouse had become an overnight stop for families on the move, it was rarely resorted to for longer-term support. In the north, provincial workhouses admitted even fewer families than those in the south, but the underlying trends were similar. Local families rarely sought relief except in cases of ill-health and while a higher proportion of families were admitted in later decades, these were invariably casual admissions.[93]

90 NDU BG Indoor Relief Registers, 1911.
91 Two-parent family groups accounted for 54 of 671 admissions: Thurles BG Indoor Relief Registers, 1870–1871.
92 284 of 2,237 admissions: Thurles BG Indoor Relief Registers, 1889.
93 In Ballymoney, for example, 4 per cent of admissions in 1850–1851 were members of two-parent family groups (14 of 369). None of the families entered more than once during the year and health problems were noted with regard to all but one family. In 1870–1871 family groups comprised just 2 per cent of admissions (18 of 948). None of the families were local and none stayed for more than two days. Local families, it would appear, were not seeking relief in the workhouse. By 1900–1901, more families were being admitted (130 of 1,456 admissions or 9 per cent), but these were all casual

The low incidence of family groups within Irish workhouses can be attributed to a number of different factors: first, two-parent families were more likely to be able to remain economically independent and were thus less vulnerable to poverty than single-parent families, or indeed single people. Second, Irish boards of guardians, like those in England, were increasingly reluctant to force families to enter, preferring to give the man outdoor relief, if a medical certificate could be obtained to sanction this.[94] At the same time dislike of the workhouse and fear of separation within it may have prevented some families from seeking admission, while others chose to split up with one parent remaining outside rather than be separated within the workhouse. Far more single-parent families were to be found in workhouses than two-parent families. Single-parent families were not a homogeneous group, however. They included widows (and widowers) with children; married women either permanently or temporarily separated from their husbands; and unmarried mothers. These groups were regarded very differently. Widows were regarded as deserving of assistance, whereas single mothers were seen as responsible, at least in part, for their situation. As the poor law commissioners noted in 1861, female pauperism was then, 'as at all times, more considerable, and is in the proportion of more than three to one in comparison with able-bodied male pauperism', but many of these were 'females who cannot obtain employment through loss of character; and no inconsiderable number of them are single females rendered destitute by pregnancy or as mothers of illegitimate children'.[95] However, even widows were expected to work if they were capable of doing so. Widows with one dependent child were not eligible for outdoor relief as they were expected to work in order to support their child.

Under the poor law system women's eligibility to relief was judged first according to their family status – whether they had a father or husband to support them – and then according to their physical status.[96] If they had no male relative to support them, were they physically capable of supporting themselves? Many people, however, questioned the relevance of the workhouse test to women. Advocating the extension of outdoor relief to

---

admissions remaining for one night. A number of families visited the workhouse more than once suggesting that officials had a relatively relaxed attitude to casual admissions: Ballymoney BG Indoor Relief Registers, PRONI, BG/5/G, 1850–1851, 1870–1871, 1900–1901.

94 Brundage notes that in England married couples with children were rarely compelled to enter the workhouse: *The English Poor Laws*, p. 122.

95 *Annual Report of the Commissioners for Administering the Laws for Relief of the Poor in Ireland, 1861*, cited in Helen Burke, *The People and the Poor Law in Nineteenth Century Ireland* (Littlehampton: Women's Education Bureau, 1987), p. 192.

96 Pat Thane, 'Women and the Poor Law in Victorian and Edwardian England', *History Workshop Journal*, 6 (1978), pp. 29–51.

widows with one dependent child in 1855, Neilson Hancock observed that the 'spontaneous and universal recognition of the principle that women ought naturally to be supported by men, implies a complete condemnation of the Poor Law doctrine of applying the workhouse test to women and children'.[97] Some years later the philanthropist and social activist, Isabella Tod, made a similar point. Widows and deserted wives, she maintained, were often:

> most respectable people, wholly unused to ordinary pauper ways, [and] it is evident that nothing can be more short-sighted than to give them only the choice between the workhouse and no help at all. A woman belonging to one of these classes is not in the least in the position of an able-bodied man; for however capable she may be, she has her hands full already, and cannot set out at once to earn her own and her children's bread.[98]

'These women', she argued, 'should be eligible for outdoor relief and not required to enter the workhouse.'

The plight of widows with children featured largely in contemporary commentary giving the impression that they formed a significant cohort within the workhouse population. Widows tended to be over-represented amongst female inmates, but the majority of these were women in their fifties or over, reflecting the economic vulnerability of women who found themselves alone and unable to support themselves. Widows made up around 20 per cent of the female admissions to Thurles Workhouse in 1870–1871, for example, when their proportion in the population was around 10 per cent. The proportion in city workhouses was higher averaging 26 per cent of admissions to NDU and 22 per cent to Belfast, and remained relatively stable over the period, while the proportion of widows in provincial workhouses appears to have declined. By 1910–1911 the proportion of widows in Thurles Workhouse had dropped to around 10 per cent of female admissions. In Glenties, however, the proportion of widows remained at around 17 per cent of female admissions. The majority were elderly suggesting that there was less support available to elderly widows in Glenties, whether in the form of outdoor relief or charitable assistance, than in other parts of the country.

Widows with children were, in fact, relatively rare in Irish workhouses and became rarer. Twenty-one per cent of widows admitted to Thurles Workhouse in 1870–1871 had children, for example, compared to just 5

97 W. Neilson Hancock, 'The Workhouse as a Mode of Relief for Widows and Orphans', *Journal of the Dublin Statistical Society*, 1 (1855), p. 85.
98 Isabella Tod, 'The Place of Women in the Administration of the Irish Poor Law', *The Englishwoman's Review*, ciii (November 1881), pp. 484–5.

per cent in 1910–1911. The decline in the number of widows with children seeking admittance to workhouses across the country was almost certainly a consequence of the rise in outdoor relief. Widows with two or more children were eligible for outdoor relief and were generally favourably regarded by boards of guardians. Southern provincial workhouses saw very few widows with children from the 1870s and the small numbers that did seek admittance were either casuals or sick. Apart from one widow who stayed for a single night with her two children in July, the only widow with children who entered Kinsale Workhouse in 1890–1891 was Anne D., whose occupation was given as 'farmer'. She was admitted with pneumonia on 10 December 1890, bringing her six children with her and stayed until 15 January 1891.[99] NDU Workhouse saw a slower but equally significant decline in the number of widows with children admitted and the virtual disappearance of widows with two or more children.[100] By 1910–1911, widows with children accounted for just 1 per cent of all widows admitted. The only widow with children who stayed for any length of time was Ellen M., a thirty-seven-year-old charwoman, who was admitted in July with her three children. She and two of her daughters were treated in hospital from where they were discharged on various dates in August and September 1911.[101]

In the north, provincial workhouses, such as Ballymoney, accommodated proportionately more widows with children in the early part of the period than those in the south, but here too numbers had dropped away by the early decades of the twentieth century. Widows with children that were admitted in these decades were almost all casual overnight admissions.[102] Belfast Workhouse, by contrast, continued to accommodate widows with children and for relatively long periods. Widows with children made up 14 per cent of all widows admitted to Belfast Workhouse in January 1864 and 20 per cent in

99 Kinsale BG Indoor Relief Registers, 1890–1891. In 1870–1871 two widows with children were admitted; Anne D., who had two children and stayed one night; and Ellen K., who had one child and was admitted three times staying seven days, nine days and then nine months: Kinsale BG Indoor Relief Registers, 1870–1871.

100 In 1860–1861, sixty-one admissions were widows with children (9 per cent of all widows), forty-one had one child and twenty had two or more. In 1890–1891, thirty-two admissions were widows with children (7.5 per cent of widows); eleven had two or more children. The average length of stay for the latter group was four months in 1871, and 2.3 months in 1891: NDU BG Indoor Relief Registers 1860–1861, 1890–1891.

101 Total of 817 admissions were widows; ten had children: NDU BG Indoor Relief Registers, 1910–1911.

102 In 1860-1861 widows made up 11 per cent of female admissions to Ballymoney. Of these, 29 per cent (eight of twenty-eight) had children and all had two or more. The average length of stay was eight months. By 1900–1901 the proportion of widows had dropped to 9 per cent (35 of 371) of whom none had more than one child. Four widows had one child. Three of the four stayed for one night; the fourth for well over a year (thirty-four months): Ballymoney BG Indoor relief Registers, 1860–1861, 1900–1901.

January 1878. The proportion had declined to 6 per cent in January 1901, but of these more than half had two or more children. The average length of stay in 1900–1901 was 3.3 months for all widows with children, but 4.6 months for those with two or more.[103] This reflected the very low rate of outdoor relief provided in Belfast; even people who were qualified and fell into what would normally be regarded as a 'deserving' category did not receive it and were forced into the workhouse as a consequence.

Over the course of the nineteenth century, the composition of workhouse populations changed, as did patterns of usage. The characteristics which featured most prominently in popular perception and commentary, such as overcrowding and family separation, became exceptional, rare events rather than common experience. Able-bodied inmates were increasingly casual visitors. Longer-term residency became confined to the physically and economically vulnerable and it is to these groups that we now turn our attention.

---

103 Admissions totalled 20 out of 146 in January 1864; 23 of 115 in January 1878; and 43 of 700 in January 1901: Belfast BG Indoor Relief Registers, 1864, 1878, 1901.

5

The Sick, Infirm and Lunatics

As the constituent elements of the workhouse population changed in the decades after 1860, so the character and function of the institution altered. As a British Medical Association Report on workhouses infirmaries noted in 1895, when the poor law was first introduced the sick were an 'unimportant section' of the workhouse population, 'Now the able-bodied have almost vanished off the land, their place being taken by infirm and aged class, and the sick.'[1] The growing emphasis within the workhouse on specialised treatment mirrored developments in England.[2] Medical matters became a regular item on the agenda of boards of guardians and while they often resisted acting on the advice of their medical officers, they found it increasingly difficult to ignore it altogether. From the later part of the nineteenth century, stricter classification and improved standards of care helped to lessen the stigma associated with workhouse hospitals.[3] Assessing developments in England, Alysa Levene has concluded that medical services for the poor were 'variable in coverage and quality', and improvements dependent on 'the initiative of individual officers and long-held expectations on entitlements as well as finance and government directives'.[4] In Ireland

---

1   'Reports on the Nursing and Administration of the Irish Workhouse Infirmaries', *The British Medical Association Reports on the Poor-Law Medical System in Ireland* (London: British Medical Journal, 1904), p. 60.

2   See, for example, Anne Crowther, 'Health care and poor relief in provincial England', in O. P. Grell, A. Cunningham and R. Jutte (eds), *Health Care and Poor Relief in Eighteenth and Nineteenth Century Northern Europe* (Aldershot: Ashgate, 2002), pp. 203–19; and M. W. Flinn, 'Medical Services under the New Poor Law', in Derek Fraser (ed.), *The New Poor Law in the Nineteenth Century* (London: Macmillan, 1976), pp. 45–66.

3   M. A. Crowther, 'Paupers or patients? Obstacles to professionalization in the Poor Law Medical Service before 1914', *Journal of the History of Medicine and Allied Sciences*, 39 (1984); and Lynn Hollen Lees, *The Solidarities of Strangers: The English Poor Laws and the People, 1700–1948* (Cambridge, CUP, 1998), pp. 278–9.

4   Alysa Levene, 'Between Less Eligibility and the NHS: The Changing Place of Poor Law Hospitals in England and Wales, 1929–39', *Twentieth Century British History*, 20 (2009), p. 325.

too, progress was uneven and subject to considerable local variation. By the early twentieth century, standards of care across the country had improved, but many workhouse hospitals remained poorly equipped and understaffed.

From the 1850s workhouse hospitals were attracting people seeking medical attention rather than relief.[5] In 1851, Dr Kirkpatrick, Medical Officer in NDU Workhouse, reported that a decline in hospital accommodation in the city, due to the withdrawal of government grants, had meant that a 'vast number of invalids' were seeking admittance to the workhouse 'solely as a hospital'. Kirkpatrick and his colleague Dr Monaghan, lobbied the board of guardians for additional medical attendance. Two additional medical officers were appointed in March at salaries of fifty pounds per annum.[6] Following the opening of workhouse infirmaries to non-destitute patients in 1862, the importance of workhouse hospitals increased. In many rural towns the workhouse infirmary constituted the only hospital in the locality.[7] In major cities the workhouse was not the only medical facility open to the poor, but it was invariably the largest. The union infirmaries in Cork and Belfast, for example, provided accommodation for more patients than all the voluntary hospitals put together.[8]

Treatment of the outdoor sick poor was provided for by the 1851 Medical Charities Act.[9] During the year ended 31 March 1909, around 650,000 cases were seen by medical officers, three-quarters at dispensaries and the rest in their own homes.[10] The combined effect of the introduction of the dispensary system and the expansion of outdoor relief contributed to a decline in the proportion of sick admissions to workhouses. This trend is evident both in annual returns and workhouse admission registers. The

---

5   In their *Annual Report* for 1855–1856 the poor law commissioners noted both the increased proportion of sick people in workhouses and the increased disposition to resort to the workhouse as a hospital: HC, 1856 [2105], p. 12.

6   NDU BG Minutes, 12 February and 12 March 1851.

7   Jeremiah Dowling recalled that Tipperary Workhouse hospital functioned as the only hospital in Tipperary town admitting many patients from the town and surrounding area. It contained around eighty beds and the nursing staff consisted of three nuns and a paid night nurse. When patients needed special attention pauper inmates assisted: Dowling, *An Irish Doctor Remembers* (Dublin: Clonmore and Reynolds, 1955), pp. 27–8, 72.

8   The later part of the nineteenth century saw the establishment of a number of voluntary hospitals in Irish cities, but these tended to be small and specialised: Voluntary Hospitals Database: (www.hospitalsdatabase.lshtm.ac.ul/).

9   Medical Charities (Ireland) Act, 1851, 14 and 15 Vic., c. 68. For the impact of this act, see Laurence M. Geary, 'The Medical Profession, Health Care and the Poor Law in Nineteenth-Century Ireland', in Crossman and Gray (eds), *Poverty and Welfare in Ireland 1838–1948* (Dublin: Irish Academic Press, 2011), pp. 189–206.

10   Census of Paupers, *Royal Commission on the Poor Laws and Relief of Distress. Appendix. Statistics Relating to Ireland*, HC, 1910 [Cd. 5244], p. 15.

proportion of admissions to Kinsale Workhouse that were noted to have some form or sickness of disability declined from 46 per cent in 1871 to 28 per cent in 1891.[11] In terms of total numbers, sick admissions remained relatively stable over the period. As the Royal Commission noted in 1909, the number had 'not materially changed during the last fifty years'. The proportion of sick and infirm inmates, however, increased. The percentage of able-bodied inmates in workhouses on the first Saturday in the year dropped from 17 per cent of the total in 1870 to 13 per cent in 1900, while the proportion in workhouse hospitals rose from 31 per cent of total inmates in 1870 to 44 per cent in 1900.[12] Within individual workhouses a similar trend is apparent. In Tralee Workhouse, for example, the proportion of inmates in hospital increased from 22 per cent in 1870–1871 to 39 per cent in 1890–1891; in Kilmallock it increased from 20 per cent in 1870–1871 to 36 per cent in 1890–1891.[13] Large city workhouses housed more able-bodied inmates and thus recorded lower proportions in hospital. In NDU Workhouse, 26 per cent of inmates were in hospital in 1880–1881; 27 per cent in 1890–1891; and 28 per cent in 1910–1911. It is important to note, however, that while the proportion in hospital was relatively small compared to rural workhouses, this should not be taken to mean that the majority of NDU inmates were healthy. In 1880–1881 in addition to those in hospital, 40 per cent of inmates were classified as infirm under medical treatment and a further 5 per cent were on a hospital diet. In all, 71 per cent of NDU inmates were on a hospital diet in 1880–1881 and 62 per cent in 1890–1891.[14] In the majority of workhouses the sick and infirm together made up between one-half and two-thirds of inmates in the decades after 1870.

If a person could not be treated in the workhouse hospital, the board of guardians could pay for them to be sent for treatment elsewhere. By the later decades of the nineteenth century this was becoming a relatively common occurrence. In December 1875, for example, a child was sent from

11 311 of 618 admissions in 1870–1871 and 291 of 911 admissions in 1890–1891, were noted to be sick or infirm: Kinsale BG Indoor Relief Registers, 1870–1871 and 1890–1891.
12 Classified return of the number of inmates in workhouses on the first Saturday of January, *Annual Report of the Local Government Board for Ireland*, HC, 1900 [Cd. 338], p. xviii.
13 The average number remaining in Tralee Workhouse at the end of the week was 410 in 1870–1871 and 417 in 1890–1891. The average number in hospital was 90 in 1870–1871 and 158 in 1890–1891. For Kilmallock, the figures were 554 and 460 remaining, and 112 and 166 in hospital: Weekly relief statistics, Tralee BG Minutes, Kilmallock BG Minutes, 1870–1871 and 1890–1891.
14 In 1880–1881 the average number remaining was 2,343: in hospital 619; infirm under medical treatment 940; and on a hospital diet 1,665. In 1891 the average number remaining was 2,651; in hospital 714; and on a hospital diet 1,651: Weekly relief statistics, NDU BG Minutes.

Kilmallock Workhouse to Steevens Hospital in Dublin for special treatment. The following month, a man suffering from cancer of the lip was sent from Kilmallock to Dublin for treatment, although the master later reported that he had failed to arrive.[15] It is possible that he absconded with money supplied as expenses. Anne S., an inmate of Westport Workhouse, was sent to Dublin in September 1901, 'on the recommendation of Dr Birmingham' for special treatment to her eyes and a sum of thirty shillings allowed for expenses.[16] Entering the workhouse became a way of accessing specialist treatment. In May 1913, a member of the Thurles Board of Guardians, P. Laffan, proposed that patients recommended for treatment in extern institutions should be 'sent direct' without having to be admitted to the workhouse. It was 'very hard', Laffan argued, to expect 'decent poor people' who required treatment in Dublin hospitals 'to come in to the workhouse for a night before going, as they had to do at present'. Most of his colleagues, however, were wary of encouraging people to seek treatment. The result, one commented, would be more people 'going up to Dublin at our expense'.[17] The legality of such referrals remained in doubt until 1917, when a judicial ruling established that the power to send people from the workhouse to an external hospital for special treatment applied only to the destitute and not to poor people, who had been admitted to the workhouse in order to obtain treatment. The latter could be treated in the workhouse, but did not qualify for external treatment.[18]

The extent to which the stigma of the workhouse discouraged sick people from entering is difficult to assess. During a smallpox outbreak in Cork city in 1872 there were fears that stories of poor care and overcrowding were preventing people from seeking treatment. It was popularly believed that it was only when the Sisters of Mercy took responsibility for nursing in the workhouse hospital that the rate of applications increased. However, given the fact that nearly 500 victims were admitted in the early stages of the outbreak there seems little hard evidence to support such stories. During the course of the epidemic 1,250 of the 3,365 known cases were treated in the workhouse, compared to 668 treated in the city fever hospital.[19] Popular prejudice against the workhouse was often exaggerated but it was not irrational. Reports of inadequate facilities and poor levels of care emerging from within the Irish medical profession in the 1890s prompted the *British Medical Journal* to send

15 Kilmallock BG Minutes, 16 December 1875 and 20 January 1876.
16 Westport BG Minutes, 21 September 1901. See also Westport BG Minutes, 6 September 1906.
17 *Nenagh Guardian*, 24 May 1913.
18 *Law Reports (Ireland)*, Kings Bench Division [1917], R. Kennelly versus Browne.
19 Colman O Mahony, *Cork's Poor Law Palace: Workhouse Life 1838–90* (Cork: Rosmathún Press, 2005), pp. 205–9.

the trained nurse and experienced hospital administrator, Catherine Wood, to investigate the state of workhouse infirmaries in 1895.[20] Having visited twenty-eight poor law unions across the country, she concluded that the vast majority of workhouse infirmaries were not fit for purpose. They were generally too small, resulting in serious overcrowding. It was not uncommon, she found, for patients to be accommodated two to a bed. Buildings were often badly designed, with common problems being damp walls, inadequate ventilation, drainage and sanitation, and insufficient and untrained staff. Wood recommended the employment of trained nurses in every workhouse infirmary; the employment of night nurses; the introduction of efficient sanitary systems including the provision of an adequate water supply and efficient methods for disposing of excreta; and the provision of day rooms; and, where possible, gardens.[21]

The official response to the BMA Report and ongoing campaign to reform the workhouse system was to stress that workhouse infirmaries were regularly inspected and did meet basic standards of hygiene and care, and that the responsibility for improvement lay with local boards of guardians rather than central government. In 1896 the Local Government Board noted that during the past year their inspectors had reported 'important improvements' in the condition and management of workhouses including the appointment of a number of assistant nurses for night duty, which had 'added materially to the comfort of inmates'. At the same time however, the financial condition of many poorer unions precluded the guardians:

> from placing the workhouses and hospitals under their charge upon the same level as regards comfort and equipment as the modern hospitals with which they have been to their disadvantage so frequently contrasted.

While anxious to promote improvements that would 'tend to lengthen the lives of the aged poor and add to the comforts of the sick', they were, they explained, bound 'to keep the difficulties [boards of guardians] encounter in their financial administration constantly before us'.[22] The central authorities placed considerable emphasis on maintaining and, where possible, improving

20 See, for example, Austin Meldon and Arthur Benson of the Irish Medical Association to the editor of the *Irish Times*, 19 July 1895. As in England, much of the pressure for reform came from the medical profession supported by social activists and philanthropists.

21 'Reports on the Nursing and Administration of the Irish Workhouse Infirmaries', p. 50, 60; and Geary, 'The Medical Profession, Health Care and the Poor Law', pp. 199–201.

22 *Annual Report of the Local Government Board for Ireland*, HC, 1896 [Cd. 8153], pp. 6–7.

the condition of medical facilities, but they were realistic about what could be achieved with limited resources.

Raising standards in workhouse infirmaries was a slow and protracted process. Poor law boards were reluctant to incur additional costs and regarded many of the circulars issued from the centre as unwarranted and unnecessary. By 1881 most workhouses had at least one paid, though not necessarily trained, nurse. All workhouses, however, continued to rely on untrained pauper attendants. The proportion of attendants to patients varied enormously. Unions in the north appear to have had the worst patient–attendant ratios. Ballycastle Infirmary, for example, was staffed by one paid nurse and two pauper assistants who cared for an average of forty-seven patients (giving a ratio of one attendant to sixteen patients); while in Glenties Workhouse infirmary one paid nurse and two assistants cared for an average of forty-three patients (ratio of one attendant to fourteen patients). Ratios in the south were better. In Kilmallock, 126 patients were cared for by four paid nurses and nineteen assistants (ratio of one attendant to six patients); while in Tralee, 200 patients were cared for by five paid assistants and twenty-two assistants (ratio of one attendant to seven patients). In other workhouses there were fewer paid attendants, but more pauper assistants. Thus in Mountmellick Workhouse one paid nurse was in charge of forty-five patients assisted by eight pauper attendants (ratio of one attendant to five patients). In the major city workhouses higher patient numbers meant that while there were more paid nurses the reliance on pauper attendants was far greater. In Belfast Workhouse Infirmary an average of 661 patients were attended by nine paid and fifty-four unpaid nurses (ratio of one attendant to eleven patients); while in NDU infirmary an average of 1,125 patients were cared for by just five paid attendants assisted by 110 paupers (ratio of one attendant to ten patients).[23]

In comparison with English workhouses, staffing levels in Irish infirmaries were relatively poor. City workhouses, such as Birmingham and Liverpool, were employing significant numbers of paid staff by the mid-1860s, giving nurse to patient ratios of one to twenty-six and one to thirty-eight.[24] In Irish city workhouses the ratio of patients to paid staff in 1881 was one to sixty-four in Cork; one to seventy-three in Belfast; and one to 225 in NDU. Furthermore, many of the paid nurses working in Irish workhouse infirmaries were nuns. The five paid nurses in Tralee Workhouse

---

23 *Return of the average number of sick persons tended in each union workhouse in Ireland during the last year for which the figures are complete*, HC, 1881 (433), pp. 2–19.

24 By 1896 this had improved to one attendant to sixteen patients for England as a whole. See, Alistair Ritch, 'Sick, aged and infirm: adults in the new Birmingham workhouse, 1852–1912' (University of Birmingham MPhil Thesis, 2010), p. 41.

Infirmary, for example, included four nuns and one midwife, while the paid staff in Thurles Infirmary included four nuns and one paid assistant.[25] Nuns were generally well educated and of impeccable moral standing, but they were not professionally trained and were unable to perform certain duties, such as night nursing.[26] During the 1870s and 1880s an increasing number of workhouse infirmaries came under the control of nuns although boards of guardians continued to rely on pauper assistants for general duties and night nursing. By 1903 a total of 325 nuns were working in eighty-five union infirmaries.[27]

Having initially opposed their appointment on the grounds that it would interfere with workhouse management, the Local Government Board was forced to acknowledge the benefits that nuns had brought. Responding to criticism of the employment of nuns in workhouses as 'prejudicial to discipline' in 1875, the secretary to the board observed that the services of nuns as hospital nurses were 'much valued by some Boards of Guardians. They have not produced so much inconvenience as was at first expected.'[28] Although nuns were generally regarded as helping to raise standards, their presence in Irish workhouses made it easier for boards of guardians to resist pressure to appoint professional trained nurses, arguing that they were not needed. Catherine Wood welcomed the 'light and cheeriness' nuns had brought into workhouses, but noted that they were not trained nurses and did not provide night nursing. Those campaigning for reform of workhouse infirmaries were careful not to criticise the nursing provided by nuns. Members of the Irish Medical Association, for example, directed their fiercest attacks on workhouses in which the nursing was 'entirely in the hands of pauper women, most of whom have come in burthened with children'.[29]

Much of the criticism of pauper attendants focused on the class of people employed. Generally 'young women with illegitimate children', they were described by Tipperary medic, Jeremiah Dowling, as being drawn 'from the lowest class, restrained by no sense either of decency or religion, loud-voiced, quarrelsome and abusive'.[30] Pauper women employed in Cork Hospital were

25 *Return of the average number of sick persons tended in each union workhouse in Ireland*, HC, 1881 (433), p. 18.
26 For a discussion of the role of nuns as workhouse nurses, see Maria Luddy, '"Angels of Mercy": Nuns as Workhouse Nurses, 1861–1898', in Greta Jones and Elizabeth Malcolm (eds), *Medicine, Disease and the State in Ireland, 1650–1940* (Cork: Cork University Press, 1999), pp. 102–17.
27 *Return showing the Number of Workhouse Infirmaries in Ireland in which Nuns are employed in any capacity*, HC, 1903 (115) pp. 4–5.
28 Banks to Burke, 6 February 1875, NAI, CSORP 1875/2360.
29 *Irish Times*, 31 May 1895.
30 Jeremiah Dowling, *The Irish Poor Laws and Poor Houses* (Dublin: Hodges, Foster and

condemned in the local press as having 'no social influence – they were mere scrubbers'.[31] Workhouse officials generally had little choice about who they employed as attendants and often struggled to find suitable people. In February 1892, the Master of Lismore Workhouse commented in his journal on the difficulty of finding attendants for the female lunatic ward, 'owing to the few able-bodied women in the house – the best being employed in the hospital'.[32] In city workhouses, where there were more able-bodied inmates, there were more candidates, although their suitability was sometimes open to question. It is difficult to determine on what criteria attendants were selected but the essential attributes appear to have been physical capacity and a willingness to undertake the tasks required. A wards maid in the lunatic department in Belfast Workhouse in 1894 described herself as 'an old jail bird', explaining that she has been a frequent visitor to the workhouse over the previous seven years during which time she had been a wards maid in a number of different parts of the workhouse.[33]

Masters of large workhouses, such as Belfast and Cork, appear to have used the appointment and deployment of attendants as a means of pauper management. In 1891, LGI George Spaight drew attention to the 'discrepancy existing in regard to the number of attendants in the different hospital wards' in Cork Workhouse, noting that in some cases 'the number of attendants and number of patients were not proportionable'. The master explained that 'the number of assistants did not necessarily depend on the number in hospital. If ten or twelve additional patients come in this week the number of assistants would not increase in the least.' Most of the assistants, Vice-Guardian William Burke commented, were drawn from the infirm class and could not be compared with properly trained paid nurses, 'because they belonged to the lost class in the community, and of course would be only anxious to do the least possible amount of work they could take on their shoulders'.[34] Many ratepayers would probably have agreed with Burke's assessment, but it was a rash remark to make publicly. Indeed his comments appear to have caused such offence that he was obliged to issue an apology the following week. His remarks, he explained, had been:

> misunderstood... He was represented to have stated that the female attendants in the various wards in the house belonged to the lost class

      Co., 1872), p. 11.
31 *Cork Examiner*, 26 April 1872, cited in O Mahony, *Cork's Poor Law Palace*, p. 208
32 Master's Journal, Lismore BG, NAI, BG/111/F3, 3 February 1892.
33 *Belfast Newsletter*, 28 November 1894.
34 *Cork Examiner*, 3 April 1891. The union was under the control of paid vice guardians
      at the time. See, Crossman and Lucey, '"One Huge Abuse": The Cork Board of
      Guardians and the Expansion of Outdoor Relief in Post-Famine Ireland', pp. 1424–8.

and that in consequence they shirked work as far as possible. He never meant to say any such thing and he would be very sorry to express himself in that way of a very deserving class of persons.[35]

Inmates lacked social capital but they were not powerless; they could not be insulted with impunity.

Many unions continued to employ pauper attendants well into the 1890s and 1900s. The primary motivation was undoubtedly financial but some boards of guardians sought to defend the practice as providing rehabilitation and training. When an inspector recommended that the Cashel Board of Guardians dispense with the services of pauper attendants, two of whom had illegitimate children, on the grounds that it was 'most undesirable that women of an immoral character should be placed in positions of trust', the guardians responded that women were mainly employed in menial work and would 'benefit from the good moral atmosphere of the wards under the guidance and instruction of the nuns'. There was, they maintained, no reason why women who had 'committed an error or more probably been led astray once in a lifetime ... should be branded for all time as infamous and unfit even for the occupation of acting attendant in a workhouse hospital'.[36] The Ballycastle Guardians had also defended the employment of unmarried mothers as attendants in the infirmary, arguing that the 'clean and neat appearance of the wards under their care shows that they are quite competent for the work expected from them'.[37] When the Local Government Board refused to sanction the appointment of a woman as a ward servant in Ballycastle Workhouse in 1901, 'owing to her being the mother of two illegitimate children', the guardians asked for permission to employ her for six months on probation, explaining that the 'woman is a good worker; she has been a farm servant, a class that is subject to very great temptation, and is not of the class to which the Local Government Board evidently refers', meaning presumably that she was not a prostitute.[38] In these cases the guardians were seeking to suit themselves and save money. Nevertheless, if the workhouse was to provide practical training as well as temporary shelter, then the guardians' attitude made more sense than that of the Local Government Board. Privileging respectability increased the status of the nursing profession, but it also operated to exclude poor women.

Throughout the 1890s the Local Government Board strove to convince

35 *Cork Examiner*, 10 April. 1891.
36 Cited in Eamonn Lonergan, *A Workhouse Story: A History of St Patrick's Hospital, Cashel 1842–1992* (Clonmel: Eamonn Lonergan, 1992), p. 159.
37 Ballycastle BG Minutes, 29 June 1895.
38 Ballycastle BG Minutes, 25 May 1901.

boards of guardians of the importance of appointing nurses with training and experience. A circular issued in 1890 described nursing as 'crucial to successful recovery. The highest skill and attention on the part of the medical officer, may be neutralized by the ignorance and incapacity of the nurse charged with the duty of carrying out his instructions.' When filling vacancies, therefore, boards should offer such salaries as would persuade qualified persons to apply.[39] Exhortation having proved ineffective the Local Government Board finally took a more proactive approach. In 1897, the board prohibited the appointment of any workhouse inmate as nurse of the workhouse and defined the latter's duties as superintending and controlling all the other nurses, assistant nurses and attendants 'subject to the directions of the Medical Officer in matters of treatment and to the directions of the master or matron in all other matters'. Paupers could still act as attendants but only if 'approved by the Medical Officer for the purpose, and ... under the immediate supervision of a paid officer of the Guardians'.[40]

Following the Local Government Act of 1898, the regulations regarding workhouse nursing were tightened further and the qualifications required of trained nurses clarified.[41] The nurse of the workhouse was responsible for nursing and feeding the sick, supervising the nursing staff and maintaining proper order and discipline in the sick wards. She was 'to carry out all reasonable directions of the medical officer, to whom and to the Board of Guardians only ... she shall be subordinate, save as regards the general disciplinary control of the Master of the Workhouse'. In an emergency the master was directed to employ fit persons to act as temporary nurses, if it appeared to the medical officer that this was 'requisite for the proper treatment of any patient or patients' until the next meeting of the guardians.[42] Empowering the master to act directly on the advice of the medical officer significantly enhanced the latter's authority and was intended to prevent boards of guardians repeatedly ignoring requests for additional nursing assistance. In February 1871, for example, one of the Medical Officers of the

39 Appointment of Nurses Circular, 10 April 1890, *Annual Report of the Local Government Board for Ireland*, HC, 1896 [Cd. 8153], p. 88.
40 Workhouse Rules – Nursing of the Sick, *Annual Report of the Local Government Board for Ireland*, HC, 1898 [Cd. 8958], pp. 67–8.
41 A trained nurse was stated to mean anyone with a certificate of proficiency in nursing and two years clinical or hospital experience. A qualified nurse was defined as a person who had obtained a certificate of proficiency in nursing from a public general hospital, a workhouse infirmary or fever hospital, or a nursing institution. Attendants were to be at least twenty-one years of age and of good health and character.
42 Workhouse Hospital Trained Nurse, 12 January 1899, *Annual Report of the Local Government Board for Ireland*, HC, 1899 [Cd. 9480], p. 741; and Order Amending General Regulations, 5 July 1901, *Annual Report of the Local Government Board for Ireland*, HC, 1903 [Cd. 1606], pp. 68–72.

NDU Workhouse, Dr Minchin, had complained of serious overcrowding in the wards occupied by the sick and infirm women which, he believed, was 'detrimental to the health of the inmates'. The guardians acknowledged that there was 'slight' overcrowding due to 'arrangement and classification of the sick and infirm inmates', but were confident that this was a temporary problem that would not occur again that year, 'now that the weather has improved'. A few weeks later, however, Minchin again complained of overcrowding in the sick and infirm women's wards, suggesting that his assessment of the situation was more accurate than that of the guardians.[43]

After 1898 the Local Government Board refused to sanction the appointment of any untrained or uncertified person as a nurse or assistant nurse in a workhouse infirmary, even in a temporary capacity. Guardians were not required to remove those already in place, however. By 1913, the total number of trained nurses employed in Irish workhouses had reached 268, together with 248 qualified nurses and 357 nursing sisters, but there were still twelve workhouses without a trained nurse.[44] Many unions continued to employ pauper attendants well into the 1890s and 1900s. With relatively few able-bodied inmates available, people were often given little choice about taking on these duties. In January 1903, the Master of Kinsale Workhouse reported an able-bodied man for refusing to work in the hospital as an assistant and subsequently ordered him to be discharged on the grounds that he had 'refused to do ordinary work'. A few months later he reported 'two able bodied women named Margaret and Mary C. for refusing to go to hospital on Monday night to mind a delirious patient'. Not surprisingly, some of those prevailed upon to act as attendants proved unsuited to the work. On 18 April 1906, the Kinsale Medical Officer 'complained the paid male attendant Edward L. for being rough to a patient'.[45]

The efficiency of any workhouse hospital depended on the medical officer and his relationship with the board of guardians. 'The benefit conferred on the poor by the hospital', one observer noted in 1869:

will depend partly on the professional character of the medical officer in charge, partly on the degree of independence which he may be able to maintain towards the guardians, partly on the certainty with which he can calculate on his orders being carried out by the subordinate officers of the house.[46]

43 NDU Minutes, 8 and 22 February 1871.
44 *Annual Report of the Local Government Board for Ireland*, HC, 1913 [Cd. 6978], p. xvi.
45 Master's Journal, Kinsale, 14 January, 15 May 1903 and 18 April 1906, CAI, BG108/F1.
46 Rev. William Anderson, 'Workhouse Hospitals in the West of Ireland', in George W. Hastings (ed.), *Transactions of the National Association for the Promotion of Social Science, Belfast Meeting 1867* (London: Green, Reader and Dyer, 1868), p. 515.

Where medical officers came into conflict with boards of guardians it was generally over money. They were spending too much on medicines or they were making too many recommendations that involved extra expenditure, whether with regard to providing hot rather than cold water baths for new admissions; or improvements in the diet; or the necessity of boarding out orphan and deserted children. The competing demands made on medical officers are evident in the response of the Medical Officer of Mountmellick Workhouse, Dr Joseph Clarke, to an order from the board of guardians in 1871 to explain 'the cause of the great increase of stimulants for the last year, as compared with 1860'. Clarke acknowledged that there had been a considerable increase despite there being 'no great difference in the numbers admitted into the hospital'. The explanation lay in the type of cases treated. Those in 1860, he explained, were generally of a mild form which did not require stimulants. In 1870, however, the cases admitted included many suffering from 'very exhaustive diseases' which required 'stimulants, tonics and nutritious diet'. Over the past year, he maintained, he had had 'to contend against the worse form of fever I have seen since the famine. I had ninety-nine cases admitted to hospital some of them heads of large, helpless families.' There had also been a great increase in the number of infirm since 1860, 'all very delicate, particularly those in the female departments and they have very often required stimulants'.[47] In justifying his actions, Clarke was careful to stress not only his professional competence, diligence and care for his patients, but also his concern to protect the financial interests of the union by ensuring that people did not remain in hospital longer than was necessary.

When assessing developments in workhouse medicine there is an important distinction to be drawn between workhouse hospitals in the major urban unions, which treated large numbers of patients and were relatively well staffed and equipped, and those in rural unions which could only accommodate a small number of patients, often under very primitive conditions. The former were often seriously overcrowded and the staff operated under constant pressure. In 1879, for example, the poor law authorities found it necessary to restrict admissions to the Belfast Union Infirmary due to the extent of overcrowding which was putting patients' lives at risk.[48] Overcrowding remained a problem, but by the early twentieth century the workhouse infirmary, which was the largest in Ireland, had developed into an important training hospital comprising obstetric, children's, consumptive, lock and lunatic wards, together with a separate

47 Mountmellick BG Minutes, 23 September 1871.
48 Inspector's Report, 23 May 1879, Belfast BG Minutes.

fever hospital.[49] The board of guardians had voted in favour of opening the
workhouse wards to medical and surgical students from Queen's College
Belfast in 1877 and a programme for nurse training was established in the late
1880s.[50] From 1901, all candidates for the position of probationer nurse were
required to pass a preliminary qualifying examination in arithmetic, writing
and spelling. They then embarked on a three-year training programme
at the end of which they were examined. Successful candidates received
a certificate of training which qualified them to be registered as trained
nurses by the Local Government Board.[51] Formerly 'an offence', the Belfast
Infirmary was described in the *British Medical Journal* in 1902, as 'one of the
best-managed and most advanced union infirmaries in Ireland'.[52]

In rural unions, the most pressing problems facing workhouse medical
officers were lack of facilities and nursing staff. In the mid-1890s, the
Medical Officer of Ballycastle Workhouse made repeated requests for the
appointment of a trained night nurse and for structural improvements, such
as the provision of a bathroom, 'as the want of such a sanitary arrangement
retards the treatment of disease and adds much to the labour of nursing'.
The guardians were unconvinced, declaring themselves 'satisfied that all
necessary attendance etc. is provided for the patients and that any further
expense in this direction would be only a waste of the poor rates'.[53] It was
only when the Local Government Board threatened to dissolve the board, 'if
the guardians do not take the necessary steps to appoint a competent trained
night nurse' that the board finally resolved to advertise for a trained nurse at
a salary of twenty pounds per annum.[54] Conditions did improve in Ballycastle
Workhouse but guardians remained wary of unnecessary expenditure. They
reacted most indignantly to an inspector's report in 1901, drawing attention
to the lack of an operating room. While 'not averse' to providing an operating
room, the guardians claimed to be more concerned about improving the
sewerage of the fever hospital, on which they were spending £150, even
though 'your inspector never discovered the need. It escaped his eagle eye.
He never reported on it.' The guardians also rejected critical comments
regarding the nursing staff, pointing out that the workhouse had two trained

49 'Special Correspondence – Belfast', *British Medical Journal*, 14 June 1902.
50 In 1887 the board of guardians agreed to appoint six suitable persons to train as nurse
   probationers: David H. Craig, 'A History of the Belfast City Hospital', *Ulster Medical
   Society Journal* (1974).
51 Belfast BG Minutes, 26 December 1877 and 2 July 1901.
52 It was noted that nursing, which was provided by ninety trained nurses, had been
   'revolutionised': 'Special Correspondence – Belfast', *British Medical Journal*, 14 June
   1902.
53 Medical Officer's Report, 17 August 1895; and Ballycastle BG Minutes, 31 August 1895.
54 Letter from Local Government Board, 1 November 1895; and Ballycastle BG Minutes
   2 November 1895.

nurses and a ward servant, 'There is scarcely a union in Ulster can excel this and yet this is only a small and poor union which however believes in doing things well.'[55] Here the guardians were seeking to demonstrate their superior understanding of local needs and interests, as well as their superior knowledge of the state of the workhouse.

The chief obstacles to improving standards of medical care were inertia on the part of boards of guardians and lack of finance. With no specific income set aside to support sick inmates or meet hospital expenses, guardians had neither incentive nor designated funds to initiate improvements.[56] Local government reorganization in 1898 provided an opportunity to remove these obstacles, at least in part. The Local Government Act made it easier for local authorities to borrow money for capital projects and under the financial regulations that accompanied the act, central government undertook to meet half the cost of officers' salaries. This included the salary of the workhouse nurse, but only if she was a qualified nurse. The act thus gave boards of guardians a direct financial incentive to appoint a trained nurse. It also empowered them to convert the union hospital into a district hospital. The aim was to create a new framework for poor law medicine that would further lessen the link between pauperism and health care. Few if any boards appear to have utilised the district hospital provision and the full impact of the changes was lost in the political upheaval that followed the Easter Rising, but a significant number of boards did take out loans in order to undertake building works and other improvements.[57]

In 1905, the Vice-Regal Commission on Poor Law Reform in Ireland circulated a questionnaire to workhouse medical officers regarding nursing arrangements and conditions in hospitals. In some unions little appeared to have changed since Woods had toured the country in 1895. The Medical Officer of the Enniskillen Workhouse described his hospital as 'far from what I would consider satisfactory. It is a relic of the barbarous past ... The guardians won't do anything.' But others referred to recent improvements. All the wards in Mount Bellew Workhouse were reported to be 'airy and well-lighted, and each has a lavatory erected within the last few years, and having all the latest sanitary accommodation'. In Trim Union the medical

55 Ballycastle BG Minutes, 20 July 1901.
56 Separate funding was provided under the Medical Charities Act to fund the dispensary system. For the LGB's use of 'economic incentives' to promote the expansion of medical services in England, see Keir Waddington, 'Paying for the Sick Poor: Financing Medicine Under the Victorian Poor Law – the Case of the Whitechapel Union, 1850–1900', in Martin Gorsky and Sally Sheard (eds), *Financing Medicine: The British Experience Since 1750* (London: Routledge, 2006), pp. 95–111.
57 See, for example, Workhouse Loans, *Annual Report of the Local Government Board for Ireland*, HC, 1903 [Cd. 1606], p. 183.

officer reported that the hospital was 'taken advantage of by large numbers of the poor of the union, and in my opinion, the prejudices which existed in the minds of the poor as to entering the workhouse infirmary do not prevail amongst them at present. Many respectable people avail themselves of the advantages which the hospital affords.' Significant progress had been made with regard to nursing; 125 out of 159 workhouse medical officers reported that nursing arrangements were satisfactory or better.[58]

Figures obtained by the Vice-Regal Commission showed that on 11 March 1905 the total workhouse population included 14,491 sick and 14,380 aged and infirm of whom 4,676 were either bedridden or ailing and feeble, out of a total workhouse population of 45,195. The commissioners estimated that of those registered as sick only a minority 'were proper cases for the sick wards'. Most of the others were aged and infirm people 'who are perhaps bed-ridden or very feeble'. Although they did not require either medical attention or skilled nursing, their presence in hospital could be 'largely attributed to a very natural, proper and humane feeling' that if aged and infirm people 'were relegated to the healthy infirm wards in many workhouses, they would not receive such attention as would enable them to spend the end of their lives in reasonable comfort'.[59] The condition of the aged and infirm was of particular concern to workhouse reformers. Speaking at a conference on Irish Workhouse Reform in London in 1896, Catherine Woods argued that, unlike the sick who tended to receive proper care as 'the doctor was in and out of the wards', there was nobody looking after the elderly and infirm.[60] Those campaigning to improve conditions made much of the vulnerability of workhouse inmates. The Secretary of the Irish Workhouses Medical Officers Association, Dr T. Hamilton Moorhead, described them as 'the forgotten people of Irish society'. There was 'no reason', he argued, 'why a sick pauper should not be attended in the same way as a sick nobleman if it was intended that a cure should be effected'.[61]

In the later decades of the nineteenth century there appears to have been a widespread perception that the workhouse system was failing to provide adequately for the sick and infirm, and a growing willingness to assert the rights of service-users. In December 1890, the Kilmallock Board of Guardians received a letter from a local resident accusing the medical officer of the workhouse of neglect of duty. It was stated that the doctor

58 Replies of Workhouse Medical Officers to Queries respecting their Hospitals put by the Commission, *Poor Law Reform Commission (Ireland). Appendix to the Report of the Vice-Regal Commission on Poor Law Reform in Ireland. Volume II*, HC, 1906 [Cd. 3203], pp. 82–100.
59 *Poor Law Reform Commission (Ireland)*, HC, 1906 [Cd. 3203], p. 23.
60 *Irish Times*, 30 April 1896.
61 *Irish Times*, 30 April 1896.

had 'turned with indifference' from a man who had walked to Kilmallock from Charleville (around six miles) on an injured leg. The doctor denied the allegation explaining that when he had examined the man he 'saw that his leg was already dressed and that there was no necessity of admitting him immediately to the infirmary and told him to come next morning to the surgery'. He acknowledged that he had not in fact seen him the following day, but this was because the man had left the workhouse. This explanation was considered satisfactory.[62] Although this patient was clearly dissatisfied, it would appear that it was lack of courtesy on the part of the doctor, rather than the actual treatment he had received, that had annoyed him.

Reformers claimed to speak on behalf of patients, but rarely acknowledged that patients were capable of speaking for themselves. People complained about the way they were treated, or not treated, and about uncomfortable conditions. Arthur Seymour, an inmate of Cork Workhouse in the 1870s, wrote a series of letters to government ministers complaining of his treatment. Seymour, who was a congenital cripple, had been admitted to the hospital in August 1877, with a sprained ankle and transferred to the infirm ward after a few days. He was readmitted to hospital a few months later suffering from piles and again transferred to the infirm ward after treatment. Having examined the entries relating to his case, LGI McCabe found him to have received 'every possible attention, appropriate diet and suitable medical treatment including a series of hot baths'. He dismissed the complaints, concluding that Seymour's threats to prosecute workhouse officers and his 'morbid suspicion of everybody about him', were evidence of an unsound mind, 'He is well educated and might be sent on his business if it were not for the fact that bodily deformity renders it difficult for him to find employment.'[63] Seymour's primary complaint was that he had not been allowed to remain in hospital where he received better treatment.

Official inspections provided regular opportunities for inmates to voice complaints. One of the reasons McCabe was sceptical about Seymour's complaint was that he had said nothing to him during recent inspections. Within the previous six months, he noted, he had visited the division Seymour occupied seven times 'and he has never addressed me'. The only matter about which he had ever complained 'was that he was not allowed to go to the Roman Catholic service one Sunday and to the Protestant service the next Sunday, and to vary his attendance at one or the other according to his whim'.[64] Complaints were also made to workhouse masters and to poor law guardians. In July 1882, the Master of Kinsale Workhouse noted

62 Kilmallock BG Minutes, 4 December 1890.
63 Frederick McCabe to LGB, 26 June 1878, NAI, CSORP 1880/12598.
64 McCabe to LGB, 26 June 1878, NAI, CSORP 1880/12598.

that a complaint had been made by a patient 'suffering from an aneurism, of neglect on the part of the night nurse ... who she says left her from about 9 pm until 2 am without attendance. The medical officer in charge is not satisfied with the night nurse.' The visiting committee of the Ballycastle Board of Guardians reported in October 1895, that a patient in the female infirm ward, 'whose bed is nearly opposite the door complained of the cold from the open door' and recommended that a porch or screen should be erected to 'prevent the cold wind from blowing on the patients confined to bed when the door is open'.[65] In this case action was taken, but boards of guardians could be slow to respond to complaints often either dismissing the matter, or postponing consideration of it until a later date.

Formal complaints against medical officers and other officials were investigated. In 1860 the poor law commissioners noted that fifty-nine medical officers had been removed or compelled to resign, following complaints made against them. The complaints had been:

> generally on the ground of neglect of duty by way of non-attendance on the patients; very frequently on the ground of habitual intemperance; and sometimes on the ground of having abused their office for immoral purposes.[66]

Boards of guardians were generally extremely reluctant to dismiss their officers unless there was clear and incontrovertible evidence of misbehaviour. Workhouse patients, as Angela Negrine observes, 'lacked any obvious power'.[67] It is likely, therefore, that only the most assertive and/or disruptive inmates made formal complaints. When an inmate of Cashel Workhouse complained in August 1898 that he had been struck with a stick by the medical officer, the guardians accepted the doctor's explanation that 'the patient referred to was the most unmanageable, disobedient and disrespectful man', and that he had done no more than examine him with a stethoscope. The following year, a hospital attendant complained to the guardians that he had found two men lying in beds that were 'wet and not in a fit state for a human being to sleep

---

65 Master's Report Book, Kinsale BG, CCCA, BG/108/FA1, 20 July 1882; and Ballycastle BG Minutes, 5 October 1895.

66 Banks to Larcom, 21 February 1860, NAI, CSORP 1860/18567. The nature of complaints remained essentially the same throughout the period. See, for example, complaints of neglect against Dr Riordan (Midleton Union) and Dr Hope (Bawnboy Union), NAI, CSORP 1893/4074.

67 Angela Negrine, 'Nursing Paupers: A Case Study of Nursing at the Leicester Workhouse Infirmary, 1850–1905' (unpublished paper), p. 25. I am most grateful to Angela Negrine for providing me with a copy of this paper.

in'. Despite the serious implications for patient welfare, the guardians once again refused to intervene.[68]

The extent to which boards of guardians owed a duty of care to sick inmates had come under legal scrutiny in 1896, when Rose Dunbar sued the Ardee Board of Guardians for damages following the death of her son Patrick, who had been admitted to the workhouse in June 1895 suffering from typhus fever. It was argued that the guardians had a duty 'to provide for his proper maintenance and treatment'. Far from doing this, however, they had 'omitted to treat the said Patrick Dunbar properly, and allowed him to remain improperly attended to', as a result of which he had died. The facts of the case were not in dispute. Dunbar had been admitted suffering from typhus fever. The doctor had examined him and had directed the master to procure extra nursing assistance as he anticipated that the patient would become delirious. The master took no action, probably because Dunbar was the only patient in the fever hospital at the time. He became violent during the night, assaulted the nurse and jumped out of the window. He was not recovered until the next day and died two days later. The master and porter were both held to be culpable and were dismissed. The case for damages failed, however, as it was held that the guardians had discharged their duty towards Dunbar by providing the hospital and staff, and that they could not be held responsible for the negligence of their officials.[69]

Inquest verdicts provide further evidence of public disapproval of inadequate care. In 1896, the Dublin City Coroner, Dr Kenny, presided over the inquest into the death of Michael K., an inmate of the NDU Workhouse who had died suddenly from heart failure. The inquest heard that Michael had been taken ill during the night and died before he could receive medical attention. The night attendant testified that 'he had never received any training as a nurse, and knew nothing at all about the treatment of the sick'. The coroner observed that the evidence showed that there was 'no night nursing in the proper sense of the word. Proper night nursing would involve the appointment of adequately trained persons, whether male or female' and criticised the Local Government Board for having 'neglected to stimulate the guardians to do what was required and what should be done'.[70] Asked to respond to the coroner's comments, the Vice-President of the Local Government Board, George Morris, insisted that far from being neglectful, officials had been 'unceasing in our efforts to get them to do what is required and the feeling of the Guardians seems to be that we expect them to do too much'. He pointed out that there were eighteen paid nurses in the NDU

68 Cited in Lonergan, *A Workhouse Story*, pp. 161–2.
69 *Law Reports (Ireland)*, Appeal 1896, Dunbar versus Guardians, Ardee Union.
70 *Express*, 9 October 1896, cutting in CSORP 1896/40871.

hospital who were 'responsible by day and night, and the night attendant who goes round every hour has a pass key to each ward and has to call the nurses or Doctor if their services are required'.[71] The crucial point however, which Morris did not address, was that night attendants received no training so that they did not always recognise when the services of a nurse or doctor were required.

The conflict between emerging ideas about appropriate standards of treatment for the sick and disabled, and the practical implications in terms of staff management and cost, is perhaps most evident in provision for lunatics, imbeciles and epileptics. The poor law made no specific provision for the insane or for the mentally handicapped. However, many people judged to be insane, imbecilic or epileptic, found themselves in workhouses due to a lack of alternative accommodation. From 1817, Ireland was provided with a network of district lunatic asylums, but accommodation was insufficient and priority was given those classed as dangerous lunatics.[72] Harmless lunatics and 'imbeciles' were, therefore, often housed in workhouses.

From the 1850s government officials began discussing the possibility of using spare workhouse accommodation to house harmless lunatics. Following a parliamentary inquiry in 1857–1858 which had recommended the workhouses should be used to house 'quiet cases of imbecility and idiocy', the poor law commissioners were consulted on the feasibility of adapting unused workhouse buildings as accommodation for lunatics.[73] Many workhouses, it was noted, had far more accommodation that they needed, whilst there was a shortage of space in lunatic asylums. In Counties Clare, Mayo and Donegal it was suggested that entire workhouses (namely Corrofin, Newport and Stranorlar) could be converted into lunatic asylums and the paupers sent to neighbouring unions. Power strongly objected to these proposals, however, arguing spare workhouse accommodation was needed to meet sudden emergencies, such as crop failures. The only practicable way of providing accommodation for lunatics within workhouses, he maintained, would be to erect a separate building within the workhouse grounds, as had

71 Morris to Under Sec, 23 October 1896, NAI, CSORP 1896/40871.
72 For district lunatic asylums, see Catherine Cox, *Negotiating Insanity in the Southeast of Ireland, 1820–1900* (Manchester: Manchester University Press, 2012); Marcus Reuber, 'Moral Management and the Unseen Eye: Public Lunatic Asylums in Ireland, 1800–1845', in Malcolm and Jones, (eds), *Medicine, Disease and the State in Ireland, 1650–1940* (Cork: Cork University Press, 1999), pp. 208–33; and Oonagh Walsh, 'Lunatic and Criminal Alliances in Nineteenth-Century Ireland', in Peter Bartlett and David Wright (eds), *Outside the Walls of the Asylum: The History of Care in the Community* (London: Routledge, 1999), pp. 132–52. For the care of dangerous lunatics, see Pauline Prior, *Madness and Murder: Gender, Crime and Mental Disorder in Nineteenth-Century Ireland* (Dublin: Irish Academic Press, 2008).
73 For the inquiry, see Cox, *Negotiating Insanity*, pp. 183–8.

been done with fever hospitals.[74] This course was subsequently adopted in a number of unions. In the late 1860s and early 1870s, Kilmallock Workhouse, for example, accommodated between twenty-five and thirty-five lunatics and idiots in 'sheds'.[75]

Further steps were taken in the 1870s to encourage the use of workhouse buildings as accommodation for lunatics and imbeciles. In 1875, legislation was passed providing for the transfer of harmless lunatics from district lunatic asylums to workhouses, subject to the approval of the Local Government Board and Inspectors of Lunatics.[76] Implementation of the act was uneven. Many boards of guardians appear to have been reluctant to accept transfers, arguing either that the individuals being transferred were not destitute and thus not eligible for relief, or that they were not from the locality and should not, therefore, be supported by local poor rates.[77] Kilmallock was one of the boards of guardians that attempted to implement the new provisions. A number of workhouse inmates who were considered to be dangerous were transferred to the district lunatic asylum and arrangements made to transfer harmless lunatics from the asylum to the workhouse, where they were accommodated in separate wards.[78] By November 1875, the number of lunatics and idiots accommodated in separate wards had risen to 126, out of a total inmate population of 628.[79] By 1881, however, the number of lunatics had dropped back to twenty-six and while this figure increased in the 1890s and 1900s it never exceeded fifty, suggesting that the higher number was found to be unmanageable. The census return for Kilmallock Workhouse in 1911 recorded forty-seven people classed as lunatics or idiots, out of a total population of 326. These were returned under a number of different descriptions including mental infirmity, mental weakness and mania. Twenty-two inmates were classified as suffering from mental derangement and fourteen from dementia.[80] Since the number accommodated in separate wards at this time was twenty-four, it is possible that those categorised as suffering from mental derangement and mania were housed separately, while those with dementia were housed with the infirm, but it may have depended on how disruptive individual inmates were.

In many rural workhouses (including Ballycastle, Ballymoney, Glenties, Thurles and Westport) no separate accommodation was provided; lunatics

---

74 Memo by T. H. Burke, 25 July 1859: NAI, OP 1859/44.
75 Kilmallock BG Minutes, 1860–1861 and 1865–1866.
76 Lunatic Asylums (Ireland) Act, 1875, 38 and 39 Vict., c. 67, s. 9.
77 Cox, *Negotiating Insanity*, p. 182.
78 Kilmallock BG Minutes, 18 and 25 November 1875.
79 The following October the number of lunatics had declined slightly to 114 out of a total population of 540. Kilmallock BG Minutes, 1875–1876.
80 The 1911 Census is available online: (www.census.nationalarchives.ie/).

and idiots were housed with ordinary inmates. A parliamentary return for the year to June 1881, noted that in Glenties Workhouse seven 'simple idiots' were housed in wards with healthy inmates, 'under the care of wardsmen and wardswomen'. Inmates who became violent or disruptive were normally transferred to the district lunatic asylum. A number of lunatics were transferred from Westport Workhouse to Castlebar District Asylum in 1906, for example, including one who had assaulted an attendant. Caring for disturbed inmates could place considerable strain on workhouse staff. In May 1906, the night nurse in the Westport Fever Hospital complained that a patient was 'constantly abusing her, using very bad language'. A wards maid made similar complaints, stating that the man was 'in the habit of using filthy language towards her' and threatened to 'resign her position if not protected'. Since the man was classed as a lunatic, however, the board decided to take no action against him.[81]

City workhouses accommodated large numbers of lunatics. Belfast Workhouse accommodated 300 lunatics in 1881 under the care of six paid and eighteen unpaid attendants, while in NDU, ninety-six lunatics and idiots were tended by pauper attendants under the supervision of two paid officers.[82] Needless to say, none of the attendants had any special training in the care of the mentally disabled or disturbed. Conditions for the insane appear to have been particularly bad in Cork Workhouse. In the late 1870s, the lunatic wards had been described as dark and gloomy; both the male and female wards were overcrowded and no occupation was provided. In 1881 the workhouse accommodated an average of 147 lunatics who were under the care of three paid attendants (one male and two female) assisted by eleven paupers (two male and nine female).[83]

By the early 1890s the number of people in Irish workhouses who were classified as lunatics was three times greater than it had been in the 1850s (see Figure 5.1). The relationship between pauperism and insanity, and between asylums and workhouses, remained confused, however. Two further parliamentary inquiries in 1879–1880 and 1890–1891 recommended the reorganisation of lunacy administration to make better provision for the lunatic poor, with district asylums concentrating on providing treatment for the insane and spare workhouse buildings being converted into asylums

81 Westport BG Minutes, 24 May and 20 December 1906. Between twelve and eighteen lunatics were housed with other inmates in Westport in the 1900s.
82 *Return of the Average Number of Sick Persons tended in each Union Workhouse in Ireland during the last Year for which Figures are complete ... and showing the Number of Paid Nurses, and Unpaid or Pauper Assistants in Charge of such Persons during the Day and Night at the present Time*, HC, 1881 (433).
83 *Cork Examiner*, 3 March and 28 May 1876; 10 and 31 August 1877, cited in O Mahony, *Cork's Poor Law Palace*, pp. 211–12.

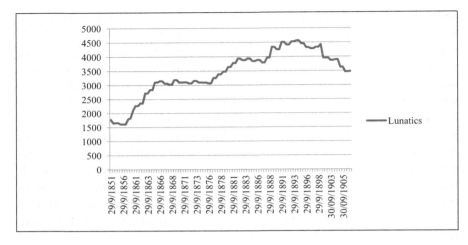

Figure 5.1   Number of persons classified as lunatics, insane persons
and idiots relieved in workhouses during each half year 1851–1907.
Source: 'Classification of Persons Relieved in Workhouses in Ireland', Annual
Reports of the Commissioners for Administering the Laws for the relief of
the Poor in Ireland and the Local Government Board for Ireland 1850–1914

for harmless lunatics and idiots who did not require special care, but no
immediate action was taken.[84] In September 1891, the Local Government
Board issued a circular on the care of lunatics in workhouses based on the
recommendations of the inspectors of lunatics. It was recommended that
paid officers should be made responsible for the care and treatment of lunatic
inmates and that mechanical restraint should not be used except by written
direction of the medical officer; separate day room and dormitory accommodation should be provided and every effort made to find employment for any
insane inmates that were able to work.[85] The circular represented an attempt
to establish minimum standards for the accommodation and treatment of the
insane, but the effect in many cases was simply to convince local guardians
that they should not be expected to provide for lunatics. The Longford
Board of Guardians repeatedly refused to improve accommodation for
lunatics, despite an inspector's report urging a number of alterations which
he considered 'essential to the comfort and well-being of this helpless class'.
The guardians maintained that 'the workhouse was not a proper place in
which to keep the lunatics', pointing out that if 'the lunatics were to be

84 Cox, *Negotiating Insanity*, pp. 186–7.
85 Circulars – Lunatics in Workhouses, *Annual Report of the Local Government Board for
Ireland*, HC, 1892 [Cd. 6801], p. 90.

removed from the house there was no need to trouble further about the wards' or their condition.[86] Deeply frustrated by the guardians' attitude, the Local Government Board directed them to reconsider, pointing out that the workhouse medical officer had reported that there was no proper accommodation for lunatics and no trained attendants, 'without which they cannot be humanely cared for nor treated. The cells provided for their accommodation are veritable black holes'. A number of guardians were in favour of doing away with the cells and appointing an attendant, as recommended by the 1891 circular, but the majority voted for them to be sent to Mullingar District Asylum. A report by the local constabulary officer noted that the guardians considered the asylum the proper place for lunatics and that this was 'where those in the workhouse should be sent'. There were, he stated, 'at present fifteen lunatics (imbeciles) in the workhouse. They are attended and looked after during the day by paupers, and at night they are locked in cells.'[87] The case highlighted the need for legislation to clarify the responsibilities of boards of guardians. Without this guardians could simply refuse to act.

Workhouse medical officers resented criticism of their role in the treatment of lunatics, since they were invariably constrained in what they could provide. The doctor in charge of the lunatic department of Belfast Workhouse, Dr McConnell, had reacted with some annoyance to a lunatic inspector's report in October 1890 which had criticised both the frequency with which patients were restrained and the level of staffing, and had recommended removing patients who were noisy, restless or destructive to the district asylum. McConnell reminded the board of guardians that he had informed them in July that seventy-two patients (out of a total of 408) required restraint or seclusion from time to time and having heard that the lunatic inspectors thought such cases should not be in workhouses, had requested the board's instructions. He had heard nothing, yet was now being criticised for restraining inmates. He pointed out that a 'complete remodelling of the wards, dayrooms, airing grounds, and greatly increased staff would be necessary', if he was not to use restraint in future, 'But if the board intend to remove all the noisy, etc., patients and retain only the quiet ones then remodelling is not necessary.' He acknowledged that the number of attendants was insufficient if patients were to be treated, 'according to latest methods and in the most humane way', but insisted that he was proud of the way the lunatic department was run, given the 'small number of attendants placed at my disposal'. He rejected the suggestion that too many patients were kept in bed explaining that this was only done when necessary

---

86 *Freeman's Journal*, 10 September 1895.
87 Report by Head Constable R. Waterhouse, 31 August 1895, NAI, CSORP 1896/15894.

for patients' health or safety. For example, epileptics were only kept in bed if they had frequent fits and this was for their own protection. Mechanical restraints were not used indiscriminately, as had been alleged. Only in cases of extreme urgency were restraints used without the written permission of the medical officer and they were discontinued as soon as possible.[88]

The problem, as guardians acknowledged, was that the Belfast District Lunatic Asylum was too small, so that it was not always possible to transfer cases from the workhouse to the asylum. There was room in an auxiliary asylum in Ballymena, but sending inmates there deprived 'their friends of the privilege of seeing them'.[89] The lunatic inspectors subsequently sought to mollify the board of guardians and their medical officer, by explaining they were not blaming any one. They were:

> careful to note that the guardians had loyally done what they considered necessary for the insane poor, and that the medical officer could not, without neglecting his other arduous duties, properly supervise the care of so large a number of the insane, who, if in a district asylum, would be under the individual attention of at least one medical officer.

They did however, reiterate their view that mechanical restraint and confinement to bed was used to a greater extent than was strictly necessary or than it would be used in an asylum.[90]

The relationship between the lunatic inspectors and Dr McConnell did not improve. Following an inspection in 1892, George Plunkett O'Farrell, submitted what he must have thought was a favourable report. He praised the efforts made by the board and its officers to care for lunatics commenting that they had acted 'liberally and benevolently towards the insane poor committed to their charge'. They had provided 'a separate and large building for their accommodation; they allow a liberal dietary; they have appointed a skilled medical officer to take special charge of the lunatic wards in addition to the ordinary workhouse nursing staff', and yet the results, he observed, were not 'entirely satisfactory'. The reduction in the use of mechanical restraint was welcome, but also demonstrated that it had been used too much previously. The number of patients confined to bed was also reduced, but was still 'excessive'. Some of those in bed were suffering from dementia, but others were epileptic or 'noisy and turbulent when up', which, the inspector observed, would not be the case in a lunatic asylum. Dr McConnell rejected both positive and negative comments. 'Restraints,' he asserted, 'were

---

88   *Belfast Newsletter*, 5 November 1890.
89   *Belfast Newsletter*, 5 November 1890.
90   *Belfast Newsletter*, 10 December 1890.

never used indiscriminately and there could not, therefore, have been an improvement in this respect'. He challenged the figures given for the number of patients confined to bed, observing that some of these were in the sick or infirm wards. The inspector's report was 'full of inaccuracies'; none of the abuses to which he had referred, 'either on this occasion or a year ago, had any existence in fact'. The board of guardians supported their medical officer, concluding that 'no better arrangements could be made than exist at present'.[91]

In subsequent years a number of deaths in the Belfast Workhouse focused public attention on the facilities provided for lunatics and epileptics.[92] Prior to 1893, deaths of lunatics in workhouses did not have to be notified to the coroner, unlike deaths in district lunatic asylums. This changed in 1893, after the MP for South Down, Michael McCartan, had raised the matter in the House of Commons, and the Local Government Board issued an order directing that all such deaths should be notified to the coroner. Opening an inquest into the death of an epileptic inmate in December 1893, the Belfast Coroner, John S. Finnigan, welcomed this development. 'Some people', he observed, 'had a general idea that institutions such as workhouses were loosely managed, and that the inmates were treated inhumanely', but recent inquests had shown that 'every attention had been paid to the deceased persons'. There were, he noted, 3,500 inmates in total in Belfast Workhouse, of whom 503 were in the lunatic department. People were admitted as destitute, then admitted to the infirmary and then to the lunatic department. Having visited the workhouse to inspect the lunatic department, accompanied by a trained nurse, he pronounced the wards to be clean and well ventilated and the patients well treated. He recommended that the lunatic department should be entirely isolated from the rest of the building and suggested two improvements: first, to have a separate ward for epileptics; and second, to increase the number of attendants. The inquest found no fault with the treatment of the deceased.[93]

Over the following years, however, inquest juries became increasingly critical of the treatment of lunatics and epileptics in Belfast Workhouse. Two issues attracted particular condemnation: first, the practice by which lunatics were transferred between the workhouse and district lunatic asylum; and second, the classification of epileptics. In January 1894, a jury recommended that violent lunatics should not be transferred from the district asylum

91 *Belfast Newsletter*, 4 May 1892.
92 For the treatment of epilepsy, see Oonagh Walsh, 'Cure or Custody: Therapeutic Philosophy at the Connaught District Lunatic Asylum', in Margaret H. Preston and Margaret Ó hÓgartaigh (eds), *Gender and Medicine in Ireland 1700–1950* (Syracuse: Syracuse University Press, 2012), pp. 81–4.
93 *Belfast Newsletter*, 30 December 1893.

to the lunatic department of the workhouse. It had transpired during the course of the inquest that whenever a violent lunatic was transferred from the workhouse to the asylum, a quiet patient was sent in exchange. In some cases this meant that someone who had been transferred as violent, was later sent back as quiet; some individuals having been transferred between the two institutions three or four times. When the guardians expressed their disapproval of the practice, they were informed by their chairman that the arrangement, which was between the medical officers of the two institutions not the boards of management, had been in place for a long time and was made necessary by the lack of accommodation.[94] It was subsequently decided that all patients being transferred from the lunatic asylum to the workhouse should go through the relieving officers to ensure that those being transferred were not only destitute, but also from the Belfast Union.[95]

Inquest juries were equally critical of the procedure by which epileptics were transferred from the main body of the house to the lunatic department. In April 1894, the coroner condemned the practice of sending epileptics to the insane department of the workhouse 'whether insane or not'.[96] The following month the board of guardians approved plans to increase the accommodation in the lunatic department, thus enabling the epileptics to be kept separate from the insane.[97] How effective the separation was came under scrutiny in late 1895, when the Local Government Board wrote to the Belfast Guardians drawing their attention to the coroner's concerns about the treatment of epileptics. This followed the inquest of a man who had been admitted to the infirmary as an epileptic and then transferred to the lunatic ward, even though he was neither insane nor of unsound mind. While endorsing separate accommodation for epileptics, the board observed that it was 'highly undesirable that such a ward should form part of the lunatic department' and recommended that the consultation held prior to the transfer of any ordinary inmate to the lunatic department should include 'at least one and in cases of difficulty more than one member of the visiting [medical] staff'.[98] When another epileptic inmate died on the lunatic ward the following year, the matter became the subject of an official investigation. In this case, however, it emerged that the dead girl was not alone epileptic, but also of unsound

---

94 Under this arrangement, which had been in place for ten or fifteen years, sixty-seven people had been transferred: *Belfast Newsletter*, 3 January 1894.
95 *Belfast Newsletter*, 7 March 1894. In December 1894 the coroner was very critical of the fact that there were forty-seven inmates in the workhouse who had been transferred from the asylum but had come from unions other than Belfast: *Belfast Newsletter*, 3 December 1894.
96 *Belfast Newsletter*, 30 April 1894.
97 *Belfast Newsletter*, 7 March and 30 May 1894.
98 MacSheahan to Clerk of Belfast Union, 29 November 1895, NAI, CSORP 1896/14048.

mind and classified as such. Confusion had arisen because when she was first admitted in April 1891 there had been 'no decided mental symptoms'. LGI Robert Agnew confirmed that epileptics were now accommodated separately from the lunatics, unless they were also classified as insane. There were sixty-six epileptics in the lunatic department, but there were also four in the body of the house and fourteen in the infirmary. However, he noted that although the guardians had agreed to improve the accommodation for epileptics and to provide a separate building with a proper recreation ground, this had not been carried into effect.[99]

When the chief secretary sought clarification of the relationship between the epileptic and lunatic wards, the Vice-President of the Local Government Board, H. A. Robinson, explained that they were separate 'in the sense that they have separate day rooms, dormitories and attendants', but were under the same medical officer and in the same wing and were 'really a sub-department of the lunatic department'. The epileptic wards had originally been set aside for sane epileptics:

but we did not think the separation sufficient, and objected to the wards for sane epileptics having any connection with the lunatic department. The wards were thereupon turned into epileptic–lunatic wards, and are still used as such, the sane epileptics being kept in the body of the house, pending the building of a detached cottage for their exclusive use.

Inmates' medical records, he acknowledged, did not distinguish between different forms of insanity or between mania, epilepsy and dementia. All insane people in workhouses were normally classed as 'lunatics and idiots'. A person who was not insane but subject to epileptic fits 'would be classed as either infirm, sick or able-bodied, as the case might be, and would be allowed to take his discharge from the workhouse at any time'. The absence of a detailed medical record, Robinson observed, was 'one of the disadvantages of keeping lunatics in places which were never intended for them', but he saw no point in establishing an inquiry on the subject since the 'only possible upshot' would be to confirm:

what we have been consistently urging on all our presidents for years past ... namely, that accommodation for epileptic lunatics, and all other insane in workhouses, is utterly unsuitable, and that there is only one

99 Report of R. Agnew, 28 July 1896, NAI, CSORP 1896/14048.

practical solution of the difficulty – to remove them from workhouses altogether.[100]

Despite universal agreement that reform was required, nothing effectual was done.[101] The 1898 Local Government Act empowered county councils to provide auxiliary lunatic asylums for chronic harmless lunatics. Such asylums could operate either as a separate asylum or as a department of the county or district asylum. They were also authorised to take over disused workhouse buildings for this purpose. As with many other parts of the act dealing with health and welfare, these provisions were permissive and enabling rather than mandatory and in most cases local authorities took no action.[102] The Local Government Board sought to keep up the pressure on county councils and in 1902 urged boards of guardians to reduce the number of insane people in workhouses by transferring the most serious cases to lunatic asylums. Some progress was made but on 31 December 1907 there remained 3,568 lunatics, idiots and epileptics in Irish workhouses, 330 more than at the end of the previous year.[103] The failure to make proper provision for lunatics highlights the central weakness of Irish local administration at the turn of the century: that of divided authority. It was far too easy for the various bodies involved, whether central or local, elected or appointed, to avoid taking responsibility and to wait for someone else to act. Poor law boards were justified in arguing that workhouses were not suitable accommodation for lunatics, but there was no justification for using this as an excuse to neglect the unfortunate individuals in their care.

By the end of the nineteenth century the permanent population of workhouses in Ireland included a sizeable proportion of elderly, infirm and sick inmates. Their care occupied the time and attention of boards of guardians and their officers to an ever increasing degree. The resulting pressures strained relations between boards of guardians and medical officers, and between local and central authorities. Medical officers complained of poor conditions and inadequate facilities and pushed for more and better trained nursing staff, boards of guardians grumbled about the cost of medicines and salaries, central government issued directives and sought to mediate between

100 Robinson to Balfour, 5 August 1896, NAI, CSORP 1896/14048.
101 The Vice-Regal Commission recommended the removal of all lunatics, idiots and epileptics from poor law institutions into specialist asylums, noting that 'the opinion is universally held that the condition of lunatics in practically every workhouse is unsatisfactory': *Poor Law Reform Commission (Ireland), Volume I*, HC, 1906 [Cd. 3202], pp. 37–40. The royal commission on the poor laws subsequently endorsed this view.
102 Cox, *Negotiating Insanity*, pp. 187–8.
103 *Royal Commission on the Poor Laws and Relief of Distress, Report on Ireland*, HC, 1909 [Cd. 4630], p. 80.

medical officers and guardians. As with other aspects of poor law administration, there was considerable local variation in the nature and quality of services provided. There were some unions in which medical officers were able to ensure that patients received effective treatment and were cared for in reasonably comfortable surroundings. There were far too many, however, in which poor law guardians found it impossible to reconcile their desire to keep rates low and adhere to the principle of less eligibility, with the requirement to provide efficient and effective medical services. As Negrine has noted with regard to England, as long as medical care was provided within the workhouse, poor law nurses and medical officers were forced to operate in 'an incongruous environment that benefited neither them nor their patients and criticism of the system that permitted this situation was entirely justified'.[104] The sick and infirm were a target group for reformers because they were seen as deserving of assistance. Other groups, including unmarried mothers, prostitutes and vagrants, were targeted because they were seen as undeserving or problematic. The following chapter examines the first two groups; vagrants are discussed in the final chapter.

104 Angela Negrine, 'Nursing Paupers: A case study of nursing at the Leicester workhouse infirmary, 1850-1905', unpublished paper, pp. 35–6.

6

Single Mothers and Prostitutes

M any of those who turned to the poor law for assistance were people whose conduct or lifestyle had excluded them from respectable society. Unmarried mothers, prostitutes and vagrants all resorted to the workhouse on a regular basis. Over the second half of the nineteenth century, declining numbers of able-bodied inmates focused greater attention on these groups as they became more visible within workhouse populations. Poor law regulations required the relief of destitution irrespective of its cause or the character of the destitute person, much to the annoyance of many guardians, officials and ratepayers. As a member of the Galway Board of Guardians complained when an elderly man was refused indoor relief on the grounds that he was not destitute, 'it was unfair that a man such as the applicant should be refused admission when "strumpets" of girls who should not be allowed in were never refused'.[1] Procedures for the admission and management of what were seen as problem groups varied according to local circumstances and sentiment. This chapter explores these variations with respect to unmarried mothers and prostitutes. In so doing, it provides both a fresh perspective on local responses to poverty and distress, and new insights into gender perceptions and attitudes to sexuality within Irish society.

Respectability and sexual morality were intimately connected. Irish women were celebrated for their purity and Irish men commended for the respect shown to women.[2] Any remnants of a more ribald recreational culture and more relaxed sexual attitudes amongst the Irish peasantry were believed to have been eradicated by the shock of the Famine, and replaced by a more disciplined social culture and stricter social mores associated with and promoted by the Catholic Church.[3] Irish society embraced the social

---

1 *Galway Express*, 14 May 1881, cited in Maria Luddy, *Prostitution and Irish Society 1800–1940* (Cambridge: Cambridge University Press, 2007), p. 60.
2 Luddy, *Prostitution and Irish Society*, pp. 1–2.
3 For pre-Famine Irish society, see S. J. Connolly, *Priests and People in pre-Famine*

values often associated with Victorian England, including a sexual division of labour and sexual double standard. Women's employment was increasingly within the home and their interests were assumed to be almost wholly domestic. While it was acceptable for men to be sexually active, this was only acceptable for women within marriage. The consequences for women perceived to have transgressed against the strict moral codes governing sexual relations, were marginalisation and social exclusion. A woman who lost her reputation, it was claimed, lost her place in society and was rejected by her family and her community. Evidence given to the Whately Commission stressed the difficulties faced by unmarried mothers.[4] The high value placed on sexual purity made its loss all the more devastating. Indeed, the fate of the unmarried mother was often represented as moral degradation and premature death.[5] Many single mothers, it was assumed, turned to prostitution having no other way of making a living. Philanthropic activity focused on young women who had had one illegitimate child, since there was thought to be a faint but real possibility of rehabilitation at this stage. Women who had had more than one illegitimate child were seen as beyond redemption. Magdalen Asylums aimed primarily to keep prostitutes off the streets, not to rehabilitate them.[6] There was limited understanding of why women became prostitutes, although the link between poverty and prostitution was noted.[7] Prostitution in England was increasingly linked to industrialisation, an association that had less relevance in Ireland, except in Belfast where employment in textile factories was believed to have a corrupting influence on young women. It was generally assumed that the path to prostitution started with a particular event or circumstance, seduction, abandonment, bad company, family estrangement, rather than an active choice. Another assumption was that prostitutes were 'feeble-minded', which again denied their agency. But whatever the reason for their actions, prostitutes were, nevertheless, held responsible for them.

It is very difficult to gauge the extent of prostitution with any accuracy.

Ireland 1780–1845 (Dublin: Gill and Macmillan, 1982). For post-Famine Irish society, see, Diarmaid Ferriter, *Occasions of Sin: Sex and Society in Modern Ireland* (London: Profile Books, 2009), pp. 11–59.

4 Cited in Liam Kennedy and Paul Gray 'Famine, Illegitimacy and the Workhouse in Western Ireland: Kilrush, County Clare', in Alysa Levene, Thomas Nutt and Samantha Williams (eds), *Illegitimacy in Britain, 1700–1920* (Basingstoke: Palgrave Macmillan, 2005), p. 127.

5 See, for example, Rosa Mulholland, *Nanno: Daughter of the State* (London: Grant Richards, 1899).

6 Maria Luddy, *Women and Philanthropy in Nineteenth-Century Ireland* (Cambridge: Cambridge University Press, 1995), pp. 97–148; and Luddy, *Prostitution and Irish Society*, pp. 76–111.

7 Luddy, *Prostitution and Irish Society*, p. 3.

Arrests for prostitution fluctuated throughout the later nineteenth century and appear to have more to do with police activity than actual numbers of prostitutes. However, there is some evidence that numbers declined in post-Famine decades before rising again in the early twentieth century.[8] Prostitution was most visible in cities and in certain parts of cities. In Belfast, the area around Millfield and Smithfield, and the docks/Shortstrand area were noted for immorality, as was the Mecklenburgh/Montgomery district of Dublin, northeast of the Custom House.[9] Outside the major cities, prostitution was most visible in towns with army barracks. However, it is likely that in all Irish towns there were women who traded sexual favours for money, food and/or lodgings. Whether they were thought of, or labelled, as prostitutes depended on social standing, the regularity of their activity and their appearance and behaviour. Street prostitutes were distinctive by their immodest and also gaudy dress, their bad language and their disorderly conduct. The typical street prostitute was a young woman from the labouring classes who had often lost one or both parents. Many gave up the work as they got older, although there are references to women working as prostitutes in their fifties and sixties. Some retired to refuges; others got married. Many became sick, either from venereal disease or poverty-related diseases, such as tuberculosis.[10] Associated with crime and disease, prostitutes were feared as a physical and moral threat, and could be harshly treated. In contrast to the unmarried mother, the prostitute was regarded as representing a problem for which there was no solution. She was a problem to be managed.

Poor law boards could not refuse or delay relief to anyone simply because their behaviour or lifestyle was objectionable. In 1863 the poor law commissioners issued a circular to boards of guardians reminding them of the duties and responsibilities of relieving officers, including that of 'visiting the cases of all applicants for relief, and of affording immediate relief in cases of urgent necessity'.[11] This was as a consequence of the death of Rosanna Doyle, a prostitute living near the Curragh Army Camp, who had died in Naas Workhouse on 19 October 1863, a few minutes after her admission. The inquest jury found the relieving officer 'guilty of neglect in not visiting and

8 Luddy, *Prostitution and Irish Society*, pp. 18–23, 242–3. See also Caitriona Clear, *Social Change and Everyday Life in Ireland, 1850–1922* (Manchester: Manchester University Press, 2007), pp. 135–7.

9 Luddy, *Prostitution and Irish Society*, p. 34; and Leanne McCormick, *Regulating Sexuality: Women in Twentieth-Century Northern Ireland* (Manchester: Manchester University Press, 2009), p. 20.

10 Clear, *Social Change and Everyday Life in Ireland*, p. 136; and Luddy, *Prostitution and Irish Society*, pp. 41–2.

11 Duties of Relieving Officers, 5 December 1863, *Annual Report*, HC, 1864 [3338], pp. 23–4.

relieving said Rosanna Doyle when informed by the police of her sickness and destitute state on the 17th inst.' As an editorial in the *Irish Times* noted in relation to the case, it was 'important that relieving officers of Poor Law Unions should know that they are bound to give immediate relief in cases of urgent necessity, and that if they neglect their duty they are liable to a charge of manslaughter'.[12] The poor law commissioners insisted that the relieving officer be dismissed, but sought to play down the wider significance of the case pointing out that it arose 'out of circumstances which are in some degree peculiar to the Naas Union, where, in consequence of the camp being formed on the Curragh of Kildare, the class of unfortunate persons, to which Rosanna Doyle belonged, habitually occupy a kind of roofless dwelling in the furze bushes'. This was not a situation with which many relieving officers were required to deal and the commissioners were anxious not to overreact, 'lest the office [of relieving officer] should fall generally into the hands of a less respectable class of persons from unwillingness to expose themselves to extreme measures in consequence of a dereliction of duty'.[13] Relieving officers needed to be aware of their responsibilities, but not overwhelmed by them.

Once inside the workhouse, the 'immoral' were governed by the same rules and regulations as the respectable poor. Unmarried mothers and prostitutes were often physically separated from other inmates and assigned to designated wards, but they were not explicitly marked out or distinguished in other ways. Mixing young and old, respectable and dissolute within the workhouse attracted widespread criticism. Workhouses, Rev. John Barry complained in the 1880s, contained people who differed from one another:

> in every conceivable way: in education, morals, manners and health. The blind and the purblind, the young and the old, the weak and strong, the wise and the idiotic, the temperate and the drunkard, the honest and dishonest, the ignorant and educated, the virtuous and vicious, are all mixed up heterogeneously together.[14]

The result, according to Lurgan Poor Law Guardian, Edward Magennis, in 1888, was 'a great amount of irregularity, degradation, self-abasement, and indeed sometimes immorality'.[15] The poor law authorities, however,

12 Report of Verdict, 24 October 1863, NAI, CSORP 1863/10089; *Irish Times*, 24 November 1863. The case is discussed in Helen Burke, *The People and the Poor Law in Nineteenth Century Ireland* (Littlehampton: Women's Education Bureau, 1987), pp. 164–71; and Luddy, *Prostitution and Irish Society* pp. 72–5.
13 Banks to Larcom, 25 November 1863, NAI, CSORP 1863/10089.
14 Rev. John Barry, *Life in an Irish Workhouse*, (Thurles, 1890), p. 75.
15 Edward Magennis, *The Irish Poor Law System; Its Evils and Its Defects* (Belfast:

rejected such allegations, insisting that while workhouses were open to all, they were also strictly regulated and that the classification system ensured that inmates were not forced to associate with unsuitable companions. Indeed, many inspectors remained convinced that workhouses provided relatively safe spaces for young women when compared to the streets or even their own homes. There was, PLI Hall declared in 1855, 'much less danger of young females becoming corrupted in the Workhouse than out of it'.[16] Criticism of the lack of effective classification was strongest in the 1850s and 1860s when workhouses were still relatively full, making it difficult to find space for separate accommodation. As PLI Lynch explained, in County Tipperary it had not been possible to separate prostitutes from other inmates, 'in consequence of the crowded state of many of the workhouses, and the omission of convenient apartments in the original plans, for a classification of this description'. Hall maintained that inmates operated their own classification system. Any 'close intimacy' with prostitutes was, he maintained, generally avoided by other female inmates and they were generally left to associate with each other both in day rooms and dormitories, 'the other women being unwilling to sleep with them'.[17] This, however, assumed that prostitutes were clearly identifiable and that, as we shall see, was not always the case.

The poor law commissioners consistently opposed the introduction of classification by character for all but a small minority of inmates. As they had explained to the guardians of SDU in 1850, 'much caution' should be used in applying any kind of moral classification and, excepting the cases of persons whose depravity is a matter of public notoriety, the guardians should not, in the opinion of the commissioners, 'place any woman in such separate wards as are contemplated unless upon the ground of serious impropriety of language or demeanour on their part, whilst inmates of the workhouse'. While it was important to 'prevent innocent persons from being corrupted by association with the incurably vicious', it was equally desirable to 'avoid the adoption of a system which might confirm evil tendencies in those who would otherwise be led by the regularity and industry of a well-conducted workhouse establishment to amend their lives and thus be ultimately restored to society'.[18]

In 1855, the poor law commissioners wrote to all boards of guardians reminding them that 'women of notoriously bad character' should be lodged in separate rooms and dormitories. At the same time, however, they urged

William W. Cleland, 1888), p. 2. See also, *Clare Journal*, 12 January 1888.

16 *Annual Report*, HC, 1854–1855 [1945], pp. 111.

17 *Annual Report*, HC, 1854–1855 [1945], pp. 109–11.

18 PLC to Clerk of SDU, 17 January 1850, NAI, CSORP 1856/12439.

boards to be careful to avoid situations in which 'unmarried females entering the workhouse pregnant, but not known to have previously led a life of infamy' would be branded with 'the character of prostitutes'. Convinced of the reformative potential of the workhouse system, the commissioners were anxious not to label people unnecessarily. This remained their position and they continued to advocate a cautious approach to the issue. When the Wexford Board of Guardians inquired in 1880 whether the master of the workhouse could keep women of bad character separate from women of good character, the Local Government Board observed that 'a separation ward should be reserved for the reception of notorious and avowed prostitutes', observing that the object of separation was 'to prevent contamination, and to relieve the women of good character from compulsory association with the depraved'. It was for the guardians 'to determine in each case whether it is for the general good that the separation should be enforced', the clear implication being that in some cases separation might not be for the general good. The board then repeated, almost word for word, the cautionary advice first given to the SDU in 1850.[19]

The approach advocated by the central authorities caused many people, Catholic clerics in particular, profound unease. Believing vice to be contagious, they argued that allowing any contact between immoral women and other inmates was to put the latter at risk of corruption. Archbishop Cullen strongly criticised the existing system of workhouse classification when he appeared before the 1861 select committee. He acknowledged that matters had improved since 1855, when the commissioners had explicitly recommended the separation of women of notoriously bad character from other women, 'still the classification is very imperfect. The presence and mixture of women with illegitimate children among young girls must tend to lower their idea of female modesty and purity.' Women of 'notoriously bad character' he argued, should not be admitted to the workhouse at all, but sent to reformatories, while mothers of illegitimate children should be kept separate from other women, since their presence was 'calculated to offer a very bad example to virtuous children or young girls, even without their saying a word to them'.[20] Significantly, moral classification formed the first item on the agenda of a public meeting on poor law reform chaired by Cullen in January 1862. It was noted that there was no provision in existing regulations for moral classification and that it was 'not usual to attempt any', so that mothers of illegitimate children mixed with the other women, 'even with those girls who, at fifteen years of age, have been removed from the

19 Banks to Clerk of Wexford Union, 2 July 1880, NAI, CSORP 1883/7984.
20 Report from the Select Committee appointed to Inquire into the Administration of the Relief of the Poor in Ireland, HC, 1861 [408], Q3970–3; 4074–8.

schools into the adult wards; and all the young women mix freely, one with another, using the same day rooms and occupying the same sleeping wards, without any regard to their previous lives, habits or associations, Such evil communications must, and do, corrupt the morals of the innocent'. The commissioners' carefully worded advice warning against the confirmation of evil tendencies was singled out for condemnation. These words, it was alleged, precluded 'any proper classification'.[21]

The Report of the 1861 Select Committee recommended that 'special attention' should be paid to moral classification. The commissioners consequently wrote to all boards of guardians inquiring what provision was made for moral classification and whether this could be improved. The replies demonstrated, according to the commissioners, first, 'that a moral classification very generally existed already, so far as to separate from the rest of the female inmates, females of notoriously profligate character'; and second, that few boards of guardians were in favour of 'the adoption of a more extensive moral classification, or of any attempt to distinguish, by different treatment or the assignment of different day rooms or dormitories, between one class and another'.[22] They also revealed a wide variety of approaches to classification from the most basic, as in unions such as Belmullet, where inmates were 'divided into four classes, viz., men, women, boys, and girls', to the relatively elaborate, as in Carlow. Here females were classed as follows: children up to fifteen years of age; girls of fifteen and upwards; nursing mothers with one child legitimate or illegitimate; aged and infirm; women with more than one illegitimate child; and notorious prostitutes. These last two classes were said to be 'kept totally apart from other females, and from each other'. In workhouses where prostitutes were accommodated separately, it was often in the female 'idiot' cells. In Banbridge, for example, prostitutes were 'kept in the female idiot cells, and the female idiots with the female adults in the infirm ward'. In Kilmallock, female inmates of 'notoriously bad character' were kept separate from other women and married women were accommodated separately from single women with illegitimate children. But while young women, 'whose character is not impeached have a separate dormitory for themselves', it was noted that the latter three classes 'all take their meals together, and sometimes work together'. This was also the case in Nenagh. As PLI Bourke acknowledged, separating the mothers of illegitimate children from other married women might be desirable, but it was not always practicable.[23]

Some boards of guardians expressed a desire to apply moral classification

21 *Reform of the Irish Poor Law* (Dublin, 1862), DDA, Cullen Papers, Poor Law.
22 *Annual Report*, HC, 1862 [2966], pp. 13–14.
23 *Annual Report*, HC, 1862 [2966], pp. 80–90; *Nenagh Guardian*, 7 September 1861.

but claimed to have found it impracticable. The Guardians of Dromore West reported that they had:

> examined all the apartments of the workhouse and do not find any which could be appropriated exclusively for the occupation of those persons [women with more than one illegitimate child] without incurring a very large expenditure for necessary alterations, which the guardians do not wish to incur.

However, there were a number of unions in which moral classification was seen as either unnecessary or problematic. The Clerk of Clonakilty Union, for example, commented that the 'prostitutes in the house conduct themselves equally well and frequently better than some of the females who have illegitimate children'. The Mohill Board of Guardians objected to moral classification on principle declaring that it was:

> no part of their duty to classify; they disapprove of any classification according to character, or reputed character; the classification should be that of age and sex, and no other; they disapprove of confining any person to separate wards under any disguise whatsoever which would be felt as a punishment for an offence, for which the individual has not undergone trial in the usual course of law.

Similarly, the Mountmellick Guardians were stated to be unwilling 'at present to make any change' in the existing arrangements 'as it might prove inquisitorial'.[24] There were, therefore, a number of deciding factors in relation to classification from the purely practical, such as the available physical space, to the strongly moral. When it came to the application of moral principles, however, what might seem simple and straightforward on paper became much more complicated in practice, when real people were involved. Most boards of guardians adopted a pragmatic approach to classification. They generally had some kind of separation ward, but this was reserved for 'hardened' or 'notorious' prostitutes. In the majority of workhouses, officials appear to have been extremely reluctant to label women as prostitutes, preferring to judge them on their behaviour within the workhouse. This was not because they were concerned for the women's welfare or feelings, or not primarily, but because it made their life easier.

Imposing too rigid a disciplinary regime within the workhouse was likely to provoke discontent and disorder. This was particularly the case in smaller workhouses where a strict moral classification involved the isolation of small

---

24 Abstract of Replies, *Annual Report*, HC, 1862 [2966], pp. 80–90.

numbers of individuals. When the Westport Board of Guardians decided to improve classification in 1861 by providing separate accommodation for the mothers of illegitimate children, the women reacted with violence and insubordination, breaking workhouse property and cutting a hole in the wooden partition separating their yard from that of other female inmates.[25] A few years later the introduction of stricter classification in Kilmallock Workhouse was greeted with an outbreak of disorderly conduct amongst the women affected. The new regime had been introduced at the urging of the local parish priest, who had written to the board of guardians calling their attention to 'the fact of two notorious prostitutes constantly resorting to the workhouse as a temporary domicile', pointing out the 'evil effects' of this practice and recommending 'a more efficient system of classification'.[26] A few weeks later the master notified the board of guardians that he had been having problems with women in the separation ward. They had been behaving badly for some days, but the previous evening they had become uncontrollable, 'they were quarrelling, cursing and screaming [and] threatened to burn the place'. He had finally had to 'take them down to the front house, and place them in the probationary ward where they now are'. This bad conduct, he believed, was owing to 'the recent changes for the better classification of persons of bad character'. On the order of the board of guardians, the women were charged with insubordination and misconduct. All five women, the master reported the following week, had been sent to jail; three for a month, one for three weeks and one for two weeks.[27]

It was not so much the classification system itself that women seem to have objected to, but changes to the system. A riot in New Ross Workhouse in February 1887 was attributed by the local constabulary inspector to 'the attempt to classify women by separating bad characters from the rest which caused great discontent'. The *London Times* reported that an order 'forbidding the inmates of the workhouse to speak or associate with the mothers of illegitimate children' had 'annoyed the women who were the mothers of such children'.[28] Used judiciously, however, classification could help to maintain order. Rewarding good behaviour was an effective means of pauper management. Thus, Celia H. was moved from the dissolute females

25 Westport divided female inmates into three classes: women of 'unblemished character; women who, not being prostitutes, have had illegitimate children, [and] common prostitutes. Each class was provided with a separate day-room, dormitory and other accommodation and not allowed to associate with each other': Westport BG Minutes, 18 April, 2 May and 11 July 1861; 30 January 1862: NLI, MS 12627.
26 Letter from Rev. Dr Downes PP, Kilmallock BG Minutes, 1 February 1866.
27 Kilmallock BG Minutes, 22 and 29 March 1866.
28 Report of District Inspector Carey, 19 February 1887: NAI, CSORP 1887/11223; *The Times*, 18 February 1887.

ward of Westport Workhouse to the ward for the mothers of illegitimate children in September 1860 in recognition of her 'improved conduct'. In June 1871, the Roman Catholic Chaplain of Thurles Workhouse recommended that Anne M. be moved from the separate ward to the infirm ward, commenting, 'I think her length of time in it joined with her good conduct entitle her to this.'[29]

Boards of guardians had no power to institute different regimes for different categories of inmates. Guardians often expressed their frustration at not being able to use workhouse rules to deter people from entering. As the Belfast PLG, Thomas Gaffikin observed in 1883, if inmates had their hair cut 'every time they came in they would not trouble us so frequently'. His chairman had little sympathy for this view, however, demanding, 'What right have you to do that? This is not a gaol.'[30] Attempts by boards of guardians to treat certain categories of inmates more harshly than others prompted swift intervention from the central authorities. When the Drogheda Guardians proposed to cut the hair of women entering the separation ward, they were informed that this would be at variance with workhouse regulations which stated that it was unlawful for boards of guardians 'to cause any distinguishing mark of disgrace, to be worn by any adult pauper, or class of adult paupers, unless such pauper or paupers shall be disorderly or refractory'.[31] A proposal by the Mountmellick Guardians to cut the hair of female tramps was similarly ruled to be unlawful unless ordered by a medical officer. In the case of male tramps, the guardians were informed that this should only be done 'for purposes of cleanliness or sanitation'.[32]

Officials in smaller workhouses often preferred to disregard moral classification, classifying inmates by age and health, and integrating prostitutes and unmarried mothers with other adult women. This had a number of advantages from the point of view of workhouse management. It avoided creating a class of disaffected women, meaning that women were less likely to be disruptive and more likely to adhere to rules and regulations. It also meant that they could be called upon to undertake tasks such as nursing and cooking. Rewards and privileges proved a more effective way of maintaining

29 Thurles BG Minutes, 20 June 1871; Westport BG Minutes, 6 September 1860, cited in Luddy, *Prostitution and Irish Society*, p. 59.
30 *Belfast Newsletter*, June 1883.
31 Precedent Book, Workhouse Inmates, Drogheda, 15472/96: PRONI, LGBD 2/1; Article 42, General Order of Regulating the Management of Workhouses, 5 February 1849. Haircutting, Luddy points out, was 'a common occurrence in the Magdalen asylums ... Having shorn hair was an obvious sign of outcast status': *Prostitution and Irish Society*, p. 60; see also Virginia Crossman, 'Viewing Women, Family and Sexuality through the Prism of the Irish Poor Laws', *Women's History Review*, 15 (September 2006), pp. 546–9.
32 Precedent Book, Workhouse Inmates, Mountmellick, 31089/96: PRONI, LGBD 2/1.

order than isolation and punishment. The Glenties Board of Guardians consistently resisted any form of moral classification. Although there was 'no separation of any woman from the others', LGI Stewart Woodhouse reported in 1883, workhouse officials were confident that there was 'no unseemly behaviour, nor indecent language on the part of any of the women'. No prostitutes had been admitted to the workhouse for many years, he explained, 'save casuals', but as they only stayed a night, 'they stop in the probationary ward. There are about ten or twelve such cases in the year.' Twelve of the sixty-seven adult women then resident in the workhouse had had illegitimate children, Woodhouse noted, but some of these had been inmates for years and their children were grown up. Guardians and officials were all agreed that 'no contamination or corrupting influence [was] exercised by any of the women who had fallen upon the others'. Woodhouse concurred in this view commenting that he had 'frequently asked destitute poor persons if they would come into the workhouse and amongst a variety of reasons given for declining, I never heard this one [fear of associating with depraved females] mentioned'.[33] What made the difference here was local knowledge. Where guardians and officials were familiar with the background and personal circumstances of the women applying for relief, they felt more confident in exercising discretion in their treatment of them. This was not possible in large workhouses with busy separation wards.

Even where the principles of moral classification were adhered to the separation between classes was often far less rigid than guardians and officials claimed. The Chair of the Belfast Board of Guardians reacted angrily to allegations published in 1879, that the workhouse was a 'nest of drunkenness, immorality and vice' due in part to defective classification. All inmates were classified, Taylor declared:

> and separate buildings are allocated to each class. Everything has been done so far as high walls and locked doors can do to prevent any intercourse between the different classes. The separation ward is a building at the rear of the workhouse grounds and is enclosed by a high wall. All unfortunate women and women having two or more

33 Stewart Woodhouse to Local Government Board, 26 and 31 March 1883, NAI, CSORP 1883/7984. Glenties was not alone in not classifying women by character. LGI H. A. Robinson reported in 1885 that women of bad character were not separated from other women in Rathdown Workhouse. The following year the Macroom Board of Guardians passed a resolution directing that 'all women in this house who are mothers of more than one illegitimate child shall in future be kept separate from all the inmates as the poor law requires', indicating that this had not been done previously: Macroom BG Minutes, 21 June 1884, CCCA, BG/115/A1; and Rathdown BG Minutes, 18 November 1885, NAI.

illegitimate children are placed in this department; they are kept entirely separate and have no intercourse with other inmates, not even in the general dining hall as their meals are all supplied to them in their own building.

Following an official inquiry into the management of the Belfast Workhouse the following year, however, the inspectors concluded that while classification was 'substantially maintained', there were aspects of the internal arrangements that entailed 'objectionable intercourse' between different parts of the workhouse and particularly between different departments. Large numbers of men and women 'pass backwards and forwards through the house from different departments, three or four times daily', the result being 'to increase undesirably the opportunities for communication between individuals of different classes'. They also recommended changes to the organisation of the nursery to separate the married and unmarried mothers. These groups, it was noted, occupied 'apartments in common and it is only when a woman comes in with several illegitimate children that she is put in the separation ward with the common prostitutes'.[34]

It was almost impossible to keep different classes entirely apart in any workhouse. Inmates passed one another in corridors and on stairs, and while making their way to and from workshops, yards and gardens. Intimacy between inmates, or between inmates and officers, was of necessity generally hidden from view. Occasionally, however, investigation of particular incidents threw light on normally secret activities. An inquiry into the pregnancy of a mentally disabled inmate of Enniscorthy Workhouse in 1873, for example, revealed that male and female inmates had been able to gain access to each other's apartments and to associate freely whilst working in the fields of the workhouse farm.[35] In 1888, the Youghal Board of Guardians was advised to make structural changes to the workhouse so as to prevent communication between the schoolboys and adult male inmates. This was a response to the discovery that two male inmates had sexually abused a number of young boys in the workhouse. The men were reported to have had 'evil communication' with nine boys, 'chiefly in the water closet of the Fever Hospital and Infirmary, the men's pump shed, the men's water closet and the top landing of the men's and boys' stairs'. The men and boys were generally kept apart, but it was discovered that the schoolmaster had allowed the older boys to go

34 Belfast BG Minutes, 18 February 1879; *Copies of the Minutes of Evidence taken at the recent Inquiry held at the Belfast Workhouse by Inspectors Bourke and Brodie, together with their Report thereon, and Final Decision of the Local Government Board*, HC, 1881 (123), pp. 1–34.
35 *Enniscorthy News*, 5 and 12 July 1873.

to their dormitories after work and before supper (between 5 and 6 p.m.) and that one of the men, Michael R., used to meet them there.[36]

In the course of the inquiry further irregularities were uncovered in Youghal. In addition to his meetings with the boys, it was claimed that Michael had also met with a female inmate, Anne S., in the pump shed 'for an immoral purpose', although she denied this. Anne had been one of a group of women who went every morning between ten and eleven to scrub the men's wards. The women were accompanied by a nun who locked them in the wards and then returned to collect them. Anne, the nun recalled, used to have her work done before the rest and was always in a hurry to get away, so she would let her go first and the others followed shortly after. Although the pump shed, which was on the way back from the men's wards, was kept locked, Michael had a key as he helped to pump water. Questioned about the matter, the master sought to deflect blame from workhouse officers, observing that:

> classification between the sexes is incomparably more perfect since the nuns took charge here, but it would seem that their utmost vigilance is sometimes to be defeated by the ingenuity of fallen specimens of human nature to be found in the workhouse. Here as to a cesspool the moral sewerage of the entire fourteen electoral divisions gravitates.[37]

Guardians and officials were quick to shift the blame for lax discipline. Lamenting the debased character of inmates was a useful cover for their own failings.

The following year, Westport Guardians were shocked to discover that two inmates, Richard B. and Anne M. had been meeting in one of the dormitories. A fellow inmate informed the authorities in November 1889, that 'they had a great meeting place made of the old men's bedroom and he used to pass up by the old men's day room, and she used to pass up by the boys school rooms'. The master and matron initially dismissed the allegation, claiming that it would have been impossible. Anne, the matron explained, was 'never up in the body of the house except when I send her with other women scouring the floors through the house, and on the two washing days' and whenever the women were at work, they were 'almost constantly under my eyes'. Her confidence was shown to be misplaced when Richard admitted

---

36 Youghal BG Minutes, 17 February 1888. Michael was found guilty of committing 'unnatural offences' and sentenced to eighteen-months imprisonment with hard labour. The other man involved was sentenced to nine months: Minutes, 17 March 1888.

37 Minutes, 24 February 1888. The guardians agreed to make the structural changes recommended and in addition to erect a water closet in the boys' yard 'with a view of making classification more perfect': Minutes, 2 March 1888.

that he had been 'keeping company' with Anne for the past year. He claimed to have met her 'several times through the house', as well as in the quarry in the workhouse grounds and in her dormitory. He acknowledged that there had been 'improper conduct' between them, but explained that Anne had asked him to marry her on a number of occasions and that he was now willing to accept her offer.[38]

Although saddened by the 'revolting state of discipline in the workhouse', the guardians were reluctant to dismiss the matron and agreed to give her another chance. The Local Government Board queried this decision, pointing out that the ease with which the couple had been able to meet was mainly due to Anne having been 'specially selected for constant employment in the various parts of the workhouse, the fact that she was a woman with three illegitimate children being apparently quite overlooked by the Master and Matron'.

The guardians were more inclined to blame the inmates, than their officers. When Richard and Anne returned to the workhouse as a married couple in February 1890, the guardians ruled that Anne, who had been 'formerly of class 3' was 'to be kept in the ward she occupied before, and is not to be permitted to occupy the same room with the other married women, and is not to be permitted to go through the body of the house'. She was understandably aggrieved about this, believing that she should be treated in the same way as other married women. The following week, the master reported that Anne was to be summoned to the Petty Sessions Court for breaking the lock of the separation ward, 'The woman persists in stating such is not her proper place in the workhouse.' She was sentenced to one-month's imprisonment. On her return to the workhouse, the guardians remained reluctant to classify Anne as a married woman, although the Local Government Board advised that they saw no objection to this 'while she conducts herself properly'.[39] The central authorities held the master and matron responsible for the lack of discipline in the workhouse. The guardians, however, persisted in regarding Anne and Richard as the real culprits.

The decades immediately after the Famine saw an increase in illegitimacy rates in Ireland, although these remained significantly lower than in the rest of the United Kingdom.[40] Within English welfare institutions, the nineteenth

---

38 Westport BG Minutes, 21 November 1889.
39 Minutes, 13 and 20 February; and 17 April 1890. The case was noted in the LGB Precedent Book as, 'a matter in which the guardians exercise their own judgement': Westport, LGBD 2/1.
40 In 1865 illegitimate birth rate was 6.3 per cent in England; 10 per cent in Scotland; and 3.7 per cent in Ireland: Kennedy and Gray, 'Famine, Illegitimacy and the Workhouse in Western Ireland: Kilrush, County Clare', in Alysa Levene, Thomas Nutt and Samantha

century saw a shift in emphasis from care of the illegitimate child to reform of the unmarried mother. At the same time, the introduction of the new poor law increased the stigma attached to illegitimacy by forcing single mothers into workhouses in order to receive relief and placing the major share of responsibility on the mothers rather than fathers of illegitimate children.[41] In Ireland, however, the poor law provided a 'safety net' for the single mother that had not previously been available.[42] Indeed, the support provided to unmarried mothers and their children in workhouses was widely believed to be encouraging illegitimacy and undermining the morals of the poor. Asked for their views on the workhouse system in 1861, Catholic priests criticised the indiscriminate nature of poor relief, as well as the corrupting influences to be found within the workhouse. Thomas Greene, Parish Priest of Athy, claimed that the number of illegitimate children belonging to his parish had increased four-fold, an increase for which he believed the workhouse system to be partly responsible. It 'affords a refuge to the mother and her illegitimate child', he remarked, 'and by diminishing the penalty of this conduct holds out an encouragement to crime'.[43] Richard Galvin reported that there were fifty-nine women in Rathdrum Workhouse who had illegitimate children. The 'shelter of the Poorhouse', he maintained, was 'a great encouragement to this class as they are enabled by the law to go in and out as they please. When they go back where they have lost character they invariably relapse.' Only a 'reformatory and more stringent rules than those of the poor law', he believed, 'could prevent this.'[44]

Poor law guardians were equally concerned about the number of unmarried mothers in workhouses and the number of illegitimate children being supported by poor rates. However, attitudes to sex outside marriage were not as clear cut as is sometimes assumed. It was recognised that not all unmarried mothers were the same and that some responsibility rested with the fathers of illegitimate children. In 1859, the Boards of Guardians of Limerick and Borrisokane had circulated a petition calling attention to 'a marked and progressive increase' that had taken place in the numbers of unmarried women seeking asylum in workhouses, who remained 'permanently chargeable to the rates as paupers after they have given birth' and calling for a change in the law so that fathers could be made to pay for

Williams (eds), *Illegitimacy in Britain, 1700–1920* (Basingstoke: Palgrave Macmillan, 2005), p. 123.

41 Alysa Levene, Thomas Nutt and Samantha Williams (eds), *Illegitimacy in Britain, 1700–1920* (Basingstoke: Palgrave Macmillan, 2005), p. 14.

42 Kennedy and Gray, 'Famine, Illegitimacy and the Workhouse in Western Ireland', p. 138.

43 Greene to Cullen, 12 March 1861: DDA, Cullen Papers, 340/1/28.

44 Galvin to Cullen, 12 March 1861: DDA, Cullen Papers, 340/1/29.

the support of their illegitimate offspring. The guardians believed that many of the women had been seduced and that some had 'lived openly in a state of concubinage with men well able but unwilling to provide for their support and that of their children'. The mothers were young and healthy, and willing to work. Most were 'betrayed into error' and were 'still innately modest and would willingly engage in honest industry was it lawful for them to leave the workhouses with a certainty that their infants would be taken care of'.[45] Asked for their comments on the petition, the poor law commissioners acknowledged that official returns showed the percentage of illegitimate children in Irish workhouses to have increased from around 8 per cent of the total in 1853 to 39 per cent in 1859, but noted that the actual number had dropped from 5,710 to 4,918, so that the statement to the effect that there had been a 'marked and progressive increase' was not borne out. The change in the proportion, the commissioners observed, was:

> probably to be explained by the fact that while the improved prosperity of the working classes has reduced the number of legitimate children dependent on the poor rates, it has had comparatively little effect upon those causes of destitution which are connected with the birth of bastard children.[46]

Figures produced by the commissioners showed Ulster workhouses to contain a higher percentage of illegitimate children than those in other provinces suggesting that there may have been a higher rate of pre-marital sex in Ulster counties and possibly even less support for single mothers within local communities.[47]

Under the Poor Law Amendment Act of 1862, boards of guardians were given powers to recover the maintenance costs of illegitimate children from the father. The following year the procedure was amended to enable boards to recover costs by civil bill process.[48] The mother was required to have identified the father in an affidavit on oath before one or more justice of the peace in petty sessions, to have appeared before the court to be examined and to have her statement supported by corroborative evidence. Many boards of guardians regarded this process as more trouble than it was worth, but some did attempt to make use of it. Even before the act was passed the

---

45 The Humble Petition of the Guardians of the Poor of the Limerick Union, n. d., NAI, CSORP 1859/9780.
46 Banks to Cardwell, 5 November 1859, NAI, CSORP 1859/9780.
47 Fifty-two per cent of children in Ulster workhouses were illegitimate compared to 35 per cent in Munster; 36 per cent in Leinster; and 39 per cent in Connaught: ibid.
48 Irish Poor Law Further Amendment Act, 1862, 25 and 26 Vic., c. 83, s. 9; Illegitimate Children Act, 1863, 26 Vic., c. 21.

Westport Board of Guardians resolved to take up the case of Ellen M. 'now in the workhouse with her illegitimate child with a view to prosecution as soon as the Bastardy Bill now before Parliament is passed'. In subsequent years the Westport Guardians required the mothers of illegitimate children to swear affidavits as a condition of remaining in the workhouse. Actually securing any money proved difficult, however. In 1865, the guardians pursued a case against a local man only to have the case then dismissed, 'the defendant having sworn on the hearing of the case that he had no means whatever of paying any portion of the amount'. A few months later the case against another man was dismissed for want of corroborative evidence.[49] Mountmellick Board of Guardians experienced similar problems. In October 1871 the Workhouse Master, James Ryan, reported that he had attended the quarter sessions at Maryborough, together with four female inmates who were mothers of illegitimate children. Two of the men named as fathers failed to appear and were fined for non-attendance, while the case against another man was dismissed 'without prejudice for want of sufficient corroborative evidence'. In only one case was a decree granted for the amount claimed.[50]

Single women who failed to conform to the ideal of female purity could be harshly treated. Bridget K., for example, was refused admission to Ballina Workhouse in March 1865, on the grounds that she was 'well dressed and consequently could not be destitute'.[51] According to Bridget, her clothes were 'more showey than valuable, they were mere flimsy gauzes', suggesting that it was her appearance and demeanour the guardians found objectionable. She had previously been an inmate for over a year but had taken her discharge earlier in the month. When asked why she sought admission, she explained that she was unable to work being in an advanced state of pregnancy and named an ex Officio Guardian, William Symes, as the father of her child. (He denied this.) She reapplied ten days later, now badly dressed, but was again refused. She was finally admitted in mid-April by which time, according to her mother, she was 'so naked and destitute that she could not appear in public'.[52] Bridget remained in the workhouse until 9 June, when she gave birth to a daughter. She died a few hours later following a haemorrhage.

49 Westport BG Minutes, 27 March 1862; 18 January and 12 October 1865; 11 January and 5 July 1866. In January 1862, 63 per cent of the children in Westport Workhouse were illegitimate (thirty-nine of sixty-two); while unmarried mothers comprised 30 per cent of the adult female inmates (sixteen of fifty-three): Minutes, 30 January 1862. Westport BG continued to pursue fathers for maintenance costs. See, Minutes, 2 January, 6 March and 3 July 1890.
50 Mountmellick BG Minutes, 28 October 1871.
51 Evidence of James Coolican PLG, Report of Dr King PLI together with evidence taken at the inquiry into the pregnancy of the late Bridget K., 31 July 1865, CSORP 1865/9459.
52 Evidence of Patrick Irwin, Chaplain, CSORP 1865/9459.

An inquiry into her death revealed that while an inmate of the workhouse she had been a regular visitor to Symes' house, leaving the workhouse on a day pass and returning with food and money. She appears to have been quite open about the relationship. In the view of PLI Charles Croker King, the fact that Bridget had 'freely exhibited' money received 'as the wages of prostitution', proved that she was 'far advanced in vice, and dead to all shame and decency'. There was no proof that she had been seeing other men, however. Claims that she had slept with the assistant schoolmaster in the workhouse, were strongly denied by him. It was Bridget's lack of shame which seems to have particularly affronted the inspector and board of guardians, as well as alienating the Catholic chaplain. King concluded that there was evidence of 'improper intimacy' between Bridget and Symes, and of poor workhouse management, but absolved the guardians and their officers from blame in relation to Bridget's death. They could not, he observed, be held 'responsible for the conduct of inmates, while removed from their immediate control'. Once outside the workhouse, inmates were 'obliged to rely on the precepts of morality and religion previously imparted to them by those whose special duty it is to watch over their moral and spiritual welfare'.[53] This comment was aimed at the Chaplain, Patrick Irwin, who had obliged the authorities to take notice of the case, although he had refused to intervene while Bridget was alive, telling her bluntly that he had no compassion for her. Irwin viewed Bridget as a victim of 'the licentiousness of a guardian of the poor', but traced her loss of character to her residence in the workhouse. She had, he claimed, been a girl of good character 'until she became an inmate of the workhouse'. Reactions to Bridget's death were revealing. None of the parties involved was willing to take responsibility; all sought to pin the blame elsewhere.

Concern about the corrupting influence of the workhouse remained a theme in social and political commentary. Referring to the number of unmarried mothers in Belfast Workhouse in 1879, Richard Hamilton argued that the institution 'afforded a strong facility to the vicious acts of those men by whose means the girls had been brought to this state, and thus produced or encouraged one of the great evils of society'. The central authorities and most guardians, however, regarded the admission of single mothers as an unfortunate necessity, insisting that responsibility for their plight lay outside not inside the workhouse. As David Taylor, chair of Belfast Board of Guardians, observed in response to Hamilton's allegations, the only

---

53 Report of Dr King, CSORP 1865/9459. Symes was severely criticised by the poor law commissioners but as he was not a paid officer they were unable to take any action against him. He was subsequently removed from the commission of the peace for counties Mayo, Sligo and Donegal: PLC to Clerk of Ballina Board of Guardians, 11 August 1865; Note to Larcom, 12 September 1865, CSORP 1865/9459.

grounds on which 'ill-conducted women' were admitted to the workhouse were destitution. They had 'nothing to do with character in considering the granting of relief, but simply to consider the question of destitution'. LGI Terence Brodie took an equally pragmatic view, commenting that:

> neither officers nor guardians can prevent women being admitted to the workhouse and being delivered there. Nor would the guardians be justified in discharging them from the house, knowing them to be destitute. When it is remembered that there are thousands of unprotected females working in factories in Belfast it is not very surprising that a small percentage should seek the workhouse as a refuge.[54]

The popular view of the workhouse remained resolutely negative, however. Spending time in a workhouse, it was commonly believed, virtually condemned young girls to single motherhood and prostitution. After 'a few years of squalid misery in the poorhouse', it was claimed in 1862, girls would 'leave the place and become prostitutes. They will lead the lives of prostitutes and die the death of prostitutes. Such has been the fate of almost all the female children in the Irish poor houses.'[55] This view was enthusiastically, if erroneously, embraced by the Vice-Regal Commission. The Commission's Report was highly critical of the role of the workhouse system in 'keeping up the numbers of this most undesirable special class of women', and allowing 'the continuation and multiplication of the class from hardened mother to shameless daughter, owing to the unnatural and unhealthy environment in which they are placed'. The commissioners claimed to have frequently found three 'illegitimate generations in the female line' when visiting workhouses and in one case four. In total, there were stated to be 2,129 unmarried mothers and 2,764 illegitimate children amongst workhouse inmates, although it was acknowledged that the number of illegitimate mothers included women of all ages, some of whom were elderly 'and their children are no longer inmates of the workhouse'.[56]

There is little hard evidence to support the commissioners' wilder claims.[57] Analysis of workhouse admission registers shows that not only had admissions of unmarried mothers declined from the 1860s, but the

54 Belfast BG Minutes, 18 February 1879; LGB to Burke (enclosing comments of LGI Brodie), 27 February 1879, NAI, CSORP 1879/3342.
55 D. Caulfield, 'Historical Statistics of Ireland', *Journal of the Statistical and Social Inquiry Society of Ireland*, 3 (1862), p. 242, cited in Luddy, *Prostitution and Irish Society*, p. 59.
56 *Poor Law Reform Commission (Ireland)*, HC, 1906 [Cd. 3202], p. 43.
57 Kennedy and Gray note that the claims are inconsistent with some of evidence collected

Table 6.1 Unmarried mothers in workhouses.

Ballycastle	1861	1871	1879	1911		
Adult women (admissions)	174	145	205	72	11	
Single mothers (admissions)	32	22	24	3	10	
Average age of single mothers	28	31	25	27	23	
Average length of stay (months)	3.3	4.1		7.75		
Ballymoney	1851	1861	1871	1891	1901	1911
Adult women (admissions)	131	147	241	156	281	240
Single mothers (admissions)	16	35	26	16	22	7
Average age	29	29	31	29	29	26
Length of stay	7.1	2.6		4.3	0.9	3.1
Belfast		Jan 1865	Jan 1878		Jan 1901	
Adult women (admissions)		319	454		604	
Single mothers (admissions)		38	89		62	
Average age		28	27		27	
Length of stay		1.6	1.2		1.3	
Glenties		1861		1891	1901	
Adult women (admissions)		105		113	114	
Single mothers (admissions)		27		6	15	
Average age		24		28	28	
Length of stay						
Kinsale			1871		1901	
Adult women (admissions)			205		306	
Single mothers (admissions)			26		15	
Average age			29		26	
Length of stay			3.4		2.4	
North Dublin	1851	1861	1871	1891		1911
Adult women (admissions)	1874	2003	2063	1260		2599
Single mothers (admissions)	63	110	148	63		113
Average age	26	26	26	26		24
Length of stay	9	5.6	5.6	4.1		2.8
Thurles		1871	1889	1901	1911	
Adult women (admissions)		217	530	455	303	
Single mothers (admissions)		14	16	19	8	
Average age		31	27	26	31	
Length of stay		2.6	0.3	1.2	4.4	

Source: Indoor Relief Registers

majority of single mothers had only one illegitimate child. Furthermore, they remained in the workhouse for months, not years, and when they left, most did not return. By the later decades of the nineteenth century relatively few unmarried mothers were being admitted to provincial workhouses (see Table 6.1). Thurles and Kinsale Workhouses saw a significant decline in the proportion of adult single women admitted who were noted to be either pregnant or accompanied by illegitimate children. Moreover, the women who were admitted often entered a number of times during the year so that the number of individual women was generally smaller than the number of admissions. In 1870–1871 for example, eight women were admitted to Thurles Workhouse with illegitimate children totalling fourteen admissions between them. In 1900–1901, eight women accounted for nineteen admissions.[58] Women who remained more than one or two nights were generally chargeable to an electoral division rather than to the union, indicating that they were resident in the locality. Provincial workhouses in the north admitted a higher proportion of single mothers than those in the south, but here too admissions dropped over the second half of the nineteenth century. The profile of the women was very similar to those in the south. They were in their twenties and the most common occupation was servant.[59] Live-in servants were particularly vulnerable to sexual exploitation. The average length of stay was in months and declined over the period in line with workhouse usage generally. In Ballymoney and Clogher Workhouses, a significant proportion of single mothers were casual inmates. Women who remained for longer than one night generally had more than one illegitimate child or were sick.[60] Women falling pregnant for the first time may well have had access to other sources of support, such as charitable institutions.

It is not difficult to find examples of multiple and multi-generational illegitimacy, but these were exceptional cases. The women concerned were often frequent visitors to the workhouse which may help to explain why they attracted more attention than their numbers warranted. Bridget L., for example, was admitted to Thurles Workhouse three times in 1900–1901. In November 1900 she entered accompanied by a son, Martin, aged four and a daughter, Bridget, aged two. The family remained in the workhouse over the

      by the commission itself: 'Famine, Illegitimacy and the Workhouse in Western Ireland', p. 139.

58 Thurles BG Indoor Relief Registers, 1870–1871, 1910–1911.

59 Seventeen out of twenty-four admissions to Ballycastle Workhouse in 1879–1880 who were registered as single women accompanied by illegitimate children were servants: Ballycastle BG Indoor Relief Registers 1879–1880.

60 Almost two-thirds of single mothers admitted to Ballymoney in 1900–1901 were casuals; and over three-quarters of those admitted to Clogher 1910–1911: Ballymoney BG Indoor Relief Registers; Clogher BG Indoor Relief Registers.

winter during which time Bridget gave birth to another daughter, Mary. She was discharged with the baby on 17 March 1901, leaving the older children in the workhouse. Mother and baby returned five days later and remained in the workhouse for a further two weeks. Bridget and all three children were discharged on 4 April. They were readmitted on 29 May and discharged the following day. Bridget returned with her daughters, but without her son in September and stayed for just under three weeks. She was also admitted twice in 1910–1911. She entered the workhouse in May from an address in Quarry Street, accompanied by three children: Bridget, Mary and Michael, whose ages were given as thirteen, eleven and eight. They remained in the workhouse for three months. Bridget's eldest son, Martin, now aged fifteen was admitted on 30 July and was discharged with his mother and siblings on 7 August. All five were readmitted on 25 August and stayed for four days. Bridget was usually described as having no occupation and once as a labourer.[61] She was undoubtedly making use of the workhouse to support her growing family, but they were far from permanent residents and her eldest son appears to have been largely independent. In Ballymoney, one woman was admitted to the workhouse in three successive census years, but here again her child appears to have become independent. Anne M., who was twenty-four years of age, entered Ballymoney Workhouse together with her baby daughter, Teresa, twice in 1860–1861. They spent much of that year in the workhouse staying from April until June and then from July to October. Anne was registered first as a weaver and then as mendicant. Ten years later, she and Teresa spent two weeks in the workhouse in June. Anne's age was given as thirty and her occupation as servant.[62] In 1880–1881 Anne entered alone and spent the winter months in the workhouse.[63] She was now forty and she was again registered as a weaver. Thus while Anne remained partially dependent on poor relief, her daughter appears to have been able to support herself.

Glenties was an exception to the general trend in that admissions by single mothers dropped between 1860–1861 and 1890–1891, but then rose again in 1900–1901. In 1860–1861, single mothers accounted for 26 per cent of admissions by adult women. Many made repeated admissions and the average length of stay was five months. In 1890–1891 single mothers accounted for just 5 per cent of admissions by adult women and the average length of stay had dropped to around six weeks. In 1900–1901 however,

61 Thurles BG Indoor Relief Registers, 1900–1901, 1910–1911.
62 We can be fairly certain that it is the same woman since Teresa was noted to be ten years old.
63 She was admitted on 29 December 1880 and remained until 17 January 1881, returning the same day and remaining until 5 May 1881: Ballymoney BG Indoor Relief Registers, 1860–1861, 1870–1871, 1880–1881.

single mothers were once again a significant presence accounting for 13 per cent of admissions by adult women. There were now two distinct groups: women who were registered as tramps and who stayed one night, some returning two or three times within the year; and other women who made longer stays, averaging fourteen months. Some were local, such as Fannie O., aged twenty-eight from Arranmore, who was admitted with her three-year-old son in July 1901 and remained until June 1904, but others were from outside the union. Bella S., for example, was a twenty-one-year-old servant from Strabane. She was admitted with her three-year-old son in August and they remained until July 1904.[64] Glenties Workhouse was also unusual in that illegitimate children were often registered under the name of the father not that of the mother, which was contrary to poor law regulations.[65] Using the name of the father may have been a way of signalling that responsibility lay with the father rather than the mother and is consistent with the more tolerant attitude towards 'immoral' women evident amongst guardians and officials in Glenties. It is possible that Bella had chosen to enter the workhouse in Glenties, rather than Strabane, for this reason.

A number of factors may account for the decline in the numbers of single mothers admitted to many provincial workhouses. National illegitimacy rates declined over the second half of the nineteenth century from 3.7 per cent in 1865, to 2.7 per cent in 1891.[66] Under the influence of the Devotional Revolution, social attitudes may have become harsher forcing single mothers to move to the relative anonymity of the city in order to find shelter and support. Alternatively, rising living standards within the farming class may have encouraged fathers to make some provision for their illegitimate children enabling single mothers to survive outside the workhouse. It is also possible that the culture within provincial workhouses became more hostile to single mothers. Stricter classification and the growing practice of separating single mothers from other women with children may have deterred women from entering some workhouses. Ó Gráda has suggested that many of the women registered as single mothers 'were really deserted wives'.[67] This, in conjunction with stricter classification, might account for the decline in numbers since deserted wives would be less inclined to present as unmarried if it meant being assigned to a separate ward. Given the relative

64 Glenties BG Indoor Relief Registers, 1860–1861, 1890–1891, 1900–1901.
65 In 1856 the poor law commissioners had written to the Westport Guardians informing them that 'in the case of illegitimate children the only parent recognised by law is the mother and that the child in question ... should be registered in the workhouse by the mother's name': Westport BG Minutes, 21 August 1856.
66 Kennedy and Gray, 'Famine, Illegitimacy and the Workhouse in Western Ireland', p. 132.
67 Ó Gráda, *A New Economic History*, p. 104.

social status of married and unmarried women, however, it seems unlikely that married women would have claimed to be single. Even in workhouses where unmarried mothers were not separated from other women there was a stigma attached to the designation. Status and reputation were very important in determining how an inmate was treated not only by officials, but also by other inmates. Furthermore, if the decline in single mothers was a reaction to a less tolerant attitude and the introduction of stricter classifi-cation, one would expect to see numbers remain high in Glenties Workhouse where a more tolerant approach was adopted. Since they dropped here too, before rising again in the early twentieth century, it is clear that classification was not the only issue involved. Popular perception notwithstanding, the majority of single mothers did not become paupers for life. They were able to leave the workhouse and maintain themselves and their child.

As one would expect, city workhouses admitted higher numbers of single mothers than provincial workhouses. The numbers admitted included young women living in the city who became pregnant, many of whom were migrants, as well as those who arrived in the city pregnant, having been forced to leave where they were living. The proportion of single mothers among adult women admissions fluctuated in both NDU and Belfast, although there is some evidence of a decline in the early twentieth century. The women were in their twenties and in NDU the most common occupation was servant, or none. Accounting for between 10 and 20 per cent of adult female admissions in the month of January in 1864, 1878 and 1901, a significantly higher proportion of single mothers were admitted to Belfast Workhouse than to NDU. This reflects the different social and economic context. There was far more female employment in Belfast and while commentators referred to the corrupting influence of factory culture, the fact that women were able to become economically independent at a relatively young age was probably more relevant. The women were again in their twenties although slightly older than those in Dublin. In Belfast the most common occupation was mill worker, followed by servant and prostitute. In January 1901 there were more prostitutes than mill workers, perhaps reflecting the contraction in female factory employment.

Some single mothers entered the workhouse from another establishment, highlighting the close interrelationship between welfare institutions. In February 1910, the NDU Board of Guardians adopted a resolution instructing their relieving officers not to admit applicants from Miss Rice's Institution, Blackhall Place, 'as such people cannot be considered as coming under the head of destitute poor'. The institution referred to was the Dublin Prison Gate Mission (DPMG), a Protestant-run reformatory. Two women from the mission had been admitted with their infants the previous week, the master reported. In both cases, 'the infants got sick, and the mothers brought them to the NDU'. If this went on, RO Lawrence Keogh commented, 'they would have to build another nursery'.[68] Having taken legal advice, however, the DPGM dismissed the guardians' resolution as unlawful and threatened to appeal to the Local Government Board 'in vindication of the rights of these poor people, who are entitled to seek the aid provided for them by the rates of Dublin'.[69] The guardians were forced to back down and women continued to be admitted from the mission. In 1910–1911, five women were admitted to NDU from Blackhall Street, or Place. Four were young, single, Protestant women all of whom were admitted with an illegitimate child. One was a young, single, Catholic woman who was admitted pregnant and whose child was subsequently born in the workhouse.[70] It would appear that women who had entered the DPGM were sent into NDU if they, or their children, required medical treatment. The workhouse was clearly not the first choice of refuge for these women, but it was an essential source of medical care. It is evident that a substantial proportion of pregnant women admitted to both NDU and Belfast were single. In 1860–1861, 70 per cent of pregnant women admitted to NDU were single, and in 1910–1911, 73 per cent. In Belfast, of the twenty-three women admitted pregnant in January 1901, seventeen were single (74 per cent). It is not surprising that married women did not see the workhouse as a place to give birth. There were a range of other options open to them particularly in the later part of the century, including a number of specialist maternity hospitals.[71]

Contemporary commentary often conflated single mothers and prostitutes, but in practice the two groups were distinct and there was only limited overlap between them. In Belfast, for example, thirty-eight admissions in January 1865 were registered as single mothers and twenty-one as prostitutes; only four admissions fell into both categories. In January 1901, sixty-two admissions were single mothers and fifty-four prostitutes; seventeen were both. We are, therefore, talking about two distinct groups of women, although they shared certain characteristics; they tended to be young and to stay for relatively long periods. Women accompanied by illegitimate children were a clearly defined group within the workhouse. Prostitutes were a much less clearly defined group. Outside the major cities,

68 *Irish Independent*, 3 February 1910.
69 DPGM Minutes, 3 February 1910, cited in Oonagh Walsh, *Anglican Women in Dublin: Philanthropy, Politics and Education in the Early Twentieth Century* (Dublin: UCD Press, 2005), p. 104.
70 NDU BG Indoor Relief Registers, 1910–1911.
71 For a recent study of maternity hospitals in Dublin, see Julie Anne Bergin, 'Birth and Death in Nineteenth-Century Dublin's Lying-In Hospitals, in Elaine Farrell (ed.), *'She Said She was in the Family Way': Pregnancy and Infancy in Modern Ireland* (London: Institute of Historical Research, 2012), pp. 91–111.

the term prostitute rarely appears in workhouse admission registers. This is not to say that prostitutes did not use the workhouse, but that they were rarely identified as such on admission. Of the nine unions studied for which admission registers are available, two (Clogher and Glenties) did not use the term at all in the years examined, while most of the others used it only very occasionally. In the north, outside of Belfast, the small number of women identified as prostitutes fell into two categories: casual admissions mainly from outside the union; and the occasional local woman who often remained in the workhouse for relatively long periods, frequently over the winter. In 1860–1861 three women were registered as prostitutes on admission to Ballymoney Workhouse, for example. Two were casuals who stayed one night. The third, Mary D., was a thirty-four-year-old woman, who was admitted twice, staying first for fifteen days and then for over a year from August until the following September.[72] Officials in provincial workhouses in the south were equally sparing in the use of the term prostitute. This was the case even in workhouses which were located in towns such as Kinsale and Thurles where there was an army barracks. In Kinsale, for example, two women were categorised as prostitutes in 1870–1871; Julia B., who was twenty-three and from Kinsale, and stayed just over two months from November to January; and Anne F., who entered hurt and stayed for over three months from January until April 1871. The term was not used in the Thurles admission registers in 1870–1871, while in 1879–1880 just two women were registered as prostitutes. These were Hannah and Susan B., both in their twenties and both Protestants from Kilkenny, suggesting that they were sisters. They stayed one night.[73]

In 1889–1890 nine separate admissions to Thurles Workhouse were registered 'prostitute', but all related to one woman, Nancy C. She had been admitted once in 1879–1880 remaining in the workhouse from January until May. On this occasion she was noted to be a widow, aged forty-five with no occupation. In 1889–1890 she was admitted nine times. Her age was recorded as fifty and she was still described as a widow, but her occupation was now stated to be prostitute. On one occasion her place of origin was given as Longford. Her stays were for the most part relatively short, generally between one day and three weeks, but she also spent the winter months in the workhouse having entered in late October and remaining until February 1890. In 1900–1901, now aged sixty, Nancy was still visiting the workhouse. She entered twice in October 1900, staying twelve days and then a little over three weeks. The term prostitute is not used in the Thurles

---

72 Ballymoney BG Indoor Relief Registers, 1860–1861.
73 Kinsale BG Indoor Relief Registers, 1870–1871; and Thurles BG Indoor Relief Registers, 1870–1871, 1879–1880.

register in 1900–1901 and here Nancy was described simply as a widow with no occupation. Having been admitted on 16 November 1900, she was never discharged and died in the workhouse in 1906. We do not know the details of Nancy's story. We do not know exactly when or why she turned to prostitution. We do know that workhouses officials felt confident in describing her as a prostitute and that she resorted to the workhouse on a regular basis, perhaps when trade was slow or she was unwell, or when the weather was bad and that she ended her days there.

Workhouses where the term prostitute was in more general use were Belfast and Cork, although its use in Cork appears to be confined to the 1860s and 1870s.[74] Under poor law regulations, decisions relating to moral classification were a matter for the board of guardians, not officials, and it is often unclear why, or on what grounds, women were identified as prostitutes.[75] Leanne McCormick plausibly suggests that reputation, appearance, demeanour, address and companions may all have played a part.[76] It is also possible that other inmates may have passed on information about individual women. The labelling of women by officials in Cork Workhouse may reflect a heightened awareness of prostitution as a result of the Contagious Diseases Acts, introduced to control the spread of venereal disease within the army. Cork, Cobh and the Curragh were 'subjected districts' under the acts which allowed for the compulsory medical examination of women suspected of being prostitutes.[77] In 1870–1871, 6 per cent of adult women admissions to Cork Workhouse were noted to be prostitutes, with an average age of twenty-eight. In roughly half the cases, the women made short stays of ten days or less. The remainder stayed for much longer periods, the average length of stay amongst this group being 9.6 months.[78]

Belfast Workhouse also admitted a significant number of women identified as prostitutes, but here there was more continuity across the period. The proportion of adult women admissions registered as being a prostitute was 7 per cent in January 1865; 11 per cent in January 1878; and 9 per cent in January 1901; their average length of stay between four and

74 'Prostitute' appears in the occupation column in 1870–1871, but not in 1850–1851, 1900–1901 or 1910–1911: Cork BG Indoor Relief Registers.

75 Banks to Clerk of Wexford Union, 2 July 1880, NAI, CSORP 1883/7984.

76 McCormick, *Regulating Sexuality*, p. 16.

77 For an analysis of the acts and the campaign to repeal them, see Luddy, *Prostitution and Irish Society*, pp. 140–55.

78 Out of a sample of 753 admissions to Cork Workhouse 1870–1871, 362 were adult women of whom twenty were noted to be prostitutes: Cork BG Indoor Relief Registers, 1870–1871. The establishment of a Magdalen Asylum in the city by Good Shepherd nuns in 1872, may help to explain why prostitutes were not identified amongst female admissions in subsequent decades. In 1911, the Asylum contained 167 inmates: Luddy, *Prostitution and Irish Society*, pp. 82, 93.

six weeks.[79] Repeat admissions were common and in a quarter of cases, the women were accompanied by children. Eliza M., for example, was admitted three times in January 1878 accompanied by her two daughters aged ten and two. They made stays of between eight and eighteen days and on each occasion returned within a day of being discharged. Similarly, Clare W. was admitted with her one-year-old son three times in January 1901, staying six days on each occasion. Mary Ann C. was admitted with her baby son, John, five times; staying between five and eight days, and again returning within a day of being discharged. It was this pattern of behaviour that particularly annoyed workhouse officials. That women did not present as prostitutes or readily accept the label, is evident from the case of Clare W., who entered Belfast Workhouse on 3 January 1901, accompanied by her baby son. She was registered as being thirty years old, married and a mill-worker, and her son as legitimate. She left two days later, returning the following day. She was now registered as single and her occupation as prostitute; her son was registered as illegitimate. It is possible that officials had made inquiries about her or had received information that caused them to change her registration. She remained for six days leaving on 12 January. She entered a further three times that month. On one occasion her occupation was registered as 'doing laundry' and she, and her son, were noted to be suffering from the effects of drink. On the other occasions she was registered as a prostitute. Having been admitted on 27 January she remained in the workhouse for a month.[80] She may have been required to remain for this length of time to stop her going in and out as frequently.

Officials in NDU did not use the term prostitute to describe women on admission. The workhouse did have a separation ward, but it is not apparent how women were assigned to it. In 1900–1901 and 1910–1911 the designation 'B' was entered in the occupation column of the admission register alongside a number of women's names. The average age of the women (thirty-three in 1901 and thirty-nine in 1911) and the addresses from which they entered, such as Tyrone Street and Mabbot Street, which were noted as 'immoral' areas, indicate that these women may have been prostitutes. In 1910–1911, 6 per cent of adult women admissions were registered with a 'B', the majority

---

79 In January 1865, of 320 admissions to Belfast by adult women, twenty-one were prostitutes; average age twenty-five, average length of stay thirty-seven days; sixteen had health problems, six were noted to have syphilis, one was insane. In January 1878, of 454 adult women admissions, forty-nine were prostitutes; sixteen were noted to have a disability, seven were venereal; average age 28.5, average length of stay forty-six days; eighty-two days for medical cases. In January 1901, 54 of 604 adult women admissions were prostitutes; average age thirty-six, average length of stay twenty-seven days: Belfast BG Indoor Relief Registers.
80 Belfast BG Indoor Relief Registers, 1864–1865, 1874, 1900–1901.

of whom stayed for relatively long periods. Excluding those staying for six days or less (21 of 159), the average length of stay was 3.3 months. As in Belfast a number of the women made repeat visits. Rosanne R., whose age was given first as thirty-nine and then as forty, was admitted five times in 1910–1911 from a variety of temporary addresses, including a landing in North King Street. Having spent most of the winter in the workhouse Rosanne made three further visits in late summer and early autumn, staying three days, seven days and then twenty-seven days. Around 20 per cent of 'B's were accompanied by children, which is similar to the proportion of prostitutes admitted to Belfast Workhouse with children. One of the reasons women sought admission to the workhouse, rather than an asylum or refuge, was that they could enter and leave with their children. Some of the women admitted to NDU were clearly familiar with the workhouse system. Kate G., who was twenty-four, was admitted with her baby daughter, Mary, who had been born in Wexford Workhouse. Anne O. was admitted in January 1911 with two children, George aged six and Christopher, who was a baby. All three had come from Balrothery Workhouse. It is possible Anne came to NDU with the intention of making provision for George since she left him behind in NDU when she was discharged with Christopher on 16 March. George was sent to the children's department of the workhouse in Cabra, where he remained until 1917 when he left to take up a situation.[81]

Separation wards were a physical manifestation of the fear aroused by female sexuality. In many provincial workhouses, these wards had few occupants. Officials were cautious about categorising women and it seems unlikely that women would have described themselves as prostitutes. Indeed, some women objected to their classification and sought to have it changed. In February 1862, three women 'classed as prostitutes' applied to the Westport Board of Guardians 'to be changed to another class'. The board, however, refused 'to do so on inquiry'.[82] Separation wards in city workhouses were busier, but officials in Belfast Workhouse appear to have been unusual in routinely describing women as prostitutes on admission. McCormick suggests that we should think of these women not as vulnerable victims, but as 'exploiting' workhouse relief.[83] This is to misunderstand both the reality of these women's lives and the operation of the relief system. They were not passive victims of circumstance, but they were victims of poverty and they were not exploiting the system, they were simply making use of it. People were entitled to enter and leave as they pleased and while guardians and officials found people going in and out annoying, they recognised that

81 NDU BG Indoor Relief Registers, 1900–1901, 1910–1911.
82 Westport BG Minutes, 6 February 1862.
83 McCormick, *Regulating Sexuality*, p. 17.

there was little they could do to stop it. Attitudes to sexual morality were complex. There was a general belief that vice was contagious and that young girls and respectable women needed to be protected from the immoral and disreputable, but there was also awareness that morality was a grey area and that over-hasty judgements could have far-reaching consequences. There was some sympathy for unmarried mothers, particularly those who were felt to be victims of male lust. Women who appeared too assertive or shameless, however, did not qualify for sympathy and were treated more harshly. As the classification system became more rigid, with less space for ambiguity, so the tendency to penalise women for 'immoral' behaviour became more pronounced.

7

Mendicancy and Vagrancy

Under the poor law system, relief was both targeted at and largely limited to the settled poor. Poor law guardians and officials sought to restrict relief as much as possible to local residents, regarding applicants who came from outside the union with suspicion and, in some cases, hostility. This is particularly evident with regard to vagrants. Vagrancy was perceived as a social problem from the early modern period. Widely associated with crime and social disorder, the mobile poor were viewed as dangerous and subversive. Vagrants were the epitome of the undeserving poor; people who could work but chose not to. Having opted out of settled society, vagrants represented a challenge and a threat to its culture and values. This was particularly evident in Ireland where attachment to land and locality was intense.[1] Attitudes to vagrancy in Ireland were in many ways typical of those displayed throughout Europe and North America, where 'institutionalization and incarceration' were widely seen as the most appropriate responses.[2] Legislation introduced in the eighteenth century empowered Irish local authorities to licence settled beggars, and confine vagrants and wandering beggars in houses of industry. At the same time, mendicity associations sought to reduce visible begging by providing aid for the deserving poor whilst denying and thus discouraging the undeserving.[3] It

---

1 This chapter draws on the concept of 'sedentarism' developed by Robbie McVeigh in relation to the traveller community in Ireland. McVeigh has noted that attachment to land and locality in Ireland is important in understanding hostility towards the traveller community whose members are regarded with 'a mixture of mistrust and envy': Robbie McVeigh, 'The Specificity of Irish Racism', *Race and Class*, 33 (1992), p. 41. See also, Mary Burke, *'Tinkers': Synge and the Cultural History of the Irish Traveller* (Oxford: Oxford University Press, 2009), pp. 4–9.

2 Paul Ocobock, 'Introduction', in A. L. Beier and Paul Ocobock (eds), *Cast Out: Vagrancy and Homelessness in Global and Historical Perspective* (Athens: Ohio University Press, 2008), p. 10.

3 Laurence M. Geary, '"The Whole Country Was in Motion": Mendicancy and Vagrancy in Pre-Famine Ireland', in Jacqueline Hill and Colm Lennon (eds), *Luxury and Austerity* (Dublin: UCD Press, 1999), pp. 121–36.

was not until 1847, however, that legislation against vagrancy was introduced in Ireland following the Poor Relief Extension Act. The Irish poor law authorities were determined to avoid the English practice of providing separate wards to accommodate vagrants, arguing that casual wards would institutionalise vagrancy in Ireland.[4] Vagrants were not accommodated separately or treated differently from other categories of paupers, although, since they generally stayed for one night only, they were kept in probationary wards and rarely admitted to the main body of the workhouse.

Over the course of the nineteenth century, the terminology used to categorise the mobile poor changed. In the early years of the Irish poor law, vagrancy was closely linked with mendicancy and begging. By the end of the nineteenth century, mendicancy in the form of the wandering beggar (most often female), was thought to have largely disappeared from Ireland. Vagrancy, personified by the figure of the tramp (most often male), was now mainly associated with crime and degeneracy. Vagrants were viewed as members of the residuum or underclass; people whose lifestyle was a choice rather than a necessity. As a consequence attitudes became harsher. Changes in terminology and attitudes are evident both in social commentary and in poor law records. The number of people described as mendicants or beggars in workhouse admission registers declined markedly from the 1850s. Admissions categorised as tramps increased over the period, although usage of the term 'tramp' was mainly confined to unions in the north. From 1869, poor law officials were required to keep a record of the number of night lodgers (people making overnight stays) accommodated in the workhouse. It was recognised that not all night lodgers were vagrants and the central authorities drew a distinction between 'ins and outs', who were people who made frequent visits to a particular workhouse, generally remaining for no more than a few days at a time and vagrants or tramps who moved around the country and used workhouses as lodging houses. With the exception of 'night lodger', which had a clear and specific meaning, all these terms – mendicant, vagrant, tramp, in-and-out – were loosely defined and highly porous. How and when they were applied depended on local custom and practice.

Mendicancy or public begging was perceived as a significant social problem in pre-Famine Ireland. Travellers often recounted their shock at being met by large crowds of beggars when they arrived in Irish market towns. Popular culture, reinforced by the teachings of the Catholic Church,

---

4 For the treatment of vagrants and casuals under the English poor law, see Lorie Charlesworth, *Welfare's Forgotten Past: A Socio-Legal History of the Poor Law* (London: Routledge, 2010), pp. 168–75; M. A. Crowther, *The Workhouse System 1834–1929: The History of an English Social Institution* (London: Batsford, 1981), pp. 247–66; and Audrey Eccles, *Vagrancy in Law and Practice under the Old Poor Law* (Farnham: Ashgate, 2012).

was believed to encourage mendicancy. In England, it was claimed, the beggar was an outcast 'whose apparent misery is ascribed to imposture or vice ... and who is relieved, not so much to satisfy his wants as to get rid of his presence'. In Ireland, by contrast, he was an accepted member of society.[5] Social attitudes to begging were not indiscriminate, however. Folk beliefs and religious teachings distinguished between local, settled beggars who were deserving of compassion and assistance; and professional, wandering beggars who were associated with criminality and vice, and were feared and disliked as a consequence.[6] Provisions to suppress mendicancy and vagrancy were included in the first draft of the Poor Law Bill but were felt to be unjustifiable given the limited nature of the measure.[7] In order to make vagrancy a criminal offence, as in England, it would have been necessary, ministers felt, to grant a right to relief. Many people, including the poor law commissioners and some boards of guardians, remained convinced that legislation to suppress vagrancy was necessary. Unless checked, the 'moral taint' of mendicancy would, the poor law commissioners predicted in 1840, 'deteriorate the entire mass of the population'. Moreover, without effective action the poor law could not operative effectively since, 'so long as vagrants shall be permitted to levy so-called charitable contributions from the public on the plea of destitution, real or fictitious, they will rarely resort to the workhouse'.[8] The availability of poor relief appeared to have done little to reduce the number of beggars. In March 1846, the Armagh Board of Guardians recorded their conviction that a vagrancy act of some kind was necessary 'to put a stop to the practice of public begging which is still extensively practiced in Ireland notwithstanding the Poor Relief Act'.[9]

The introduction of outdoor relief in 1847 provided the opportunity to legislate. Under the Vagrant Act wandering abroad and begging became an offence punishable by one-month's imprisonment, as did going from one poor law union to another for the purpose of obtaining relief.[10] The Act appears to have had little immediate impact. Local officials were often reluctant to initiate prosecutions, being more concerned to ensure that the mobile poor remained mobile and did not form a charge on their particular union. In 1853, the poor law commissioners issued a circular warning against

5 N. W. Senior, 'Mendicancy in Ireland', *Edinburgh Review*, 77 (1843), p. 400.
6 Peter Gray, *The Making of the Irish Poor Law 1815–1843* (Manchester: Manchester University Press, 2009), pp 15–16, 70; Geary, 'The Whole Country Was in Motion'; Niall Ó Ciosain, 'Boccoughs and God's Poor', p. 7.
7 Gray, *The Making of the Irish Poor Law*, pp. 171, 179–80.
8 *Annual Report*, HC, 1840 [245], p. 38; and Geary, 'The Whole Country was in Motion', p. 131.
9 Armagh Board of Guardians Minutes, 3 March 1846, PRONI, BG/2/A/3.
10 Vagrant Act, 1847, 10 and 11 Vic., c. 84.

the practice of issuing discharged paupers 'who were desirous of proceeding to distant parts of the country' with documents which they might use to obtain food and lodging from workhouses along the way. This practice, it was noted, 'is open to very serious objection, not only on account of its tendency to encourage mendicancy but also as promoting a direct breach of the third section of the Vagrant Act'.[11]

In the early 1850s the social disruption caused by the Famine was evident in many parts of the country. Describing the state of Waterford in 1851, local MP, H. W. Barron, declared that such was the multitude of dispossessed and displaced people 'wandering about the country as beggars or thieves ... that the farmers cannot sleep at night lest their houses should be broken into and robbed'.[12] By the later 1850s, however, the situation appeared to have improved. In 1856 the poor law commissioners cited the almost total disappearance of deaths by the wayside as evidence of a 'material diminution of pauperism and mendicancy in Ireland'. But while mendicancy was reported to have 'materially abated' in many districts, it had not disappeared. In more prosperous counties, the commissioners concluded, 'the evil still exists in a considerable degree' and in others there was 'a strong probability of its revival'. What was needed, they argued, was 'uniform and sustained action' on the part of the constabulary to enforce the Vagrant Act, pointing out that there might not be 'a more convenient time for the repression of mendicancy than a time when the number of offenders is comparatively small, and when conviction of mendicants would not cause inconvenience to the gaols'.[13]

Asked to comment on the extent of mendicancy in 1856, most poor law inspectors described it as on the decline, attributing this to the improved state of the country. A number distinguished between different classes of vagrant or mendicant. Reporting from the northwest, Richard Bourke identified four classes of mendicant: professional beggars; vagrants; people rendered destitute by the Famine, who were 'wandering through the country preferring a life of mendicancy to the restraints of the workhouse'; and the dependents of men who had gone to England or Scotland in search of work. Bourke noted that the third and fourth classes, which were most closely linked to economic conditions, had practically disappeared so that 'with but few exceptions, the only beggars to be met with in this district belong to the professional classes'. Mendicants, he suggested, would remain 'as long as indiscriminate alms-giving continues to be the practice of the middle orders

11 Circular 30 May 1853, reprinted in 'Vagrancy in Ireland', *Appendix to the Report of the Departmental Committee on Vagrancy, Volume III*, HC, 1906 [Cd. 2892], p. 87.
12 *Hansard 3rd series*, cxv, 1276, 8 April 1851.
13 *Annual Report of the Commissioners for Administering the Laws for the Relief of the Poor in Ireland*, HC, 1856 [2105], p. 14.

of this country'.[14] There were conflicting reports on the state of professional mendicancy, which was the category that caused most concern. In the southwest, rising prosperity was said to be encouraging people to leave the workhouses to 'seek a living by begging through the country'. In Ulster, by contrast, Henry Robinson recorded a decline in the number of mendicants. The existence of the poor law had, he believed, 'to a considerable extent checked the system of alms-giving,' providing less encouragement for people to 'seek a livelihood by begging'. Where the Vagrant Act was enforced, as in Belfast, the reduction in the number of beggars was 'particularly to be observed'.[15] What might appear as contradictory – in some areas greater prosperity appeared to have reduced mendicancy while in others it had encouraged it – was in fact a reflection of the regional character of welfare provision. Ulster's minimalist welfare regime created a climate in which expectations were low, as well as levels of relief, while in the more prosperous midland and eastern counties, which relied on a casual labour force, attitudes to the mobile poor were more tolerant and treatment more generous.

More rigorous enforcement of the Vagrant Act, the poor law commissioners believed, would provide an effective check on mendicancy and vagrancy. This did not, however, prove to be the case. Prosecutions for vagrancy were on the rise from the 1860s but did little to curb what was perceived to be a growing problem. The number of prosecutions for begging and other offences rose from around 2,000 in 1870 to over 4,000 in 1889. Prosecutions for vagrancy offences were highest in cities, particularly Dublin, and lowest in the west. Leinster routinely returned significantly higher figures than other provinces; Connaught the lowest.[16] Social anxiety, which had previously centred on wandering beggars, increasingly focused on the figure of the tramp. One of the major differences between tramps and beggars, at least in popular perception, was that whereas beggars were thought to avoid workhouses as much as possible, tramps made use of them, even planning their routes according to the availability of convenient and accessible workhouses. Anxious to discourage people from utilising workhouses as temporary lodgings, the poor law commissioners had issued a circular in 1857 warning boards of guardians that workhouse regulations should be enforced for all admissions. Not subjecting overnight admissions to the ordinary

14 Report from Richard Bourke, *Annual Report of the Commissioners for Administering the Laws for the Relief of the Poor in Ireland*, HC, 1856 [2105], pp. 50–1.
15 Report from W. P. O'Brien; Report from Henry Robinson, HC, 1856 [2105], pp. 52–3, 56–7.
16 *Judicial Statistics, persons proceeded against summarily*. For the proportion of vagrancy offences 1866–1914, see Caitriona Clear, *Social Change and Everyday Life in Ireland, 1850–1922* (Manchester: Manchester University Press, 2007), pp. 178–9.

discipline of the workhouse, the commissioners observed, had 'a direct and obvious tendency to encourage vagrancy' since 'persons who may adopt a wandering and vagrant mode of life' could 'always calculate with certainty upon obtaining an asylum for the night'. Such people would, however, be deterred from applying for admission, 'when it becomes known that all parties, when admitted, will be searched, washed, and clothed in workhouse dress' and not allowed to leave without performing a task of work.[17] Strict adherence to workhouse regulations remained the official solution to almost all vagrant-related problems.

Public concern about vagrancy was most evident in southeastern counties. In the early 1860s there was reported to be a particular issue along the east coast where, according to PLI Hamilton, vagrancy appeared to be 'a regular profession'. Groups of tramps or vagrants tended to arouse alarm. Hamilton referred to 'parties' travelling 'systematically about the country from union to union bringing disease and bad habits with them. They are not of a very destitute class, and the masters have described them to me as militia men, discharged East Indian soldiers, ticket of leave men, blind men, persons who frequent races, fairs, etc., etc.' They never remained more than one night and never visited a workhouse more than once a year.[18] They were also, it appeared, becoming adept at avoiding the police. The Master of Lismore Workhouse reported that 'suspicious characters of this class' generally applied for admission late in the evening, arriving at the workhouse 'by means of paths through the fields' and leaving 'in the same manner thus avoiding passing through the town and escaping the observations of the police'. He recommended that a constable should attend the workhouse each morning at the time when paupers took their discharge. This would discourage 'idle vagabonds' from seeking admission 'and would confine relief more than at present to a class of night lodgers who are compelled to seek shelter from circumstances not under their control'. However, the Inspector General of the Constabulary, Sir Henry Brownrigg, objected to this idea suggesting instead that workhouse masters should inform the police of any suspicious characters.[19]

In response to what was described as 'the increase in professional vagrancy, and to the inconvenience caused by it in many unions', the poor law commissioners issued another circular on the subject in 1868. They reminded boards of guardians of the provisions of the Vagrant Act which included the offence of 'going from the union in which he had been resident

17 Circular, 6 August 1857, in Mooney, *Compendium*, pp. 398–400.
18 Quoted in Banks to Larcom, 18 September 1862, NAI, CSORP, 1875/18978.
19 Isaac Flower, Master of Rathdrum Workhouse to PLC, 30 August 1862; note by Sir Henry Brownrigg, 17 October 1862: CSORP, 1875/18978.

to some other union for the purpose of obtaining relief', and pointed out
that enforcement of the provisions of the act did not necessarily involve the
refusal of relief. Indeed applying for and obtaining relief could be material
elements in a prosecution, 'If, therefore, a night-lodger be known to have
offended against the act and the offence can be proved', workhouse officials
could 'on his taking his discharge from the workhouse, apprehend and take
him before a Justice or deliver him to the police'.[20] The circular appears
to have been effective in encouraging boards of guardians to take a more
proactive approach; and prosecutions increased. However, it soon became
apparent that some boards were adopting an overly zealous approach. In
1869, the commissioners were obliged to issue a further circular pointing
out that being a stranger in the union and applying for and obtaining relief
was not, in itself, an offence. There needed to be something to indicate
that a person had arrived in the union with the intention of obtaining
relief. Boards of guardians and their officers, the commissioners warned,
needed to distinguish between tramps and vagrants, whose intention could
be presumed, 'not only from their coming there and applying for relief and
obtaining it, but from other circumstances known regarding them personally'
and 'cases in which the applicant for relief has been overtaken by misfortune
or want while passing through the country on lawful business'.[21] Once again,
union officials were being asked to achieve an almost impossible task; to
take a strong stand against vagrancy whilst being alert to cases of temporary
distress and keeping an open mind about the intentions of visiting strangers.

The commissioners returned to the issue of vagrancy repeatedly in the
years 1868 to 1871. But while they advocated a more general enforcement
of the Vagrant Act, they were anxious not to exaggerate the extent of the
problem. They reacted angrily to an observation in the judicial statistics for
1869 that the restricted system of outdoor relief in Ireland was 'among the
causes of an excess of vagrancy in Ireland'. The number of vagrants and
tramps known to the police in Ireland was 12,626 compared to 33,191 in
England and Wales. Taking relative population into account, the commissioners acknowledged that this suggested an excess in Ireland of 'no less
than 3,892'. As they pointed out, however, there was a much heavier police
presence in Ireland. Workhouse relief, the commissioners insisted, tended
'to diminish mendicancy and vagrancy, inasmuch as persons so relieved
have all their wants supplied and cannot be abroad begging'. Outdoor relief,
on the other hand, 'fails to supply all the wants of the recipients, and a
large number of them, therefore, being at liberty to go where they please,
naturally supplement their means of livelihood by wandering abroad and

20 Circular, 28 November 1868, in Mooney, *Compendium*, pp. 400–1.
21 Circular, 5 November 1869, in Mooney, *Compendium*, pp. 403–4.

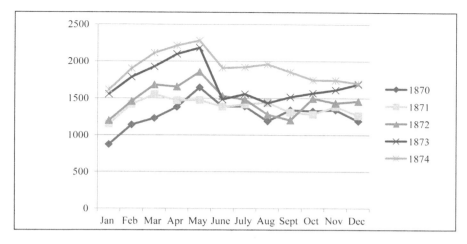

Figure 7.1   Admissions of night-lodgers 1870–1874.
Source: Return showing the total number of Night-Lodgers (Casuals) relieved
in the Workhouses in Ireland in the first week in each month from the 6 March
1869 to the first week in December 1874, inclusive: CSORP 1878/18978

begging'. The key to the suppression of both vagrancy and mendicancy,
they maintained, lay in 'the withholding of alms, and rests, therefore in the
hands of the public itself and in the exercise of individual discretion on the
part of every member of society'.[22] Weekly figures for the number of night
lodgers relieved in workhouses were returned from 1869. These followed,
the commissioners noted in 1870, a seasonal pattern rising in the winter
and falling in the summer (see Figure 7.1). Whilst acknowledging that 'the
power of obtaining with ease and impunity a night's lodging in every union
workhouse affords great facilities to professional vagrants', the commissioners were hopeful that 'this branch of the vagrant system has now been
placed under effectual restraint'.[23]

The tramp issue did not go away, however. In the mid-1870s there were

22 Extracts from *Annual Report of the Poor Law Commissioners for 1869*, NAI, CSORP
    1875/18978. Returning to the comparison with England in 1871, the commissioners
    noted that prosecutions for vagrancy offences in England were 'largely in excess of
    those in Ireland, estimated relatively to the population' while far fewer casuals were
    relieved in workhouse (5,430 on 1 January 1870 in England, compared to 174 in Ireland).
    They were thus 'compelled to conclude that there is a far greater number of vagrants
    in England than in Ireland relatively to the population': Extracts from *Annual Report of
    the Poor Law Commissioners for 1871*, CSORP 1875/18978.
23 Extracts from *Annual Report of the Poor Law Commissioners for 1870*, CSORP
    1875/18978.

reports of tramps 'infesting' parts of the country and complaints about the 'tramp system'. In December 1874, the *Irish Times* claimed to have received several letters from different parts of Leinster regarding the 'extraordinary increase' in the number of tramps in the region. The language used to describe their activities was calculated to instil fear. Tramps were said to 'prowl about' in gangs; one of the gang might claim to be 'a tinker, or a mender of umbrellas, or a ploughman wanting work'; women, 'nearly in a state of nudity', were used to allay suspicion. The women would approach a house first, 'and once in the men come up and force their way in; the trade is a very lucrative one'.[24] There were similar reports from County Sligo where 'idle, ill-disposed individuals' were said to be wandering the country, 'whose only object in life is plunder'. According to the *Sligo Champion*, many of the murders and burglaries committed in the county the previous year could be 'attributed to tramps who, having no fixed place of residence or a desire to earn their livelihood by industry or honesty, prowl about the country praying on their neighbour's property and hesitating at no means however foul to accomplish their evil designs'. Readers were warned to be on the alert and to suppress their natural sympathy for the poor. Tramps deserved no quarter, 'clothed though they may be in the garb of poverty and suffering in order to elicit the commiseration of an easily-deceived public'.[25]

As with other aspects of poor law administration, there were evident tensions between different branches of local government. Police and magistrates complained that poor law officials were not doing enough to discourage vagrants, while boards of guardians complained about magistrates failing to commit people sent before them on vagrancy charges and lack of co-operation from the police. When the Resident Magistrate, T. W. Fitzgerald, wrote to the Chairman of Boyle Board of Guardians in 1874, alerting him to the fact that a number of crimes committed in the area had been traced to tramps and observing that 'the boards of guardians can do much by prosecuting such persons in every instance where they seek relief at their respective poor houses', the clerk of the union commented that this had been tried some years before and the resident magistrate had declined to act. The master then interjected that the chairman 'gave directions some time ago to send for the police; that has been done but nothing came of it'.[26] In England, where vagrancy prosecutions were heard by ordinary magistrates,

24 Cutting from *Irish Times* (n. d.), in Fitzgerald to Under Secretary, 3 December 1874, CSORP 1875/18978.
25 Cutting from *Sligo Champion* (n. d.), in Fitzgerald to Under Secretary, 16 December 1874, CSORP 1875/18978.
26 Fitzgerald to King Harman, 23 November 1874; Report of Boyle Poor Law Meeting, *Irish Times* (n. d.), in Fitzgerald to Under Secretary, 3 December 1874, CSORP 1875/18978.

the same officials were responsible both for the control and punishment of vagrants, and for poor law administration. The interconnectedness of these two branches of administration, Lorie Charlesworth has argued, meant that when a pauper sought aid 'he or she risks rather more than a refusal'.[27] In Ireland, where vagrancy cases were often heard by resident magistrates, who had no connection with poor law administration, less interconnection meant less risk.

Refusal of relief could be challenged, but this too involved risk. In December 1870, Philip Doyle complained first to a magistrate and then to the poor law commissioners that 'although he was in a destitute state, he had been refused relief by the guardians of the North Dublin Union'.[28] The case was reported in the *Freeman's Journal* and prompted an investigation by the board of guardians. On 21 December, Relieving Officer, Daniel Gilligan, reported that having inspected his books, he found that Philip had first applied for relief in March and had been admitted provisionally. He had taken his discharge after a few days, leaving the workhouse before his case was considered by the admission board. He had claimed to be living in Church Street, although this proved to be false and to have spent the previous nine months in Liverpool. He applied again in August and was again admitted provisionally. He was admitted fully the following week and left three days later. He then spent some months in London, returning to Dublin in the autumn. He had applied to the workhouse master late on a Saturday night and was admitted, but was rejected by the admission board the following Monday and discharged. He applied again in December and was again rejected. It was then he had made his complaint. The relieving officer stated that he had informed Philip that if he got a 'dispensary district note of illness that I would admit him. He told me that he would not go to the dispensary but would break the windows of my house that night.' Having heard the relieving officer's report, the board of guardians resolved that the man should be prosecuted as a vagrant. The following week Gilligan 'reported that he had had Philip conveyed to the police station on that night and laid a charge against him of having several times broken the Vagrant Act. He remained there that night and was brought up next morning for trial. Mr Campbell, Reliving Officer of the South Dublin Union and I proved severally that Doyle was in the habit of frequently going from one Union to the other and remaining but two or three days in either, on which evidence he was committed by Mr O'Donnell and sentenced to one months imprisonment with hard labour.'[29]

27 Charlesworth, *Welfare's Forgotten Past*, p. 172.
28 *Freeman's Journal*, 13 December 1870.
29 NDU Minutes, 28 December 1870. See also, 14 and 21 December 1870.

Philip was clearly well acquainted with the poor law system knowing how and when to apply for relief. By making a complaint he was able to cast himself as a victim and put pressure on workhouse officials. In his initial complaint, Philip stated that 'he was starving, and that he absolutely required relief', prompting the magistrate, C. J. O'Donnell, to remind the guardians that their officials 'incurred a great responsibility in refusing relief to a destitute person; they might become amenable to a charge of manslaughter should a person die who claimed and was refused relief'.[30] Although Philip's complaint exposed him to the risk of prosecution, and was to land him in jail, he achieved his immediate objective, forcing NDU officials to admit him while the complaint was investigated. He spent the period from 14 to 21 December in the workhouse, which he may have regarded as a victory, of sorts.

When consulted about the need for further legislation in 1875, the Local Government Board sounded a cautious note, pointing out that the number of casual poor was far from excessive and considerably lower than in England, judging from the number of night lodgers accommodated in workhouses and casual wards. The number of night lodgers relieved in England and Wales was stated to be twice that in Ireland, even though the number of workhouse inmates was only about three times the number in Ireland, while the population of England was four times that of Ireland. The board reiterated their opposition to casual wards and stated their preference for 'the treatment of all applicants for relief as destitute poor under one and the same system of workhouse management and regulation'.[31] They did, however, agree to issue yet another circular, drawing the attention of boards of guardians to the previous circulars on tramps and casuals, 'asking them to co-operate with constabulary in taking descriptions and recommending that, as was the practice in England, able-bodied males who stayed one night should be required to break stones before they left and women to pick oakum'.[32]

The dangers inherent in an overzealous approach became evident in 1875 in relation to the case of John L. who was committed to Limerick Gaol under the Vagrant Act and died there before the expiration of his sentence. John had been admitted to Glin Workhouse on 4 June and subsequently prosecuted under the Vagrant Act and committed to gaol. On investigation it was discovered that he was a member of the Limerick Militia and had been on his way to join his regiment for training. The case was raised in Parliament and became the subject of an inquiry under LGI Richard Bourke.

30 *Freeman's Journal*, 13 December 1870.
31 Banks to Burke, 11 February 1875, CSORP 1875/18978.
32 Circular, 31 March 1875, CSORP 1875/18978.

Relieving Officer, Maurice Fitzgerald, explained that John had applied for relief:

> and as he did not belong to this Union and was not able to give a satisfactory account of himself and appeared strong and healthy, and the country at that time infested with that class of people, I thought it my duty ... to prosecute him as a vagrant.

Fitzgerald explained that John had said nothing about being in the militia until he was arrested and even then had said nothing about being on his way to training. Having previously been criticised for granting too much provisional relief, the relieving officer felt he had no option but to prosecute. He had been informed that 'in the case of strong men able to work', it was 'a great neglect of my duty not taking them before a magistrate and letting him deal with them ... I acted under the instruction of the Board'.[33] Bourke concluded that in prosecuting John, the relieving officer was carrying out the verbal orders of the board of guardians. The circumstances connected with John's application for relief, he observed:

> differed in no respect from those of an ordinary traveller seeking shelter and food for the night ... [and] no special circumstances were relied on in support of the charge beyond the facts of the man having applied for relief and received it, and not 'belonging to the Glin Union'.

Twelve other people, he noted, had been prosecuted to conviction in the union under similar circumstances in the previous nine months. Bourke was highly critical of the 'impropriety' of the course pursued by the board of guardians in allowing the relieving officer such discretionary power, adding that he could:

> scarcely conceive a person less fit to exercise it judiciously than Mr Fitzgerald. Besides his youth and inexperience he appears to me to want the necessary capacity for distinguishing between the class of vagrants coming before him, and his one idea of duty appears to be to confine all relief to persons living in the union or natives of it.

However, he noted that John's case seemed no different from that of any ordinary tramp of the class which the board of guardians seemed to have been deliberately authorising their officers to prosecute: 'Tramps

---

33 Evidence of Maurice Fitzgerald, 16 July 1875, NAI, CSORP 1875/12889.

of this class come one day and go the next and if the direct order of the guardians to prosecute were required in each case most of the offenders against this part of the Vagrant Law would go away unpunished'. It was for the magistrate to judge whether the evidence proved the offence, 'which depends altogether on the purpose and intention with which the accused acted'.[34] Determining intention, however, was a highly subjective process.

Conflict between magistrates and boards of guardians continued to hamper efforts to suppress vagrancy. Despite general agreement that vagrancy was a problem and that action should be taken, there was little agreement on the best way to achieve this. The central difficulty was that so much depended on subjective judgments; poor law officials were required to make judgements about the veracity and moral character of those applying to them for relief; magistrates were required to assess the evidence presented to them and apply the law. All were conscious that there were cost implications. In 1878, the Portumna Board of Guardians complained bitterly to the Local Government Board when the Resident Magistrate, Major Percy, discharged two men who had been taken before him as vagrants. The men had been admitted to the workhouse on the night of 4 April:

> and as they had all the appearances of being professional tramps, and not being able to give a satisfactory account of themselves, he had them taken before Major Percy RM who refused to commit them unless the expenses attendant on their removal to the County Gaol, Galway, were defrayed from the poor rates.

The men were discharged with a caution. Major Percy explained that, having carefully inquired into the case, he had concluded that the men were not 'professional tramps' and being unwilling to incur the expense of sending them to Galway Gaol, had exercised his discretion and discharged them. He had, he declared, 'never refused to commit a professional tramp or vagrant when proved to be so', but thought that the custom adopted in other unions, 'viz that of obliging the tramps to take a bath on admission and compelling him to do half a day's work for his night's lodging would have equally if not more a deterrent effect when known as committing to gaol at heavy expense'.[35]

The following year the Navan Board of Guardians complained that their efforts to discourage vagrancy were being frustrated by local magistrates. The workhouse master had reported that eighteen night lodgers had been

---

34 Report of Richard Bourke, 17 July 1875, CSORP 1875/12889.
35 Percy to Under Secretary, 26 April 1878: NAI, CSORP 1878/8462.

sent before the magistrates. Two had been committed for trial on vagrancy
charges and the rest discharged. An explanation was sought from the resident
magistrate who maintained that the evidence presented, which rested on the
'fact of their having obtained relief in this workhouse on a former occasion'
was insufficient. One woman, Eliza B. who was accompanied by her two
children, had stated that she had been several times in the workhouse
without being prosecuted and had 'fairly assumed that no prosecution would
be instituted against her on this occasion'. Had she 'been told when applying
for admission that she would be prosecuted the next day, she would not have
made use of the house'.[36] Here again the resident magistrate and workhouse
master appear to have been applying different criteria as to what constituted
vagrancy. Workhouse officials tended to overlook isolated or occasional
overnight stays, only taking action against people who made repeated visits.
Resident magistrates, on the other hand, looked for consistency of approach,
assuming that if someone met the criteria for a vagrant they should be
prosecuted immediately.

That enforcing the regulations with regard to baths and work was not
in itself an effective deterrent, is evident from the experience of officials
at Lismore Workhouse, County Waterford. In May 1888, the master noted
in his journal that 114 tramps had sought lodgings in the workhouse in the
last week: sixty-nine men; twenty-four women; and twenty-one children,
prompting the board of guardians to direct that every able-bodied tramp
should be compelled to break the prescribed number of stones. The very
high number of admissions was partly a product of the season – numbers
generally peaked in May – and of the location of the workhouse, but may
also have reflected a tendency on the part of the master to designate people,
particularly women and children, as tramps who might not have been so
designated in other workhouses. Later that month, the master reported that
a tramp had been taken to the police station with the intention of prosecuting
him for insubordination, after he had refused to break any stones. A
magistrate could not be found, however, and the man was let off with a
caution. Nevertheless, the 'fact of the constabulary being called', the master
believed, had 'a salutary effect, for the number of tramps is since reducing'.[37]
The following spring the issue resurfaced, and once again the workhouse
rules were strictly enforced. A number of those admitted were reported to be
too feeble or delicate to do any work, suggesting that these were hardly the
'idle vagabonds' of popular mythology.[38]

Complaints about tramps continued to be voiced, most regularly from

---

36 Plunkett to Burke, 28 August 1879: NAI, CSORP 1879/15103.
37 Master's Journal Lismore, 16 and 30 May, 1888: NAI, BG 111/F3.
38 On 29 May the master recorded that of twenty-one tramps admitted, eight were unable

unions along the east coast and on routes out of Dublin. In 1893 an editorial in the *Kildare Observer* called for more severe legal sanctions to deal with vagrants. The 'tramp nuisance', the paper argued, was becoming a significant social problem, the worst aspect of which was the presence of tramp children who 'brought up in the midst of poverty and wretchedness ... and breathing an atmosphere of corruption and vice during their early lives ... as a natural consequence, inherit all the evil ways of their parents'.[39] Subsequent correspondence on the subject warned against confusing professional tramps with itinerant beggars, who went 'from house to house soliciting arms'. The latter 'were not only tolerated but encouraged by the peasantry'. The best way to discourage tramps, it was suggested, was not to give money to itinerants. Some years later, convinced that Kildare unions were 'being made the victims ... of hordes of tramps', the *Observer* called for a law of settlement, arguing that it was unfair that ratepayers in Kildare should be obliged to support vagrants from other parts of the country. The Naas and Celbridge Unions, it was claimed, were being 'continually victimised by the vagrant class' and their workhouses 'used as halfway houses at which tramps coming from or going to the city get housed and fed and at the expense of the ratepayers ... while the districts from which those persons originally belonged to are well rid of them and benefit accordingly'.[40]

In the early twentieth century, the figure of the tramp came to act as a focus for public concern about degeneracy and social decay. In a typically alarmist account, the writer and social activist, Laura Stephens, described the tramp as a drain on and danger to society, 'a genuine parasite, living at the cost of his host', surviving by intimidation at best and criminality at worst. Anyone 'who has lived in the country', Stephens claimed, 'will know how the visits of well-known tramps strike terror into the hearts of farmers' wives and cottagers living in lonely places. Not only was the tramp 'dirty and degenerate', but he was also 'rearing up a crop of dirty and degenerate children, the tramps of the coming generation'. Despite laws against vagrancy, the 'tramp evil', she claimed, showed no sign of abating. Stephens advocated the introduction of labour colonies together with powers to remove children from tramp parents and place them in the care of the state. Only by such

to break stones being too feeble and disabled – all got baths: Master's Journal Lismore, 29 May 1889.

39 *Kildare Observer*, 15 July 1893. For the increasing importance attached to child welfare within social commentary and social activism, see Sarah-Anne Buckley, 'Found in a "Dying" Condition: Nurse Children in Ireland, 1872–1952', in Elaine Farrell (ed.), *'She Said She Was in the Family Way': Pregnancy and Infancy in Modern Ireland* (London: Institute of Historical Research, 2012) pp. 145–62; and Maria Luddy, The Early Years of the NSPCC in Ireland', *Eire-Ireland*, 44 (2009), pp. 62–90.

40 *Kildare Observer*, 17 July 1893, 24 February 1900.

measures could 'any effective blow be struck at the root of vagrancy, which now flourishes in a rank growth and spreads out its poisonous branches on every side'.[41] Similar views were common in social commentary of the time both in Ireland and England, and reflected a growing tendency to pathologise social problems such as long-term poverty and homelessness.

There were some dissenting voices. J. M. Synge published a very different and highly romanticised, account of vagrancy in Wicklow in 1906. Synge, who saw much to celebrate and even to envy in the tramp lifestyle, was careful to make a distinction between vagrants or tramps and mendicants or professional beggars. The former were physically fit and many lived to a great age. They made no pretence or plea of infirmity when begging and rarely committed crimes. Synge claimed that he had 'never seen a tramp who was drunk or unseemly. If they are treated with tact they are courteous and forbearing, and if anyone does not give them the recognition they think due to them in Wicklow, they are content to avenge themselves with a word of satire.' The workhouse system, Synge noted, was central to the maintenance of the tramp system in County Wicklow. He acknowledged that a 'few of these people have been on the road for generations; but fairly often they seem to have merely drifted out from the ordinary people of the villages, and do not differ greatly from the class they come from'. Vagrancy, in his view, was often a positive choice and reflected a sense of pride and independence as well as a lack of resources.[42]

Newspaper commentary continued to reflect ambivalent views on vagrants. There was a general feeling that something needed to be done about vagrancy, coupled with awareness that not all itinerants were professional tramps. A report in the *Irish Independent* on measures being taken by the Lurgan Board of Guardians to deal with the tramp nuisance in 1905, noted that the medical officer had divided tramps into three classes: professional tramps; drunken and lazy individuals who either could not or would not work; and people genuinely seeking work. The latter, the paper argued, deserved help while the former should be committed to 'a real workhouse' and only released on proof of industry and reformed habits.[43] A few years later the *Independent* reported that a proposal by the Ballymoney Board of Guardians to use cold baths as a 'punitive engine' against tramps had been opposed by one member of the board 'as an act of torture'.[44] Other boards

41 Laura Stephens, 'The Tramp', *Dana*, 11 (March 1905), pp. 339–43.
42 J. M. Synge, 'The Vagrants of Wicklow', *Collected Works*, Vol. II, (Washington: Catholic Press of America, 1982), pp. 202–8.
43 *Irish Independent*, 11 March 1905.
44 *Irish Independent*, 8 March 1909.

of guardians shared this reluctance to adopt a punitive regime, although the motivation was often official lethargy as much as concern for pauper welfare.

As the Local Government Board acknowledged in a memorandum submitted to the departmental committee on vagrancy in 1906, while workhouse regulations stated that all persons should be subject to the normal rules regarding searching, clothing, discipline and diet, these rules were 'we regret to say, very often not adhered to. The regulations regarding the giving of baths is evaded in every possible way, on the plea of ill-health etc., and the porters appointed in many workhouses are often physically unfit to adopt stringent measures with the troublesome class of inmate.' Regional differences were again highlighted. In western districts, in addition to professional tramps, the vagrant class was reported to include local beggars. These were generally 'unoffending poor persons who have lost their homes and frequent the country and small towns where they were originally known when in better circumstances'. Beggars were 'not unpopular with country people and seldom interfered with by the police'. Professional tramps, on the other hand, were said to be widely disliked. Rare in the extreme west, they were reported to be common in eastern and midland counties where they levied 'a kind of blackmail, people being only too glad to get rid of them for a trifle either in food or money'. Such people were, however, very difficult to prosecute under the Vagrant Act, as they usually claimed to be looking for work. 'This difficulty in obtaining convictions', the memorandum concluded, 'together with the leniency towards the genuine beggar before referred to, accounts for the comparatively small number of prosecutions of workhouse casuals in Ireland under the Vagrany Act [sic].'[45]

The poor law authorities continued to play down the issue of vagrancy, but were forced to acknowledge public disquiet. In their 1906 Annual Report, the Local Government Board noted that while the number of individual night lodgers or casuals admitted to workhouses 'seems small in proportion to the population of the country', the average number of individuals seeking admission was increasing year on year. The figure for 1905–1906 was 879 compared to 745 the previous year; and 535 in 1894–1895.[46] This class was said to form a significant presence in workhouses in the eastern, northern and midland counties where 'the professional tramp abounds. These persons are constantly moving from one workhouse to another, seldom remaining more than a night in the same place and in their wanderings visit many workhouses during the course of a year.' There was, the board admitted, 'a

---

45 'Vagrancy in Ireland', Appendix to the Report of the Departmental Committee on Vagrancy, Volume III, HC, 1906 [Cd. 2892], p. 86.
46 In 1872–1873, the average number had been 287: *Annual Report*, HC, 1873 [Cd. 794], p. 16; 1906 [Cd. 3102], p. 525; and 1895 [Cd. 7818], p. 15.

very general feeling throughout the country that the present condition of the law dealing with vagrants is unsatisfactory'.[47] Boards of guardians increasingly saw little point in attempting to prosecute vagrants. With so much stress on the dangers posed by tramps, containment was seen as the priority. In 1911, Naas guardians criticised the workhouse master for prosecuting too many tramps arguing that this was a waste of time and money, and might be counter-productive. As the Chairman, George Wolfe, commented, it was safer to have tramps 'inside the walls of this place than going into haystacks, for you can't tell what may occur'. The cost of maintaining tramps in the workhouse, his colleague, Thomas Lacey, observed, 'would not be half as much' as that of prosecution. Their relieving officer agreed. The workhouse, he pointed out, 'was made for those people, but the hay ricks and farmyards were not', adding that some people might be 'found dead on the roadside if not admitted'.[48]

The Vice-Regal Commission devoted special attention to vagrants and tramps. In their report they drew a distinction between casuals, by which they meant people 'frequently in receipt of indoor relief in the same workhouse', who were mainly to be found in cities and vagrants who were people 'living a wandering life without a home'. On 11 March 1905 there were reported to be 813 casuals in Irish workhouses and 878 vagrants or tramps. Not only were casuals distinct from vagrants, in the view of the commission, but tramps could also be distinguished from other itinerants. No 'person of perception', it was claimed, 'could mistake tramps for anything but what they are'. Unlike the situation in England and Scotland, where there was, they acknowledged, a genuine difficulty in telling tramps from tradesmen and labourers 'honestly looking for work', in Ireland there was very little casual employment so that itinerant workmen or tradesmen were 'few in comparison with the habitual tramps'. The commission estimated that there were around 2,000 tramps in Ireland and that this number included four or five males for every female.[49] When the figures returned for the different provinces are examined, however, it would appear that there was some confusion between the different categories. In Munster workhouses there were reported to be 440 casuals and 231 tramps, compared to 147 casuals and 366 tramps in Leinster workhouses.[50] Even allowing for the fact that the more geographically remote Munster unions were rarely included on

47 *Annual Report of the Local Government Board for Ireland*, 1906 [Cd. 3102], p. xv.
48 *Kildare Observer*, 23 December 1911. See also, 16 December 1911.
49 *Poor Law Reform Commission (Ireland). Report of the Vice-Regal Commission on Poor Law Reform in Ireland. Volume I*, HC, 1906 [Cd. 3202], pp. 52–4
50 Return No. 4: Classification ... of Healthy Workhouse Inmates According to Character, and Estimates as to the Number of Casuals and Vagrants, *Poor Law Reform Commission (Ireland). Appendix to the Report, Vol. II*, HC, 1906 [Cd. 3203], p. 16.

tramp itineraries, it seems unlikely that the disparities were really that great. It seems more likely that some of those categorised as casuals in Munster were being returned as tramps in Leinster. Given the extent to which people moved around the country, it is also possible that the same people were being classified differently in different unions.

The underlying causes of vagrancy were stated to be 'drunkenness (most of all) and other vicious habits'. Asked to comment on the causes of destitution among casual inmates, workhouse masters most commonly cited idleness, laziness or thriftlessness and 'addicted to drink', though a number also gave 'want of employment' as a cause.[51] Having, as it was claimed, met hundreds of tramps and talked to them, the commission concluded that they spent their lives:

> in trudging along by daylight without any definite purpose or business to influence their movements, except that the greatest number keep to the direct roads between workhouses. Some vagrants frequent one area or group of counties and become familiar with their district and its possibilities for gifts or blackmail.

They recommended that labour houses should be established for this class, financed by central government and under the control of the Prisons Board, but that relieving officers should be empowered to provide food and lodging in cases of genuine working men seeking employment. Two classes that were not to be sent to labour houses were old and infirm people, 'well known in a locality who exist on the charity of friends and neighbours', and itinerant musicians and other entertainers.[52]

All the evidence received, it was claimed, was 'most hostile to tramps'. Witnesses, 'almost without exception' were said to be in favour of 'depriving this class of their liberty to march around the country terrorizing women … and to escape any regular exertion for self-support'.[53] This was not in fact the case. William O'Hare from Belfast, for example, had argued that the tramp question was widely misunderstood and the extent of the problem greatly exaggerated. The total cost of accommodating night lodgers throughout Ireland, he pointed out, was around £1,600 over the year or £400 per province. James Hore, the Chairman of Wexford Urban District Council,

---

51 The masters of twenty-two workhouses gave 'want of employment' as a cause of destitution among casuals: Ballina; Ballinasloe; Balrothery; Baltinglass; Carrick-on-Shannon; Castlebar; Claremorris; Cork; Drogheda; Kenmare; Larne; Lisnaskea; Macroom; Mohill; Mullingar; Naas; NDU; Roscommon; Skull; Strabane; Strokestown; and Tipperary: Return No. 4, HC, 1906 [Cd. 3203], p. 16.
52 *Poor Law Reform Commission (Ireland)*, HC, 1906 [Cd. 3202], pp. 55–6.
53 *Poor Law Reform Commission (Ireland)*, HC, 1906 [Cd. 3202], p. 54.

agreed observing that the average number of tramps in Wexford Workhouse was 'four a night. They come in and get a crust of bread or stirabout and are discharged in the morning and the cost is very little.' If they were not given accommodation in the workhouse, they would sleep rough 'in hayricks or other places, where they are likely to do damage'. It was impossible, he remarked, to change a man's behaviour by legislation alone, 'It is just like temperance; you cannot make him good by Act of Parliament.' Hore rejected the idea that all tramps were feckless, insisting that some were genuinely looking for work. He had 'known a steady tradesman to start off from his work where he had good employment and go on a tour round the workhouses of Ireland and come back again'. 'Some vagrants,' another witness remarked were 'very deserving people that go about through no fault of their own'.[54]

Poor law regulations, official discourse and much contemporary commentary assumed that there was a clear distinction between tramps and vagrants, and other casuals. However, poor law records indicate that these categories were far more porous than was often claimed. The term vagrant did not appear in any of the workhouse registers examined, although it was used by guardians in discussion, particularly in relation to people being prosecuted for vagrancy. Workhouse masters were not required to classify people as vagrants or casuals on admission, so there was often no indication in the admission registers that an individual was regarded as a vagrant. Outside Ulster, the term tramp was rarely used in workhouse registers. In contrast to their colleagues in the north, officials in southern unions appear to have been cautious about labelling people, whether as tramps or prostitutes. The decline in mendicancy and subsequent growth in vagrancy noted in official reports was reflected in some workhouse registers. In the immediate post-Famine decades significant numbers of people were designated as beggars or mendicants on admission. By the later decades of the nineteenth century, this was no longer the case.

The term mendicant, which was common in the mid-nineteenth century, appears to have fallen out of usage more quickly in unions in the three southern provinces than in Ulster. It was used in Cork Workhouse in 1850–1851, for example, but not in 1870–1871 or 1900–1901. Out of a sample of 1,665 admissions in 1850–1851, 314 were classed as 'mendicant' or 19 per cent. These fell into two main groups, adult women (193 admissions) and teenage boys (73 admissions). The women were predominantly either widowed or single, the latter being considerably younger than the former. The average age of the single women was twenty-five, compared to fifty-one

54 *Poor Law Reform Commission (Ireland). Minutes of Evidence taken before the Vice-Regal Commission on Poor Law reform in Ireland. Vol. III*, HC, 1906 [Cd. 3204], Q11269-73; 20288-309; 23576.

218 POVERTY AND THE POOR LAW IN IRELAND

for widows.[55] The relatively high number of mendicants can be attributed to the impact of the Famine and reflects the number of people left alone to fend for themselves. A much smaller number of admissions to NDU, just 0.2 per cent, were identified as 'mendicant'. A slightly greater number (0.7 per cent) were described as beggars.[56] The profile of these admissions was similar to that of mendicants in Cork Workhouse; the majority being women who were either widowed (average age forty-three) or single (average age twenty-one). Of the nine male admissions, all but one was aged fifteen or sixteen. There was one child among the individuals classified as beggars. This was ten-year-old Anne F., who was admitted with her mother, Eliza, an unmarried servant and her eight-year-old brother, Denis. Their place of origin was given as Malahide and their address as Sheriff Lane. They were described as ragged and dirty and Eliza had dysentery. Anne was apparently contributing to the family income and it was probably her mother's illness that bought the family into the workhouse. All three entered on 4 December and were discharged 13 December. The majority of those registered as beggars in NDU in 1850–1851, were sick, infirm, disabled or pregnant, and their average length of stay was 2.5 months. Beggars were not casual visitors, therefore, only resorting to the NDU Workhouse when they needed access to medical or other care. In later decades, 'beggar' was no longer used as a description in NDU. Mendicant continued to be used, but only very occasionally. It appeared in the NDU admission register twice in 1860–1861, for example, five times in 1880–1881 and just once in 1910–1911. Of five admissions described as mendicants in 1880–1881, four were aged sixty-eight or over.[57]

No one was described as a tramp in NDU registers although it is clear from other evidence that tramps were being admitted.[58] At a board meeting in 1887, the clerk was reported as referring to the number of tramps admitted to the workhouse from the Night Asylum as the cause of much expense, prompting one guardian to suggest that providing less in the way of whiskey, snuff and tobacco would help to discourage them.[59] The presence of the Night Asylum had long been a cause of annoyance to the North Dublin Guardians who believed that vagrants, and others, entered the asylum in order to gain entry to the workhouse. Guardians complained of people from the south-side of the city who 'came across the Liffey, spent a night or two

---

55 Cork BG Indoor Relief Registers, 1850–1851, 1870–1871, 1900–1901.
56 Out of 5,119 admissions, eleven were described as 'mendicant' and thirty-four as 'beggar': NDU BG Indoor Relief Registers, 1850–1851.
57 NDU BG Indoor Relief Registers, 1850–1851, 1860–1861, 1880–1881, 1910–1911.
58 It would appear from Mary Daly's analysis that tramps were identified in the registers of South Dublin Union. She found that 47 per cent of male inmates in 1880 were tramps who were accommodated for a single day: *Dublin: The Deposed Capital*, p. 89.
59 *Irish Times*, 27 January 1887.

in the asylum on the north-side and then claimed admission to the North Dublin Workhouse', although, as LGI William O'Brien pointed out, people did not need to have spent time in the asylum to establish a claim, 'Any destitute person coming to them was entitled to admission into the house.' The guardians continued to feel aggrieved, however, convinced that the asylum operated to their disadvantage. Numbers in the NDU Workhouse were rising while those in the SDU were decreasing, one guardian observed and this 'was attributable to the fact that persons who were really resident on the south-side get into this house from the Night Asylum'.[60]

In poor law terminology 'mendicant' seems to have had a broader meaning than either 'beggar' or 'tramp' and encompassed a wider constituency. Twenty per cent of admissions to Kinsale Workhouse were categorised as mendicant in 1870–1871, comprising seventy-one females and fifty-four males.[61] Many appear to have resided in the union and the average time spent in the workhouse was 2.4 months for women and 2.2 months for men. These were clearly neither casuals nor itinerants. As in other unions, people admitted to Kinsale Workhouse as mendicants appear to have been without families or other support networks. Of the 125 admitted in 1870–1871, 100 were widowed or single and there were only two married couples in the cohort. There was a significant age difference between sick, infirm or disabled adults whose average age was fifty-nine and those who were able-bodied whose average age was thirty-six. By 1880–1881 the proportion of admissions to Kinsale, categorised as mendicant, had dropped to 6 per cent. Here again the majority were widowed or single and the able-bodied were significantly younger than the sick and infirm.[62] However, able-bodied mendicants were now mainly casual admissions who remained a single night. Those registered as sick or infirm remained longer, and four of the nine women registered as sick or infirm died in the workhouse. In 1890–1891 just one admission was categorised as mendicant. This was a sixty-year-old woman who remained for two months. There was also one male tramp admitted who stayed one night. In 1900–1901 none of the people admitted was described as either mendicant or tramp. However, since over half of all admissions were categorised as 'casual', it seems reasonable to assume that

60 *Freeman's Journal*, 23 November 1876. See also, *Freeman's Journal*, 28 October 1874.
61 The total number of admissions was 620: Kinsale BG Indoor Relief Registers, 1870–1871.
62 Sixty-seven of 1,100 admissions (thirty-five female; thirty-two male); forty-eight were widowed or single; the average age of able-bodied mendicants was thirty-three; the average age of sick mendicants was sixty-five: Kinsale BG Indoor Relief Registers, 1880–1881.

at least some of these would have been described as mendicants in earlier decades or as tramps in some other unions.[63]

The decline of mendicancy coincided with a rise in vagrancy, but it should not be assumed that mendicants were simply being reclassified as tramps or vagrants. Despite the growing reference to a tramp problem, 'tramp' was rarely used as a defining category in admission registers outside the north. The exception, at least among the unions examined here, was Thurles in 1870–1871. Of 671 admissions that year, 216 were registered as tramps. Of these, 100 were also noted to have a trade or profession and were presumably regarded as looking for work. With the exception of a small number who needed hospital treatment, none of the 'tramps' remained for more than one night. In contrast to those described as mendicants in other unions, the Thurles tramps were predominantly able-bodied men and while the majority were single, the group included fourteen married couples, six with children.[64] In all, thirty-seven tramps were admitted with children. In Thurles, unlike most other unions where the term 'tramp' was used, the children of tramps were not classified as such in the register. If children are included, the tramp cohort totalled 270 admissions or 40 per cent of admissions. The relatively high proportion of women and children among the cohort confirms the impression that many of these were not 'professional tramps'.

On 20 June 1871, the Master of Thurles Workhouse, Edward Walsh, reported that he had prosecuted an able-bodied tramp named John McG., who had been admitted on a ticket from the relieving officer. The magistrates had sentenced the man to one-month's imprisonment with hard labour. John, who was described in the register as twenty-four years of age, single and 'badly clad', had been admitted on 11 June and discharged the following day. His prosecution seems to have had a deterrent effect since there were no more admissions of able-bodied men that were classified simply as tramps, although men described as 'labourer and tramp' or 'slater and tramp', or 'carpenter and tramp' continued to be admitted, as did female, sick and disabled tramps. John F., for example, who was a cripple, was admitted on 21 September and discharged the following day. On 19 September the master reported that 'two able bodied tramps admitted on tickets from the Relieving Officer on Saturday night last left the house when told they would be prosecuted'.[65] In Thurles, therefore, officials were drawing a clear

---

63 Kinsale casuals were largely working-age men. Of 706 casual admissions in 1900–1901, 479 were adult men with an average age of forty-three; 142 were adult women (average age forty) and eighty-five were children. The vast majority remained one night: Kinsale BG Indoor Relief Registers, 1890–1891, 1900–1901.

64 Twenty-nine of 216 were noted as being sick or disabled. There were 151 males and 65 females: Thurles BG Indoor Relief Registers, 1870–1871.

65 Thurles BG Minutes, 20 June and 19 Sept. 1871.

distinction between itinerant men and women, and those they believed to be professional tramps. But while only the latter were liable to be prosecuted as vagrants, the former were admitted for a single night and not encouraged to remain longer. The practice adopted in Thurles in 1870–1871 was unusual, however, and was subsequently discontinued. The designation 'tramp' does not appear in any of the other Thurles registers examined suggesting that it came to be regarded as inappropriate.

People admitted to workhouses in the north of the country were more likely to be designated as 'mendicant' or 'begging' in the post-Famine decades or as 'tramp' in the early decades of the twentieth century, than those admitted to workhouses in the southern provinces. But, as with other aspects of relief administration, there were also significant differences between unions in the north. Officials in Ballymoney, for example, unlike those in Ballycastle and Glenties, did not describe people as tramps in the workhouse register. The term mendicant was regularly applied, however, and remained in use until the early twentieth century, although the number and proportion of admissions described in this way declined. In 1850–1851, mendicants made up 40 per cent of admissions to Ballymoney Workhouse.[66] As in other unions, women significantly outnumbered men among this group and stayed for longer periods, and there were few married people. Almost three-quarters of adult mendicants were ill or infirm. These individuals were older than the able-bodied but the age differential was not as great as in Cork or Kinsale. By 1870–1871 the proportion of mendicants had dropped to 5 per cent, predominantly widowed or single women.[67] Children made up 29 per cent of the cohort, compared to 32 per cent in 1850–1851. Just six adult men were registered as mendicants in 1870–1871. Three of these were elderly men who stayed between a week and three months. The other three were much younger, in their late twenties or early thirties. None stayed more than two days. The term mendicant was still being used in 1900–1901 but it accounted for just 2 per cent of admissions, most of whom were casual admissions who stayed one night.[68] The gender balance was now relatively even (eighteen admissions by women compared to seventeen by men), but the women were more likely to make repeat admissions. A small number of those admitted as mendicants in 1900–1901 stayed for relatively long periods. These included three seventy year olds (one single woman and two widowers) and three men in their forties. Patrick M. was admitted eight times in all. He generally stayed for one night but also made two longer stays of two to three

66 148 of 369 admissions: Ballymoney BG Indoor relief Registers, 1850–1851.
67 Fifty-one of 948 admissions: Ballymoney BG Indoor relief Registers, 1870–1871.
68 Thirty-five of 1,456 admissions; twenty-nine were casual admissions who stayed one night: Ballymoney BG Indoor relief Registers, 1900–1901.

weeks. Robert H. and James W. both made extended stays of just under and just over a year. These men had somehow managed to establish a claim to entitlement, although how they did this is unclear.

Officials in Ballycastle and Glenties used both 'begging' and 'tramp' as occupational categories. The second term gradually displaced the first, but they were not synonymous. Furthermore, while there were similarities between those registered as beggars in Ballycastle and Glenties, and those designated mendicants in other unions, the profile of these groups differed in some important respects. Those described as 'begging' included more children and more able-bodied adults. In 1860–1861, out of 452 admissions to Ballycastle Workhouse, one-third were registered as 'begging'; fifty-nine of these were children (38 per cent), twenty-five illegitimate. Women outnumbered men by more than two to one and were on average slightly younger.[69] They also tended to remain in the workhouse for longer periods. The average length of stay for adult women beggars was 4.4 months, compared to 2.4 months for men. Women beggars appear to have comprised two distinct groups: elderly women many of whom died in the workhouse; and younger women with children. Twenty-five of the adult women were aged sixty-five or over, fourteen of whom died in the workhouse. With one exception, all of these elderly women beggars were sick or infirm. Of the adult men, three-quarters were elderly or sick, infirm or disabled, or both. Ten years later, the number of admissions registered as 'begging' had declined to less than one-fifth.[70] Men remained in the minority among the adults and while the average age of female beggars remained similar to that in 1861, that of males had increased to seventy-one. By 1900–1901, the proportion of admissions recorded as begging had dropped to just 4 per cent, comprising two men and ten women with an average age of seventy-three, all but one of whom was sick.[71] There were no beggars recorded in Ballycastle Workhouse in 1910–1911. As with 'mendicant' elsewhere, 'begging' fell increasingly out of use as an occupational category in Ballycastle, becoming reserved for a small number of mainly elderly and/or infirm individuals.

By the end of the 1870s, 'tramp' was also being used as an occupational category in Ballycastle. In 1879–1880, around 1 per cent of admissions were noted to be tramps.[72] Tramps were predominantly male (ten men to one woman) and were much younger than beggars, with an average age of just twenty-seven. By 1900–1901 tramps accounted for around one-quarter of

69 156 admissions were described as 'begging'. The average age of adult women beggars was fifty-three compared to fifty-seven for men: Ballycastle BG Indoor Registers, 1860–1861.
70 Seventy of 398 admissions: Ballycastle BG Indoor Registers, 1870–1871.
71 Twelve of 294 admissions: Ballycastle BG Indoor Registers, 1900–1901.
72 Eleven of 814 admissions: Ballycastle BG Indoor Registers, 1879–1880.

admissions to Ballycastle Workhouse, with the same proportion recorded in 1910–1911. The majority were not resident in the union but were from the north, as was the case with beggars.[73] While adult male tramps outnumbered women by around four to one in 1900–1901, in 1910–1911 their numbers were roughly equal (forty-seven admissions by adult women compared to forty-nine by adult men), with married couples making up 40 per cent of the cohort in 1910–1911, compared to 11 per cent in 1900–1901. None of the tramps admitted in either 1900–1901 or 1910–1911 stayed more than two nights, except in isolated cases where the individual was sick or injured. Children comprised 17 per cent of the cohort in 1900–1901 and 14 per cent in 1910–1911. Tramps were thus less likely to be admitted with children than beggars in earlier decades or mendicants in other unions. Ballycastle Officials appear to have exercised their discretion in identifying tramps, since there were a number of people who might be thought to fit the tramp profile who were not registered as tramps. Almost all of the people admitted in 1910–1911 whose residence was given as somewhere outside Ulster were working-age men who remained one-night only. Nine were identified as tramps; seventeen as labourers; and eleven as tradesmen of various kinds.[74] Officials were thus able to distinguish, at least to their own satisfaction, between men who were looking for work and tramps.

A decline in begging and corresponding rise in tramping was also evident in Glenties Union. In 1860–1861, 31 per cent of admissions were described as 'begging', the majority single or widowed adult women, together with a small number of mostly elderly men.[75] Children made up 40 per cent of the cohort. As in Ballycastle, the adult women were divided by age; around a third were elderly women in their late sixties and older, the remainder were much younger women in their twenties and thirties most of whom had children, the majority illegitimate. Nearly three-quarters of those registered as beggars stayed for at least a month and over half for three months or more. In 1890–1891 begging was still occupying a significant minority of admissions (21 per cent). There was now a more even gender balance, thirty-nine admissions by adult men and forty-six by adult women, and there were fewer women with children and fewer elderly women.[76] The average length of stay had dropped markedly. Over half of those registered

73 Seventy of 294 admissions in 1901–1901 were described as tramps and 111 of 409 in 1910–1911; fourteen came from outside Ulster in 1900–1901 and thirteen in 1910–1911: Ballycastle BG Indoor Registers, 1900–1901, 1910–1911.
74 These included baker, blacksmith, cooper, dealer, mason, painter, printer, tailor and weaver: Ballycastle BG Indoor Registers, 1910–1911.
75 Seventy-two of 229 admissions: Glenties BG Indoor relief Registers, 1860–1861.
76 Eighty-five of 405 admissions; women aged sixty-six plus made up 22 per cent of admissions by adult women beggars; of those aged sixty-five and younger, half entered

as begging remained less than a week, with only 27 per cent staying for a
month or more. By 1900–1901 the proportion of beggars among admissions
had declined to 5 per cent all, with the exception of one single mother and
two illegitimate children, aged sixty or over.[77] Slightly more than half of
all admissions were now described as 'tramp' in the occupation column.[78]
The vast majority were designated 'no fixed abode' and all except two of
these stayed a single night. Men outnumbered women by three to one, with
children making up around one-quarter of the cohort, the vast majority
legitimate. In 1900–1901 three tramps were described as being drunk on
admission, suggesting that the remainder were sober. It would be unwise to
read too much into this, but it does support Synge's claim that drunkenness
among tramps was relatively rare.

Mendicancy and begging were clearly connected, although the terms
appear to have had slightly different meanings in different unions. Generally
speaking, 'mendicant' appears to have been a description of a state, being
reliant on alms, while 'begging' described an activity. The number of people
falling into these categories declined over the period and the terms beggar or
begging and mendicant were used increasingly rarely. Tramp had a range of
meanings and there was little consistency in the way the term was used across
the country. The same family could be designated tramps in one workhouse
and not in another. John and Margaret M., together with their two small
daughters aged five and two stayed a single night in Ballymoney Workhouse
on 8 March 1901. John was in his late fifties and Margaret in her forties.[79]
His occupation was given as slater and it was noted that the family had come
from Limavady. The following month the family spent a night in Glenties
Workhouse where their occupation was given as tramp and their residence as
no fixed abode. In the observation column they were described as 'ragged'.
In September they spent a night in Ballycastle Workhouse having come from
Belfast. They were all described as tramps. On 21 October, the family was
admitted to Belfast Workhouse where John's occupation was given as slater
and Margaret's as mill worker. Here they were all described as destitute. They
stayed two nights and departed on 23 October. The family appeared to have
confined their travels to the north of the country, confirming the impression of
the Vice-Regal Commission that tramps tended to remain in a particular area.

While the term 'tramp' was increasingly used to define a lifestyle that
had not been categorised in this way in earlier decades, it was not applied

with children; children made up 20 per cent of the cohort: Glenties BG Indoor relief
Registers. 1890–1891.

77 Eighteen of 385 admissions: Glenties BG Indoor relief Registers, 1900–1901.

78 198 of 385 admissions: Glenties BG Indoor relief Registers, 1900–1901.

79 John's age was variously given as fifty-eight, fifty-seven or fifty-six and Margaret's as
forty-eight, forty-seven or forty.

indiscriminately. In 1890–1891 Joseph and Mary G. travelled around the country with their five children moving from workhouse to workhouse and never staying more than two nights. They spent the night of 18 September 1890 in Kinsale Workhouse, for example, stayed in Glenties Workhouse 23 to 25 November and were admitted to Clogher Workhouse on 15 April 1891, Ballymoney on 21 April and Clogher again on 28 August, remaining one night on each occasion. Joseph was always registered as a mason and presumably presented and was accepted as looking for work. In order to avoid being categorised as a tramp and potential vagrant, men such as Joseph needed a plausible story and a respectable appearance. 'Tramp' was a subjective and elastic term that officials used in different ways. The cumulative effect, however, was to marginalise and criminalise vulnerable people who in previous decades had been regarded and treated more tolerantly.

Despite official statements regarding the ease of identifying tramps, a significant proportion of those described as tramps on admission to the workhouse did not fit the profile of the habitual or professional tramp. Men outnumbered women, but they did so by around three to one, significantly less than the figure of four or five to one cited by the Local Government Board and the Vice-Regal Commission. Moreover, apart from the length of time they remained in the workhouse, there was little to distinguish women and children identified as tramps in the early twentieth century, from those identified as mendicants or beggars in earlier decades. The change in terminology was the result of a change in attitudes and both reflected and reinforced a growing unwillingness to provide homeless or itinerant paupers with more than the most minimal levels of support.

The tramp problem was not really a tramp problem at all. The problem lay in a shortage of regular, secure employment and poor relief system that had become increasingly restrictive. Relieving officers and workhouse masters became so reluctant to admit people other than as casuals that the only way people could access the relief system was by using workhouses as temporary lodging houses. The mobile, unsettled poor were forced to remain mobile. Those who condemned tramps and vagrants failed to consider or acknowledge that it was settled society and the strong localism of the poor law system that promoted and perpetuated vagrancy. To assume that people only resorted to workhouses under duress was to misunderstand the nature of the post-Famine poor law system. The real issue was not that the respectable poor were forced into workhouses but that many of those who sought admission were only allowed limited access. The factors that influenced patterns of relief were rooted not in individual need but in the structures of the relief system; the kind and amount of relief that was on offer. This was not a system shaped by the needs of the poor. It was a system that reshaped how the poor lived.

Conclusion

The poor law never acquired popular legitimacy in Ireland. It was too expensive, too inefficient, too associated with British rule and with memories of the Famine. Following independence, the workhouse system in the south was swept away as part of a reorganisation of local government and social welfare that saw the abolition of poor law boards and workhouses, and the introduction of home assistance administered by boards of health and public assistance. Workhouse buildings were generally converted into hospitals or county homes. The latter provided institutional care for the elderly and infirm, and chronic invalids, together with, in some cases, lunatics, epileptics, single mothers and children. The workhouse system and its administrators could be safely consigned to the past, one chapter in the larger story of oppression and misrule. But as this study has shown, the system of poor relief that operated under the Irish poor law was a system that reflected the culture and values of Irish society. If the system was harsh and limited, this was not only because the principles enshrined in the legislation were harsh, but also because its administration reflected popular notions about entitlement and eligibility, the belief that relief should be restricted to local people and denied to strangers, and that anyone capable of working should be expected to do so. Many of the assumptions made about the Irish poor law have been shown to be false. The poor law was not synonymous with the institution of the workhouse. By the end of the nineteenth century, substantial numbers of people were being relieved in their own homes. Only a minority of relief recipients were forced to enter the workhouse. Workhouses accommodated few families and few able-bodied people. They could be difficult to access and difficult to remain in for any length of time. They were, however, important sites of medical treatment and care.

Much of the detailed discussion within this study has focused on systems and procedures. These have not been examined in isolation, however, but in the context of their human consequences: how they impacted on individuals. We have seen how disapproval of certain lifestyles contributed to the deaths of Rosanna D., Bridget K. and John L. Information on individual paupers derives primarily from investigations into and discussion of cases of misman-agement or neglect. In one sense such cases are the tip of the iceberg. John Barry claimed that anyone who made a complaint against poor law officials was 'marked out for punishment', so that 'few paupers will complain of the grossest outrages perpetrated on them'. Complaints that were made, he believed, were either ignored or subjected to pointless inquiry. The truth never emerged because paupers were frightened and officials protected each other. This was an exaggeration, but Barry's observation that workhouse inmates were so 'ground down and made so mean' by the workhouse system that they were more likely to inform on each other than complain, no doubt contains a kernel of truth.[1] Boards of guardians often displayed more concern for the welfare of their officials than of the workhouse inmates for whom they were responsible. Focusing exclusively on cases of abuse or mistreatment will produce a distorted picture, however. We know far more about occasions on which the system failed than when it succeeded. We have little information about the people for whom poor relief provided much needed but temporary support and who went on to rebuild their lives. The evidence presented here suggests that the workhouse system played an important role in helping Ireland recover from the Famine. Workhouses provided vital support for relatively long periods for vulnerable people who had lost their livelihoods and/or their families, as well as providing for 'deserted' wives and single mothers.

Social disruption caused by the Famine was of particular concern to Catholic clerics who were alarmed by the apparent weakening of established moral conventions evidenced by the rise in illegitimacy. The campaign to reform the poor law spearheaded by Archbishop Cullen in the 1860s was motivated as much by concern for the moral as well as the physical welfare of the poor; what he and his colleagues most objected to in the existing system was the absence of moral criteria for the granting and management of relief. In subsequent decades the Catholic Church was largely successful in ensuring that strict moral codes governed the organisation of almost all aspects of Irish society, but particularly those relating to education and welfare. Behaviour and reputation became crucial factors in determining entitlement to a range of welfare services including poor relief. While the Church never embraced the poor law system and would have preferred welfare provision to be entrusted either to religious orders and congregations or to voluntary organisations, it became less overtly hostile to it. A measure of acceptance was aided by the growing extent of Catholic influence as the

---

1 Rev. John Barry, *Life in an Irish Workhouse* (Thurles, 1890), pp. 10–11, 72.

number of Catholic poor law guardians and officials steadily increased in the later decades of the nineteenth century.

Historians of early modern poverty have located the origins of many enduring attitudes and beliefs in an ever-receding past. Modern historians, Anne Scott has observed, too often assume that 'the phenomena they observe began in their period, whereas they often had an earlier origin'.[2] There has been a similar tendency amongst Irish historians to assume that the phenomena they observe are peculiar to Ireland, when in fact they are common to many Western European countries. A persistent theme within writing on the poor law has been the difference between the poor law systems of England and Ireland. Yet, close examination of relief practices reveals just how similar basic attitudes and responses were. This is particularly evident with regard to the notion of 'belonging' which has long been stressed as a central element of poor relief administration in England. Despite the absence of a law of settlement in Ireland, a desire to limit relief to those who belonged to the union was also a feature of the Irish poor law and one that became more pronounced in the post-Famine period as Irish poor law administration became more responsive to local interests. Snell's analysis of the impact of belonging on relief administration has many echoes in Ireland.[3] Lack of knowledge about individual applicants made it more difficult for administrators of city poor law unions, for example, to make judgements about what constituted involuntary poverty. Those administering relief in rural areas were more alert to personal circumstances and more understanding of individual needs, but also more influenced by gossip and reputation. It is equally clear that in Ireland, as elsewhere, there were limits to belonging; it conferred the right to apply for relief, but not necessarily to receive it.

There were significant differences in the way the poor law system operated in different parts of Ireland; levels of relief were highest in the southeast and lowest in the north. These differences reflected regional economies but also social and cultural attitudes. Here too there are similarities to England where the industrial regions of the north developed more restrictive welfare regimes than the mainly agricultural south. There is much more to be discovered about the nature and extent of regional variations, and the relationship between local labour markets and poor relief. Equally important, however, were differences within regions. As we have seen, individual unions developed their own relief practices whether it was the identification and classification of tramps in Thurles or the resistance to moral classification in

2 Anne M. Scott, 'Experiences of Poverty', in Anne M. Scott (ed.), *Experiences of Poverty in Late Medieval and Early Modern England and France* (Farnham: Ashgate, 2012), p. 14.
3 Snell, *Parish and Belonging*.

Glenties. Even neighbouring unions could operate in very different ways. To investigate this further we need to know more about the local circumstances in particular unions and more about the individuals responsible for relief administration.

The Irish poor law, like the English, established rights and obligations, and created expectations. The more established the system became, the stronger the sense of entitlement. By the early twentieth century there was a general feeling that the poor law system needed reform. Costs were rising yet the support available was judged neither adequate nor appropriate. The tendency to blame the inadequacies of the system on its English origins and to problematise particular groups of poor people, such as vagrants and prostitutes, whose existence could be blamed on the presence of British soldiers and the pernicious influence of England, discouraged serious strategic thinking about the organisation of social welfare and encouraged lazy prejudice.[4] Claiming a state of victimhood for the nation obscured the needs of the most vulnerable members of society. This study set out to explore the working of the relief system. It has examined the strategies adopted by the poor and the propertied, and has revealed the extent to which applying for relief was a process of negotiation. The operation of the poor law has much to tell us about the way people thought about social relationships and responsibilities, about the rights and duties of individuals and about the nature, meaning and limits of community.

---

4 Luddy, *Prostitution and Irish Society*, pp. 156–193; and Ben Novick, *Conceiving Revolution: Irish Nationalist Propaganda During the First World War* (Dublin: Four Courts Press, 2001), pp. 132–69.

Note on Statistics and Sources

Annual Statistics

Analysis of trends in relief over the period 1850 to 1914 was conducted using a database compiled from the statistical tables of expenditure and relief printed as Appendices to the Annual Reports of the Poor Law Commissioners and subsequently the Local Government Board. Returns of relief and expenditure under the poor law underwent various changes over the period. Figures for the number who received relief, both indoor and outdoor, in each union were initially included in the expenditure returns. From 1858, the average daily number relieved in each workhouse was included in the returns. From 1867 figures for relief were presented separately from those for expenditure. From 1872, all relief figures were provided in one table which included figures for the collective number of days for all persons relieved in the workhouse during the year and the average number of days of relief to each workhouse inmate, in addition to the average daily number in the workhouse. Information was also given on the cost of 'provisions, necessaries, and clothing' and the average weekly cost per pauper relieved.

Following the passage of the Local Government Act 1898, the expenditure tables changed reflecting the reduced responsibilities of poor law boards. A number of categories of union expenditure, such as sanitary expenses, were dropped as these now became the responsibility of district councils. The relief tables remained unchanged. During the implementation of the Act, the end of the administrative year was temporarily moved from 30 September to 31 March. Figures returned for 1899 were the figures for the half year from 1 October 1898 to 31 March 1899. The figures for the next three years 1900–1902 were for the year to 31 March. The returns presented in 1905 reverted to the practice of using 30 September as the cut-off for yearly statistical returns and also included the figures for the year to 30 September for 1903 and 1904.

Indoor Relief and Outdoor Relief Registers

These registers are the handwritten ledgers in which details of relief were given. For the purposes of this study, databases were compiled containing the details of all those entered on the registers in the period from 1 October to 30 September for the following unions and census years:

Ballycastle

1860–1861 (454 admissions)
1870–1871 (398 admissions)
1879–1880 (814 admissions)
1900–1901 (294 admissions)
1910–1911 (409 admissions)

Ballymoney

1850–1851 (369 admissions)
1860–1861 (545 admissions)
1870–1871 (948 admissions)
1880–1881 (1,520 admissions)
1890–1891 (654 admissions)
1900–1901 (1,456 admissions)
1910–1911 (1,389 admissions)

Clogher

1870–1871 (577 admissions)
1890–1891 (572 admissions)
1910–1911 (3,247 admissions)

Glenties

1860–1861 (229 admissions)
1890–1891 (405 admissions)
1900–1901 (385 admissions)

Kinsale

1870–1871 (620 admissions)
1880–1881 (1,100 admissions)
1890–1891 (911 admissions)
1900–1901 (1,092 admissions)

North Dublin[1]

1850–1851 (5,119 admissions)
1860–1861 (4,112 admissions)
1870–1871 (4,625 admissions)
1880–1881 (8,050 admissions)
1890–1891 (3,330 admissions)
1910–1911 (7,491 admissions)

Thurles[2]

1870–1871 (671 admissions)
1879–1880 (1,111 admissions)
1889 (calendar year/2,237 admissions)
1900–1901 (2,065 admissions)
1910–1911 (1,202 admissions)

Due to the high number of admissions the following registers were sampled by recording every tenth entry:

Cork

1850–1851 (1,665 admissions)
1870–1871 (753 admissions)
1900–1901 (1,000 admissions)
1910–1911 (802 admissions)

North Dublin

1900–1901 (1,286 admissions)

Belfast

For Belfast, all the entries for the following months were recorded:
October 1864 (497 admissions)
January 1865 (730 admissions)
January 1878 (1,241 admissions)
October 1900 (1,577 admissions)
January 1901 (1,549 admissions)
April 1901 (1,353 admissions)
July 1901 (1,376 admissions)

Outdoor Relief Registers

Antrim[3]

1875 (43 entries)
1885 (76 entries)

Ballycastle

1900–1901 (50 entries)

Ballymoney

1860–1861 (34 entries)
1865 (48 entries)
1870–1871 (89 entries)
1875 (74 entries)
1880–1881 (83 entries)
1885 (80 entries)
1890–1891 (62 entries)
1895 (52 entries)
1900–1901 (60 entries)
1910–1911 (52 entries)

Enniskillen

1865 (2 entries)
1875 (25 entries)
1885 (21 entries)
1895 (26 entries)

Rathdown

1865 (7 entries)
1875 (159 entries)
1885 (763 entries)

Notes

1 Some names and other details were illegible due to water damage. This occurred in 1870–1871 (a few first names were illegible), 1880–1881 (340 entries out of 8,050); 1890–1891 (142 out of 3,440); and 1910–1911 (5 out of 7,491). The database for NDU 1890–1891 ends mid-year (20 May 1891) which is where the register ends. The next register is missing.
2 Since admission registers for 1880–1881 and 1890–1891 were not extant the nearest available year was used.
3 Data for Antrim, Ballymoney (1865, 1875, 1885 and 1895), Enniskillen and Rathdown had been obtained for an earlier project using calendar years.

Bibliography

A. **Manuscript Sources**

Ballymoney Museum, Ballymoney
Ballymoney Board of Guardians Records: Accounts of Paupers Relieved

Cork City and County Archives, Cork
Cork Board of Guardians Records: Indoor Relief Registers
Kinsale Board of Guardians Records: Minute Books, Indoor Relief Registers,
    Master's Journal, Master's Report Book
Macroom Board of Guardians Records: Minute Books
Youghal Board of Guardians Records: Minute Books, Out-Letters

Donegal County Library, Letterkenny
Glenties Board of Guardians Records: Minute Books, Indoor Relief Registers

Dublin Diocesan Archives, Dublin
Cullen Papers

Kerry County Library, Tralee
Tralee Board of Guardian Records: Minute Books

Laois County Library, Portlaoise
Mountmellick Board of Guardian Records: Minute Books

Limerick County Library, Limerick,
Kilmallock Board of Guardian Records: Minute Books

National Archives of Ireland, Dublin
Chief Secretary's Office Registered Papers
Lismore Board of Guardian Records: Master's Journal

North Dublin Board of Guardian Records: Minute Books, Indoor Relief Registers
Rathdown Board of Guardian Records: Minute Books, Outdoor Relief Registers

National Library of Ireland, Dublin
Larcom Papers
Westport Board of Guardians Minute Books

Public Record Office of Northern Ireland, Belfast
Antrim Board of Guardian Records: Outdoor Relief Registers
Belfast Board of Guardian Records: Minute Books, Indoor Relief Registers, Outdoor Relief Registers, In-Letters
Ballycastle Board of Guardian Records: Minute Books, Indoor Relief Registers, Outdoor Relief Registers
Ballymoney Board of Guardian Records: Minute Books Indoor Relief Registers, Outdoor Relief Registers
Clogher Board of Guardian Records: Minute Books, Indoor Relief Registers, In-Letters
Enniskillen Board of Guardian Records: Minute Books, Outdoor Relief Registers
Local Government Board Precedent Book

Tipperary Local Studies Library, Thurles
Thurles Board of Guardian Records: Minute Books, Indoor Relief Registers

University College Dublin
National Folklore Collection

B. Parliamentary Papers
Annual Reports of the Commissioners for Administering the Laws for the Relief of the Poor in Ireland
Report from the Select Committee Appointed to Inquire into the Administration of the Relief of the Poor in Ireland, HC, 1861 [408]
Annual Abstract of Return of the Number of Able-Bodied Persons who have Received Provisional Outdoor Relief in Cases of Sudden and Urgent Necessity ... from Relieving Officers in every Poor Law Union in Ireland ... from the Year 1858 to the present time, HC, 1867 (427)
Correspondence etc. relative to duties of relieving officers (Ireland), HC, 1867 (581)
Annual Reports of the Local Government Board for Ireland
Poor Law Union and Lunacy Inquiry Commission (Ireland), HC, 1879–1880 [Cd. 2239]
Copies of the Minutes of Evidence taken at the recent Inquiry held at the Belfast Workhouse by Inspectors Bourke and Brodie, together with their Report thereon, and Final Decision of the Local Government Board, HC, 1881 (123)

Return of the Average Number of Sick Persons tended in each Union Workhouse in Ireland during the last Year for which Figures are complete ... and showing the Number of Paid Nurses, and Unpaid or Pauper Assistants in Charge of such Persons during the Day and Night at the present Time, HC, 1881 (433)

Appendix to the Report of the Departmental Committee on Vagrancy, Volume III, HC, 1906 [Cd. 2892]

Report of the Vice-Regal Commission on Poor Law Reform in Ireland. Volume I, 1906 [Cd. 3202]

Poor Law Reform Commission (Ireland). Appendix to the Report, Vol. II, 1906 [Cd. 3203]

Poor Law Reform Commission (Ireland). Minutes of Evidence taken before the Vice-Regal Commission on Poor Law reform in Ireland. Vol. III, 1906 [Cd. 3204]

Royal Commission on the Poor Laws and Relief of Distress, Report on Ireland, HC, 1909 [Cd. 4630]

Royal Commission on the Poor Laws and Relief of Distress. Minutes of Evidence (with Appendices) relating Ireland, HC, 1910 [Cd. 5070]

Royal Commission on the Poor Laws and Relief of Distress. Appendix. Statistics Relating to Ireland, HC, 1910 [Cd. 5244]

C. Newspapers

Anglo-Celt
Ballymoney Free Press
Belfast Newsletter
Cork Constitution
Cork Examiner
Enniscorthy News
Freeman's Journal
Irish Independent
Irish Times
Kildare Observer
Nation
Nenagh Guardian
People (Wexford)
Tralee Chronicle

D. Contemporary Works

Anderson, Rev. William. 'Workhouse Hospitals in the West of Ireland', in George W. Hastings (ed.), *Transactions of the National Association for the Promotion of Social Science, Belfast Meeting 1867* (London: Green, Reader and Dyer, 1868).

Barrett, R. M. *Guide to Dublin Charities* (Dublin: Hodges, Figgis and Co., 1884).

Barry, Rev. John. *Personal Experiences in Clonmel Workhouse* (Clonmel, 1887).

———. Life in an Irish Workhouse (Thurles, 1890).

The British Medical Association. Reports on the Poor-Law Medical System in Ireland, the Case of Irish Dispensary Doctors, and the Nursing and Administration of Irish Workhouse Infirmaries, *British Medical Journal*, (1904).

Cameron, Sir Charles A. *How the Poor Live* (Dublin: John Falconer, 1904).

Dowling, Jeremiah. *The Irish Poor Laws and Poor Houses* (Dublin: Hodges, Foster and Co., 1872).

———. *An Irish Doctor Remembers* (Dublin: Clonmore and Reynolds, 1955)

Hall, W. H. B. *Gleanings in Ireland after the Land Acts* (London: Edward Stanford, 1883).

Hancock, Neilson W. 'Should Boards of Guardians Endeavour to make Pauper Labour self-Supporting', *Transactions of the Dublin Statistical Society*, 2 (1851).

———. 'The Workhouse as a Mode of Relief for Widows and Orphans', *Journal of the Dublin Statistical Society*, 1: 84–91 (1855).

Magennis, Edward, *The Irish Poor Law System: Its Evils and Its Defects: An Address Delivered at a Meeting of the Guardians of the Lurgan Union, on Thursday, 12th. January, 1888, when Proposing a Resolution Calling for an Inquiry into the Working of the Poor Laws in Ireland with a View to Their Abolition or Alteration to a System More in Accord with the Disposition, Habits and Wishes of the Irish People* (Belfast: William W. Cleland, 1888).

Mooney, Thomas A. *Compendium of the Irish Poor Law* (Dublin: Alex, Thom and Co., 1887).

Nicholls, Sir George. *A History of the Irish Poor Law* (London: John Murray, 1856).

O'Hanlon, W. M. *Walks Among the Poor of Belfast and Suggestions for their Improvement, Belfast 1853, republished with a foreword by Andrew Boyd* (Menston: Scolar Press, 1971).

Senior, N. W. 'Mendicancy in Ireland', *Edinburgh Review*, 77: 391–411 (1843).

Stark, Archibald G. *The South of Ireland in 1850; The Journal of a Tour in Leinster and Munster* (Dublin: James Duffy, 1850).

Stephens, Laura. 'An Irish Workhouse', *The New Ireland Review*, 13: 129–34 (1900).

———. 'The Tramp', *Dana*, 11: 339–43 (1905).

Synge, J. M. 'The Vagrants of Wicklow', *Collected Works*, Vol. II, (Washington: Catholic Press of America, 1982).

Tod, Isabella. 'The Place of Women in the Administration of the Irish Poor Law', *The Englishwoman's Review*, ciii: 481–9 (November 1881).

Williams, George D. *Dublin Charities: Being a Handbook of Dublin Philanthropic Organisations and Charities* (Dublin: John Falconer, 1902).

E. Secondary Works

Beier A. L. and Paul Ocobock (eds), *Cast Out: Vagrancy and Homelessness in Global and Historical Perspective* (Athens: Ohio University Press, 2008).

Breathnach, Ciara. *The Congested Districts Board of Ireland, 1891–1923: Poverty and Development in the West of Ireland* (Dublin: Four Courts Press, 2005).

——. 'Smallholder Housing and People's Health, 1890–1915' in Ciara Breathnach (ed.), *Framing the West: Images of Rural Ireland 1891–1920* (Dublin: Irish Academic Press, 2007).

Brundage, Anthony. *The English Poor Laws 1700–1930* (London: Palgrave, 2002).

Burke, Helen. *The People and the Poor Law in Nineteenth Century Ireland* (Littlehampton: Women's Education Bureau, 1987).

Carroll, Lydia. *In the Fever King's Preserves: Sir Charles Cameron and the Dublin Slums* (Dublin: A. and A. Farmar, 2011).

Cassell, Ronald D. *Medical Charities, Medical Politics: The Irish Dispensary System and the Poor Law 1836–1872* (Woodbridge: Boydell Press, 1997).

Charlesworth, Lorie. *Welfare's Forgotten Past: A Socio-Legal History of the Poor Law* (London: Routledge, 2010).

Clark, Anna. 'Wild Workhouse Girls and the Liberal Imperial State in Mid-Nineteenth Century Ireland', *Journal of Social History*, 39 (2005).

——. 'Orphans and the Poor Law: Rage against the Machine', in Virginia Crossman and Peter Gray (eds), *Poverty and Welfare in Ireland 1838–1948* (Dublin: Irish Academic Press, 2011).

Clarkson, Leslie. 'The Modernisation of the Irish Diet, 1740–1920', in John Davis (ed.), *Rural Change in Ireland* (Belfast: Institute of Irish Studies, 1999).

Clear, Caitriona. *Social Change and Everyday Life in Ireland, 1850–1922* (Manchester: Manchester University Press, 2007).

Cousins, Mel. *Poor Relief in Ireland 1851–1914* (Bern: Peter Lang, 2011).

Cox, Catherine. 'Medical Dispensary Service in Nineteenth-Century Ireland: Access, Transport and Distance', in Catherine Cox and Maria Luddy (eds), *Cultures of Care in Irish Medical History, 1750–1970* (Basingstoke: Palgrave Macmillan, 2010).

——. *Negotiating Insanity in the Southeast of Ireland, 1820–1900* (Manchester: Manchester University Press, 2012).

Craig, David H. 'A History of the Belfast City Hospital', *Ulster Medical Society Journal*, 43: 1–10 (1974).

Cronin, Maura. *Country, Class, or Craft?: The Politicisation of Nineteenth Century Cork* (Cork: Cork University Press, 1994).

Crossman, Virginia. 'The New Ross Workhouse Riot of 1887: Nationalism, Class and the Irish Poor Laws', *Past and Present*, 179: 135–58 (May 2003).

——. 'Viewing Women, Family and Sexuality through the Prism of the Irish Poor Laws', *Women's History Review*, 15: 541–50 (2006).

――. *The Poor Law in Ireland 1838–1948* (Dundalk: Economic and Social History Society of Ireland, 2006).

――. *Politics, Pauperism and Power in Late Nineteenth-Century Ireland* (Manchester: Manchester University Press, 2006).

――. 'Cribbed, Contained and Confined? The Care of Children Under the Irish Poor Law 1850–1920', *Eire-Ireland*, 44: 37–61 (2009).

――. '"Facts Notorious to the Whole Country": The Political Battle over Irish Poor Law Reform in the 1860s', *Transactions of the Royal Historical Society*, xx: 157–70 (2010).

――. 'Attending to the Wants of Poverty: Cullen, the Relief of Poverty and the Development of Social Welfare in Ireland', in Dáire Keogh and Albert McDonnell (eds), *Cardinal Paul Cullen and his World* (Dublin: Four Courts Press, 2011).

―― and Peter Gray (eds). *Poverty and Welfare in Ireland 1838–1948* (Dublin: Irish Academic Press, 2011).

―― and Donnacha Seán Lucey, '"One Huge Abuse": The Cork Board of Guardians and the Expansion of Outdoor Relief in Post-Famine Ireland', *English Historical Review*, cxxvi: 1408–29 (December 2011).

Crowther, M. A. *The Workhouse System 1834–1929: The History of an English Social Institution* (London: Batsford, 1981).

Daly, Mary E. *Dublin – The Deposed Capital: A Social and Economic History 1860–1914* (Cork: Cork University Press, 1984).

Driver, Felix. *Power and Pauperism: The Workhouse System 1834–1884* (Cambridge: Cambridge University Press, 1993).

Eccles, Audrey. *Vagrancy in Law and Practice under the Old Poor Law* (Farnham: Ashgate, 2012).

Elliott, Marianne. *When God Took Sides: Religion and Identity in Ireland – Unfinished History* (Oxford: Oxford University Press, 2009).

Feingold, William L. *The Revolt of the Tenantry: The Transformation of Local Government in Ireland 1872–1886* (Boston, Mass: Northeastern University Press, 1984).

Fraser, Derek (ed.). *The New Poor Law in the Nineteenth Century* (London: Macmillan, 1976).

Geary, Laurence M. '"The Whole Country Was in Motion": Mendicancy and Vagrancy in Pre-Famine Ireland', in Jacqueline Hill and Colm Lennon (eds), *Luxury and Austerity* (Dublin: UCD Press, 1999).

――. *Medicine and Charity in Ireland 1718–1851* (Dublin: UCD Press, 2004).

――. 'The Medical Profession, Health Care and the Poor Law in Nineteenth-Century Ireland', in Virginia Crossman and Peter Gray (eds), *Poverty and Welfare in Ireland 1838–1948* (Dublin: Irish Academic Press, 2011).

Gray, Peter. *The Making of the Irish Poor Law 1815–43* (Manchester: Manchester University Press, 2009).

Green, David. *Pauper Capital: London and the Poor Law, 1790–1870* (Farnham: Ashgate, 2010).

Gribbon, H. D. 'Economic and Social History, 1850–1921', in W. E. Vaughan (ed.), *A New History of Ireland: Ireland under the Union 1870–1921* (Oxford: Oxford University Press, 1996).

Hooper, Glenn. *Travel Writing and Ireland, 1760–1860 Culture, History, Politics* (Basingstoke: Palgrave Macmillan, 2005).

Jordan, Alison. *Who Cared? Charity in Victorian and Edwardian Belfast* (Belfast: Institute of Irish Studies, n. d.).

Kennedy, Liam and Paul Gray, 'Famine, Illegitimacy and the Workhouse in Western Ireland: Kilrush, County Clare', in Alysa Levene, Thomas Nutt and Samantha Williams (eds), *Illegitimacy in Britain, 1700–1920* (Basingstoke: Palgrave Macmillan, 2005).

King, Steven. *Poverty and Welfare in England 1700–1850: A Regional Perspective* (Manchester: Manchester University Press, 2000).

—— and Alannah Tompkins (eds), *The Poor in England, 1700–1850: An Economy of Makeshifts* (Manchester: Manchester University Press, 2003).

Laragy, Georgina. 'Poor Relief in the South of Ireland, 1850–1921', in Virginia Crossman and Peter Gray (eds), *Poverty and Welfare in Ireland 1838–1948* (Dublin: Irish Academic Press, 2011).

Lees, Lynn Hollen. *The Solidarities of Strangers: The English Poor Laws and the People, 1700–1948* (Cambridge: Cambridge University Press, 1998).

Levene, Alysa, Thomas Nutt and Samantha Williams (eds), *Illegitimacy in Britain, 1700–1920* (Basingstoke: Palgrave Macmillan, 2005).

Lonergan, Eamonn. *A Workhouse Story: A History of St Patrick's Hospital, Cashel 1842–1992* (Clonmel: Eamonn Lonergan, 1992).

Lucey, D. S. 'Poor Relief in the West of Ireland 1861–1911', in Virginia Crossman and Peter Gray (eds), *Poverty and Welfare in Ireland 1838–1948* (Dublin: Irish Academic Press, 2011).

Lucey, Donnacha Seán. 'Power, Politics and Poor Relief During the Irish Land War, 1879–82', *Irish Historical Studies*, xxxvii: 584–98 (November 2011).

Luddy, Maria. *Women and Philanthropy in Nineteenth-Century Ireland* (Cambridge: Cambridge University Press, 1995).

——. '"Angels of Mercy": Nuns as Workhouse Nurses, 1861–1898', in Greta Jones and Elizabeth Malcolm (eds), *Medicine, Disease and the State in Ireland, 1650–1940* (Cork: Cork University Press, 1999).

——. *Prostitution and Irish Society 1800–1940* (Cambridge: Cambridge University Press, 2007).

Martin, Kathleen Callanan. *Hard and Unreal Advice: Mothers, Social Science and the Victorian Poverty Experts* (Basingstoke: Palgrave Macmillan, 2008).

McCormick, Leanne. *Regulating Sexuality: Women in Twentieth-Century Northern Ireland* (Manchester: Manchester University Press, 2009).

O'Brien, Gerard. 'The Establishment of Poor-Law Unions in Ireland, 1838–43', *Irish Historical Studies*, xxiii (1982).

——. 'Workhouse Management in Pre-Famine Ireland', *Proceedings of the Royal Irish Academy*, 86C (1986).

——. 'Cosherers, Wanderers and Vagabonds: The Treatment of the Poor and Insane in Ireland', *Saothar* 13: 45–8 (1988).

Ó Ciosáin, Niall. 'Boccoughs and God's Poor: Deserving and Undeserving Poor in Irish Popular Culture', in Tadgh Foley and Sean Ryder (eds), *Ideology and Ireland in the Nineteenth Century* (Dublin: Four Courts Press, 1998).

O'Connor, John. *The Workhouses of Ireland: The Fate of Ireland's Poor* (Dublin: Anvil Books, 1995).

O'Dwyer, Martin. 'Fr. John Barry – The Pauper Priest 1841–1920', *Boherlahan-Dualla Historical Journal*, pp. 67–72 (2000).

Ó Gráda, Cormac. *Ireland: A New Economic History 1780–1939* (Oxford: Oxford University Press, 1994).

O Mahony, Colman. *Cork's Poor Law Palace: Workhouse Life 1838–90* (Cork: Rosmathún Press, 2005).

O'Neill, T. P. 'The Catholic Church and the Relief of the Poor', *Archivium Hibernicum*, 31: 132–45 (1973).

Purdue, Olwen. 'Poor Relief in the North of Ireland 1850–1921', in Virginia Crossman and Peter Gray (eds), *Poverty and Welfare in Ireland 1838–1948*, (Dublin: Irish Academic Press, 2011).

Robins, Joseph. *From Reflection to Integration: A Centenary of Service by the Daughters of Charity to Persons with a Mental Handicap* (Dublin: Gill and Macmillan, 1992).

Snell, K. D. M. *Parish and Belonging: Community, Identity and Welfare in England and Wales 1700–1950* (Cambridge: Cambridge University Press, 2006).

Thane, Pat. 'Women and the Poor Law in Victorian and Edwardian England', *History Workshop Journal*, 6: 29–51 (1978).

Walsh, Oonagh. 'Lunatic and Criminal Alliances in Nineteenth-Century Ireland', in Peter Bartlett and David Wright (eds), *Outside the Walls of the Asylum: The History of Care in the Community* (London: Routledge, 1999).

——. *Anglican Women in Dublin: Philanthropy, Politics and Education in the Early Twentieth Century* (Dublin: UCD Press, 2005).

——. 'Cure or Custody: Therapeutic Philosophy at the Connaught District Lunatic Asylum', in Margaret H. Preston and Margaret Ó hÓgartaigh (eds), *Gender and Medicine in Ireland 1700–1950* (Syracuse: Syracuse University Press, 2012).

Welshman, John. *Underclass: A History of the Excluded, 1880–2000* (London: Hambledon Continuum, 2006).

Williams, Karel. *From Pauperism to Poverty* (London: Routledge, 1981).

Williams, Samantha. *Poverty, Gender and Life-Cycle under the English Poor Law 1760–1834* (Woodbridge: Boydell Press, 2011).

Index